The New Asian Immigration
in Los Angeles
and Global Restructuring

In the series
Asian American History and Culture
edited by Sucheng Chan and David Palumbo-Liu

*A list of books in the series appears
at the back of this volume.*

The New Asian Immigration in Los Angeles and Global Restructuring

Edited by Paul Ong, Edna Bonacich, and Lucie Cheng

Temple University Press
Philadelphia

Temple University Press, Philadelphia 19122
Copyright © 1994 by Temple University
All rights reserved
Published 1994
Printed in the United States of America

The paper used in this publication meets the
minimum requirements of American National
Standard for Information Sciences—Permanence
of Paper for Printed Library Materials,
ANSI Z39.48-1984 ∞

Library of Congress Cataloging-in-Publication Data

The New Asian immigration in Los Angeles and global
restructuring / edited by Paul Ong, Edna Bonacich, and
Lucie Cheng.
        p.   cm. — (Asian American history and culture)
    Includes bibliographical references.
    ISBN 1-56639-217-9 (cloth: alk. paper)
    ISBN 1-56639-218-7 (paper: alk. paper)
    1. Immigrants—California—Los Angeles.
2. Asians—California—Los Angeles. 3. Asian
Americans—California—Los Angeles. 4. Los Angeles
(Calif.)—Emigration and immigration. 5. Asia—
Emigration and immigration. 6. Los Angeles (Calif.)—
Economic conditions. 7. Los Angeles (Calif.)—Social
conditions. I. Ong, Paul M. II. Bonacich, Edna.
III. Cheng, Lucie. IV. Series: Asian American history
and culture series.
JV6926.L67N49   1994
305.895'079494—dc20   93-49863

Contents

Preface

This volume is, in a sense, a sequel to *Labor Immigration under Capitalism: Asian Workers in the United States before World War II* (Berkeley: University of California Press, 1984), edited by Lucie Cheng and Edna Bonacich. As the title indicates, that work focused on the history of Asians in the United States in the pre–World War II era, when Asian immigrants were primarily laborers, subject to exclusion, denial of citizenship, and racial oppression. Our primary goal there was to formulate a theoretical understanding of Asian immigration in the context of a developing global capitalism. We saw the immigration of Asians to the United States not simply as a product of discrete pushes and pulls in the homelands and receiving country, but as a more systematic phenomenon. In particular, we attempted to link U.S. imperialism in Asia with dislocations that spurred emigration. At the same time, we tried to show that a changing U.S. capitalist economy, particularly on the West Coast, created a demand for a semicoerced labor force that could be filled by these emigrants.

Even as we were conducting that research, we recognized the need for a follow-up study of post–World War II Asian immigration. Meetings were held by a group of scholars at the Asian American Studies Center at the University of California, Los Angeles, in the mid-1980s to get such a study off the ground, but we let it languish. We renewed the interest in 1989 when Paul Ong joined us and we formed a new team of researchers.

From the start we knew that the new Asian immigration is, in many ways, different from the old. No longer were workers the primary immigrants; now middle-class people, including professionals and entrepreneurs, were arriving in large numbers. Moreover, the response by the United States to the new immigrants was no longer one of exclusion and overt racial subordination. Our theories regarding Asian immigration, therefore, needed to be expanded to cover these changes.

Our approach still starts with the effects of global capitalism on Asian immigration. We continue to believe that immigration needs to be understood within this larger context. Since World War II, however, global capitalism has undergone considerable growth and change. Not only has the world economy become much more globally integrated, but the role of Asia in that economy has shifted dramatically as well. No longer are Asian countries subject to Western and particularly U.S. dominance; instead, they have become formidable competitors in the world market. Concomitantly, Asian emigrants are no longer primarily displaced peasants, although there remains a significant component of working-class Asian immigrants accompanying the middle-class migrants.

The new immigration began formally with the passage of the Immigration and Naturalization Act of 1965. Before the enactment of this legislation, immigration from Asia had been subject to harsh restrictions. Asia had been singled out for unique treatment in this regard. The shift in law was not simply a product of U.S. recognition of a clearly discriminatory policy, but also a reflection of the changing world order. Asia could no longer be treated in a humiliating manner, particularly when U.S. interests in the continent were expanding dramatically. The change in law that opened the gates to the new immigrants is thus in important ways a result of the globalizing economy.

In this work we use the concept of "restructuring," especially of the Pacific Rim economy. Restructuring is another term for the rapid global economic integration that is taking place. As we see it, the new Asian immigration is not only a product of the restructuring of the Pacific Rim region, but also a force that is contributing to that restructuring. The region is experiencing large-scale growth in trade relations, in capital flows in both directions, and in accompanying political involvements. The movement of people is a concomitant of these flows and in turn plays an important part in them. Immigration, trade, investment, economic aid, political and military involvement all go hand in hand. It is this larger context, the restructuring of the Pacific Rim, that provides the theoretical framework for this study.

Unlike *Labor Immigration under Capitalism*, which centered on

Asian immigration into California and Hawaii, the current study concentrates more narrowly on the new Asian immigration in Los Angeles. We made this choice because the new immigration is far larger and more complex than the old; we could not hope to cover the entire new immigration experience. Rather than spread our coverage too thin, we decided to develop a locational focus. Los Angeles was chosen because it is, indeed, the major center of the new Asian immigration (although we recognize that there are multiple secondary centers as well) and is an important node in the emerging Pacific Rim economy, a "global city" for the region. Thus a study of Los Angeles links the analysis of restructuring to immigration.

Another reason for the focus on Los Angeles is that it enables us to link macro- and microlevel forces. To put it another way, we can combine the global or regional level with the local level and consider how the two interact. This study, however, does not deal much with individual, subjective experiences. Rather, we emphasize how social forces affect processes such as immigration and the economic and political adaptation of immigrants. Despite this "structural" emphasis, we are very concerned with how these social forces and processes play themselves out in the experience of people. Limiting our research to one urban area enables us to develop a more concrete account of the experiences of the new Asian immigrants.

Most of the research reported in this book was conducted before the Los Angeles urban uprising of 29 April to 1 May 1992. The uprising brought the city's new Asian immigrants to the nation's attention, as Korean stores became one of the targets of attack. Unfortunately, we are not in a position to elucidate this event, but this volume may help provide some background for understanding it. The uprising did not come as a surprise to the authors of this book, who could see conflicts brewing. Moreover, we do not believe that the occurrence marks the end of such conflicts. Our hope is that this volume will contribute to an understanding of the role being played by the new Asian immigrants in Los Angeles, that it will point to contributions as well as to areas of conflict, and that it will serve in the efforts being made to resolve the problems.

This book is divided into four parts. Part I presents our basic approach and sketches out the major issues under study. We lay out the general idea of restructuring, particularly as it is manifested in the Pacific Rim region, and relate it to Asian immigration. Part II analyzes developments in Asia since World War II as they affect emigration and conditions in the United States that led to changes in immigration policies. Here we also describe the new immigrants, their settlement patterns, and their class characteristics.

In Part III we turn to the economy of Los Angeles and the role the new immigrants are playing in it. We focus on two industries—garment and health care—and the Chinese-Vietnamese ethnic economy. Our subjects range from the professionals, managers, and workers to the entrepreneurs. While we do not claim this section to be all-inclusive, we attempt to present in it a spectrum of economic activities representative of Asian immigrants in California.

Part IV examines some of the political ramifications of the new Asian immigration, including the involvement of the immigrants in the politics of a suburban area, conflicts with other nonwhite groups, and competition for public funding. Our focus is the impact of post-1965 Asian immigration on the distribution of and struggle for power and resources in the local community.

The contributors to this volume have been trained in different disciplines, including sociology, economics, anthropology, urban planning, and history. We share the belief that an adequate understanding of Asian immigration must be multidisciplinary. Although we try to develop a common language and style, years of professional practice make it difficult to shed the idiosyncrasies of our respective disciplines. We aim more to lay out lines of future investigation than to give a comprehensive account. This book should be seen, therefore, as an orientation or framework that we hope will stimulate more research.

In the course of researching and writing this book, we have benefited from the participation of many individuals and organizations. First and foremost are the numerous informants and interviewees who provided the basis for our explorations. These individuals are acknowledged separately in each chapter. Organizations that provided funding for the project include the University of California at Los Angeles and the University of California at Riverside academic senates, the UCLA Asian American Studies Center, and the Center for Pacific Rim Studies. We are indebted to Sucheng Chan and an anonymous referee for their insightful comments and to Suzanne Hee, Phil Okamoto, Glenn Omatsu, and Karen Umemoto for editing and pulling together the manuscript.

Part I
Introduction

1. The Political Economy of Capitalist Restructuring and the New Asian Immigration

Paul Ong, Edna Bonacich, and Lucie Cheng

Since the mid-1960s, immigration from Asia has been renewed on a large scale. The only other period that witnessed a similar influx started with the gold rush in the mid-nineteenth century and extended to 1934; during this time, thousands of Asians immigrated to the United States. Coming primarily from China, Japan, and the Philippines, they were mostly single men from rural villages, seeking to make money to support families in their home countries and in some cases hoping eventually to return in an improved economic position. Many of them worked as unskilled laborers in the mines, railroads, fields, canneries, and service industries of Hawaii and the West. Some were able to bring wives, establish families, and move into business and farm ownership, creating settled Asian American communities (Chan, 1991; Cheng and Bonacich, 1984; Takaki, 1989).

The early Asian communities faced considerable hostility from the surrounding society. Efforts were quickly made to curtail immigration from each of the Asian countries of origin, so that the scale of immigration was cut to very modest numbers. For those who did manage to come, anti-Asian agitation took the form of segregation, denial of citizenship, restrictions on land-ownership, physical abuse, and even massacre. The height of anti-Asian action was reached during World War II, when more than one hundred thousand Japanese Americans were evacuated from the Pacific Coast and put in concentration camps.

For two decades after the war, the local Asian American communities developed without any significant new immigration. De facto exclusion remained in place, singling out Asia as the sole continent from which immigration to the United States was unacceptable. This exclusion was eliminated in 1965 with the passage of a new immigration act that equalized immigration rights for all nationalities. The change of law prompted a new wave of Asian immigration to the United States.

The new Asian immigrants are different from the old in several important respects. Although they include people from such earlier sources as China and the Philippines, new sending countries have emerged, most notably South Korea, India, and Vietnam. No longer constrained by exclusion laws, the new immigrants are coming in much larger numbers than before. Women constitute a far higher proportion than in the past and now make up the majority of immigrants from some countries. And a substantial number are from urban, educated, middle-class backgrounds. These immigrants come to the United States as professionals, managers, and entrepreneurs.

Some of the shift toward higher-educated, professional immigrants is a product of U.S. immigration law, which gives preference to highly trained people. Still, the law alone cannot explain why the United States is pursuing immigrants with these skills, nor can it account for the fact that so many of them are coming from Asia. These new trends need to be explained.

It is important to note that not all the new Asian immigrants are middle-class professionals and managers. Indeed, Asian communities often reveal a class polarization. At one end are the well-off groups we have mentioned, and at the other are people working in low-skilled, minimum-wage, service-sector and manufacturing jobs, or who are unemployed. Although the median income of several of the Asian communities is relatively high, Asians suffer twice the poverty rate of the dominant society.

Much international migration theory has focused on the movement of unskilled labor from poor, underdeveloped countries to the core countries of Europe and North America. Some of the new Asian immigration reflects these old patterns. But the new professional-managerial stratum does not. Old theories are not very helpful in understanding the new conditions, and we must devise more adequate explanations.

The purpose of this volume is to describe and explain the new Asian immigration. Other authors have examined this subject (e.g., Fawcett and Carino, 1987; Gordon, 1990; Light and Bonacich, 1988; Mangiafico, 1988; Portes and Rumbaut, 1990; Riemers, 1985; Weiner, 1990), providing many useful insights. Our approach tends to differ from theirs in stressing the importance of placing the immigration in the context of the restructuring of global capitalism, particularly in the Pacific Rim area. Other authors, notably Alejandro Portes and Robert Bach (1985) and Saskia Sassen (1988), have looked at immigration in this context, but they focus on the movement of labor and do not give much attention to the new professional-managerial immigration. This volume contributes to the expansion of migration theories by including the movement of professionals and managers and examining that movement in terms of global restructuring.

Capitalist Crisis and Restructuring

Capitalist development is never even but proceeds in fits and spurts, partly due to a chronic condition of anarchy in capitalism as a system. Capitalism's reliance on the "free market" allows for uncontrollable swings and imbalances as investors and workers rush from one speculative opportunity to the next. While the business cycle is the most obvious fluctuation in the economy, there are also long-term swings. The distinction between the two types of cycles is the scope of change. When the economy heads into a recession within a business cycle, the change is characterized by a decreased level of economic activity, while societal structures remain largely intact. In long-term cycles a downturn not only affects the level of economic activities, but also precipitates a crisis.

A crisis within a capitalist system means a breakdown in productive expansion and accumulation. It is characterized by a falling rate of profit and an increasingly dysfunctional superstructure, that is, the set of social and political institutions that supports capitalism (Gordon, Edwards, and Reich, 1982; Kolko, 1988). To overcome this crisis, it is necessary to restructure the whole of society. Of course, the distinction between long-term and business cycles is not absolute. Even business cycles force some modification of social and political institutions and relationships. Business cycle–induced changes are more marginal and evolutionary, however.

What distinguishes a long-swing crisis is the large-scale and pervasive dislocation of capital and labor. Many existing industries and workers are cast aside permanently, rather than being temporarily underused and unemployed, as during a recession. There is no single cause for an economic crisis, and it often has noneconomic dimensions. The economic changes overrun the social and political structures and the prevailing ideology that had previously stabilized and supported economic relationships. Consequently, it is necessary to construct a new set of structures and to adopt another dominant ideology. The incongruities between emerging economic realities and preexisting societal structures force a wholesale redefinition of industrial organization and employer-worker relationships. The changes are interlinked and mutually reinforcing, leading to a rapid and discontinuous transformation of capitalism from one stage to another.

Capitalism has proved to be extremely robust, having survived a number of crises in its long history. This robustness comes from the fluidity of capital, which is manifested in a realignment of investments in response to the emerging economic realities. New capital eventually flows to those sectors and economic activities that will help reestablish profits. This pattern leads to widespread abandonment of existing industries. The most obvious response is withdrawing from markets where producers are no longer competitive. The realignment also includes other adjustments short of abandonment. Quantum changes in prices for inputs, for example, make some plants obsolete and some regions no longer competitive, leading not only to plant closures but also to the relocation of plant operations. Innovation is used to increase competitiveness, both through higher productivity and through the creation of new markets. Labor costs are reduced by incorporating lower-wage workers and by increasing work effort. New forms of inter- and intrafirm organization emerge to minimize risk, increase responsiveness in the face of uncertainty, lower production costs, reestablish economies of scale, and recover market power.

These adjustments exact tremendous social costs, not only in terms of abandoned capital but also in the dislocation of workers and the disruption of communities. This "creative destruction" is

occurring on a grand scale today as capitalism reconstitutes itself.

Restructuring is not merely an economic phenomenon. It has
generated changes that go beyond the realm of past experience.
Confusion about the proper policy sets in as older policies become ineffectual and even counterproductive. Existing economic
and social policies that were part of the older stage of capitalism
come under increasing fire. This policy crisis is resolved through
a political realignment in which ideologies and parties once on
the sidelines displace the existing order.

Thus far, political restructuring has almost never challenged
capitalism as an economic system. The idea of a centrally
planned economy is not considered a real alternative by the capitalist powers, and in the current case, the events in Eastern Europe and the Soviet Union have pushed this concept into greater
disrepute. Even though, at times, the government accommodates
labor and popular protest by adopting certain social policies, the
state is intrinsically linked to the system and must pursue capital
accumulation. The state must operate within the constraints of
capitalist necessities. The goal of the state is, at bottom, to protect and enhance profit. All that an economic crisis can do is
force the state to enact a new political agenda, one still within
the bounds of capitalist ideology, to help the economy not only
to survive but to thrive once again.

Ultimately, political restructuring entails class struggle. The
current crisis provides the capitalist class an opportunity to reas-
sert itself in the political as well as the economic arena. Although
capital never relinquished its hegemony in the state, before the
current crisis labor and social movements often were able to
extract concessions from the state. Capitalist actions during restructuring aim at reversing these trends, with the goals of lowering labor costs, imposing greater discipline on the work force,
and cutting social entitlements.

Although capitalism defines the range of state action, specific
outcomes are not predetermined, because profitability in capitalism can be reestablished under a large number of societal structures. In this sense, tomorrow's history is not already written,
since there is more than just one possible path to reconstruction.

The "openness" of capitalism to alternative paths provides an arena for a struggle over ideologies that can be fought within a democratic electoral process. Although it is true that the debate is confined to ideas that do not threaten to overthrow the economic system, the question of which set of ideas will emerge as dominant has important implications for people and communities. This process of political restructuring is not without flaws; it is fraught with ideological swings and counterswings. While it is useful to view the economic and political responses as two separate phenomena, they are nonetheless interconnected.

The precise nature of economic and political responses to crisis is particular to individual nations, because preexisting institutions influence restructuring. The reconstruction of a new political economy never starts from scratch. Instead, the process draws on a legacy of historically created institutions that are unique to each country. Some institutions are more amenable to new conditions, emerging stronger and directing events along a path consistent with their principles. These institutions are able to impart their own particular visions so long as profitability is restored. Some institutions are not congruent with the new order but can survive by transforming themselves. Those that are incongruent and intransigent are eventually pushed aside.

Globalization and the Asian Challenge

The current crisis in capitalism began to emerge in the advanced capitalist countries in the 1960s. The welfare state had shifted the balance of power from capital to labor, threatening the profit rate. This shift was manifested in powerful industrial unions and in rising tax rates that covered expanding social services. To avoid these pressures, capital from the developed countries started relocating some of its activities, first to less-developed regions within their own countries, with lower levels of unionization, and then abroad to less-developed countries.

This globalization marked a new stage in the world economy. Capital from developed countries was already active in the less-developed world, primarily in the extraction of raw materials. The current crisis has led capital to shift manufacturing enterprises to the developing countries. In essence, capital is seeking out new recruits for industrial production around the globe. Frequently peasants and often young women, these workers are first-generation proletarians who are more easily controllable than experienced workers and are employed at low wages.

The movement of capital to developing countries does not necessarily entail high levels of direct investment. In many industries the shift has been implemented by various types of contracting relationships. For example, in the apparel industry, companies often arrange to have their garments manufactured in other countries without investing any money. Nevertheless, they control both the designing and marketing ends of production and arrange for the more labor-intensive aspects of production to be done abroad. These goods are produced mainly for export to the developed countries, which provide lucrative markets for these manufactured exports.

Meanwhile, the developed countries have experienced "deindustrialization" (Bluestone and Harrison, 1982), as the number of manufacturing jobs has declined. What has emerged is a "new international division of labor" (Fröbel, Heinrichs, and Kreye, 1980), with industrial production increasingly shifted to developing countries and with the developed countries focusing more on providing business services to global enterprises. This restructuring world economy has had drastic consequences for countries such as the United States.

What started as an exploitation of less-developed countries by the advanced economies and transnational corporations (TNCs) has been transformed into competitive challenges from semi-autonomous emerging economies. Although advanced economies and TNCs exert a tremendous amount of control over Third World nations, the control is never absolute. Development often creates a foundation for nationalist drives that are beyond the influence of the core countries. This process has produced forces that disrupt the very order that fueled capitalist expansion.

Overdependency by developed countries on foreign sources for energy gave OPEC nations the potential for monopolistic action through cartels. Export-driven industrialization turned developing economies in Asia into global competitors. And decolonization partially freed Third World nations to act in their own national interests. Starting in the early 1970s, the internal economies of the advanced nations have been increasingly disrupted by developments abroad. Some disruptions were abrupt, such as the oil-price shocks of 1973 and 1979. Others have been more continuous but have accelerated over time, such as the unrelenting increase in market competition in manufactured goods. Of course, not all Third World nations were able to emerge as economic challengers and competitors. For example, Latin American countries failed to form even short-run cartels and suffered setbacks in their efforts to industrialize. But even their failure created problems for advanced nations in the form of a growing Third World debt crisis.

The economic development of Asia is of particular relevance to the studies in this volume. Before the 1960s, industrial production was dominated by the developed countries of Europe and North America. Now some previously underdeveloped countries, many of them in Asia, are engaging in manufacturing. The rise of Japan as one of the world's leading economic powers is the prime example of this shift, but of increasing importance are the newly industrializing countries (NICs). In most of these countries, several factors—the expanding world economy; a special relationship with the United States, which was seeking alliances in the Pacific region against the Soviet Union and China; a weak civil society with no powerful groups to challenge the state; and a population that has long held values of thrift and hard work—converged to allow a strong, authoritarian state to emerge to guide economic development.

Leading the group is Japan, which was nurtured out of postwar disaster by the United States to stave off Communist threat. With lavish amounts of foreign aid in the late 1940s and 1950s, a generous share of the U.S. domestic market, little expenditure for national defense, and the opportunity to serve as a major supplier for U.S. military operations in Korea and Vietnam, Japan was able to create the first economic miracle in Asia. Its focus on manufacturing for export was to become the magic wand for the NICs in the 1960s.

The Asian NICs are generally seen to be Hong Kong, Singapore, South Korea, and Taiwan (Bradshaw et al., 1988; Deyo, 1987; Galenson, 1985; Gereffi and Wyman, 1990; Hamilton, 1983). All experienced their great economic growth from the mid-1960s through the 1980s. Although some Latin American countries, especially Mexico and Brazil, have also been referred to as NICs, their growth has not been sustained to the same extent as in the Asian NICs (Gereffi and Wyman, 1990).

Several factors were critical to the success of the Asian NICs, especially South Korea and Taiwan. Coming out of a long period of colonization by Japan after World War II, both countries benefited from a special relationship with the United States as it struggled for hegemony with the Soviet Union in the Pacific region. The United States provided large amounts of foreign aid to these countries during the 1950s and 1960s, helping stabilize their economies and guaranteeing the survival of their authoritarian governments. South Korea and Taiwan, faced with possible extinction by their Communist counterparts, rallied their populations behind an anti-Communist ideology, accompanied by urgings of austerity. U.S. aid made it possible for the states to develop autonomously, thus laying the basis for effective state intervention in economy and society, as they pushed for export-led industrialization in the 1960s at the insistence of the United States (Gereffi and Wyman, 1990, 374–375).

The expanding world economy in the 1960s also provided a niche for the other two Asian NICs, the entrepôt city-states of Singapore and Hong Kong. A strong authoritarian state in Singapore supplied the political and social stability necessary to attract foreign private investments. Hong Kong's proximity to China provided a source of cheap labor that gave the colony a comparative advantage in pursuing labor-intensive manufacturing. In addition, a well-developed organizational infrastructure and a close partnership between the colonial government and the banks made Hong Kong the financial and service capital of the region.

Confucianism, a powerful cultural heritage in all these Asian countries, was a significant contributing factor in their rapid economic development in at least two ways. Its praise of thriftiness and self-denial led to a savings rate that is the highest in the world. In addition, the Confucian work ethic has made the labor force willing to endure the world's longest working hours.

Besides the "four little tigers," or "minidragons," as the Asian NICS are sometimes called, other Asian countries, such as Thailand, Indonesia, Malaysia, India, and the Philippines, are trying to pursue the same development course. Primarily, that means entering the global economy by manufacturing for export. Typically, the strategy involves strong state participation in the development process, an effort to attract foreign capital, and enclave development in the form of free trade zones (FTZS). The regimes are often authoritarian and tend to support a "free market" capitalist ideology, despite active state intervention in the economy. Their ideology is consonant with the conservatism espoused by Western restructuring economies.

China is a latecomer in the process of world capitalist incorporation. Although still engaging in a socialist discourse, the Chinese state is following a path of development similar to that pursued by the NICS. The sheer size of the Chinese economy is bound to have a great impact on global restructuring and to pose serious challenges to the world system.

Entry into the world market is usually based on a "cheap labor" strategy. The competitive advantage of the developing country lies in its low-cost labor, which is used to attract foreign investment and to undercut prices on the world market. The authoritarian regimes help maintain this advantage by promising to control labor and by limiting social spending (Deyo, 1989). In other words, they focus on capital accumulation at the expense of public consumption and the development of trade unions.

In a restructuring world economy, however, a cheap labor strategy is inevitably short-term, because there are always new, even poorer or more repressive countries ready to take their place at the bottom. Consequently, the NICS, and other new entrants, have had to seek alternative means to maintain their industrial growth. Like the West, they are moving production to other countries where labor costs are lower than their own. Japan has moved its more labor-intensive industries to Indonesia. Taiwan and South Korea, having succeeded in becoming the major suppliers of global garment demands, are relocating their manufacturing plants to countries such as Indonesia, Thailand, and Guatemala, where cheap labor is still abundant. Asia now has its own internal patterns of international investments and runaway shops.

As part of an effort to move up the ladder of technological innovation, many Asian developing countries are promoting higher education. Some students are sent to the developed industrial countries, such as the United States, for advanced training. Others are trained at home, often in schools developed under the aegis of advisers from the advanced capitalist countries. As a result, a highly educated stratum of trained technicians and professionals exists in many Asian countries. These people have become an important element in the new Asian immigration to the United States.

More recently, as the Asian countries have emerged from their peripheral status within the world economy, their focus on scientific and technical innovation is luring back many of their professional expatriates from the United States. This phenomenon has three consequences. For the developing Asian countries, the return of highly educated and experienced people helps relieve a significant shortage of professionals in selected fields. For the United States, the departure of these highly trained professionals with experience in the most advanced areas of research presents a potential threat. Finally, for the world system as a whole, the frequent movement back and forth of professionals contributes to the internationalization of the professional-managerial stratum (Cheng and Evans, 1991).

The rise of Asian developing countries acts as an independent force on global restructuring. These nations have been active players, leading rather than merely following the developments in the world capitalist system. Although there are myriad ties between them and the advanced core states, they have the capacity to pursue a course of development somewhat independent of the needs and actions of the developed countries of the West. Restructuring is, to an important extent, being imposed on countries such as the United States by challenges from Asia.

The Crisis in the United States

For the United States, the cumulative changes brought about by the global reordering, along with its own endemic problems, have produced economic chaos, policy confusion, and heightened social tensions. The growing penetration of imports, the bulk of which come from East Asia, can be readily seen in national accounting data. Imports accounted for only 5.7 percent of the gross national product (GNP) in 1969, but two decades later they accounted for 14.8 percent of the GNP (U.S. President, 1991). Because global development is highly uneven, the resulting competition and challenges from abroad are concentrated in manufacturing. Imported merchandise as a percentage of the domestic manufacturing component of the GNP increased from 13.9 percent in 1969 to 50.6 percent in 1988. Some sectors of the economy have come under considerable pressure, other sectors have been sheltered from changes, while still others have benefited. This unevenness forces a restructuring of the economy and society.

Some obvious economic consequences include stagnation, a slow-down in productivity growth, high inflation, rising unemployment, and economic dislocation. In the late 1970s, the combination of a slow-down in GNP growth and double-digit inflation driven by increasing oil prices produced stagflation. The U.S. economy escaped stagflation in the early 1980s, but only by suffering the worst recession since the Great Depression. Inflation was tamed by pushing unemployment rates above 10 percent by the last quarter of 1982. Although the subsequent business recovery proved to be one of the longest experienced by the United States, it was followed by another recession, which has continued into the early 1990s, especially in California.

The current crisis should also be seen as a crisis in the continued accumulation of capital and profits. During the mid-1960s, the rate of return to U.S. capital averaged 9 percent per year, but by the late 1970s it had fallen to below 6 percent per year (Bowles, Gordon, and Weisskopf, 1986). Profitability can be increased by two basic strategies. One involves cutting labor costs or disciplining the working class. The other entails increasing efficiency through reorganization and investment in new technology. Both strategies are being pursued in the current restructuring efforts. The question of how the burden of the crisis is shared between capital and labor is determined not only by market forces but also by the actions of the state.

Attack on Labor. Reducing labor costs is the simpler, more direct strategy of the two. It involves laying off redundant workers, lowering wages, lengthening the working day, and generally squeezing the workers harder. One clear effect of restructuring is the large number of workers dislocated when capital abandons plants and industry. In the 1970s, when increased international competition and energy-price shocks hit many industries, millions of experienced workers were displaced. The dislocated workers of this period were not readily reabsorbed, and those from industries in which import penetration was the greatest tended to suffer long periods of unemployment (Kruse, 1988). Although the rate of dislocation slowed in the 1980s, millions more were displaced even as the economy began to recover from the worst downturn since the Great Depression. During the back-to-back recessions of 1980 and 1981–1982, 5.1 million experienced workers were displaced, and from 1985 to 1989, another 4.2 million were dislocated (Herz, 1991). Although there are no statistics yet on workers who have been displaced by the downturn of the early 1990s, the number will likely reach the same levels experienced a decade earlier.

At the same time as the widespread layoffs, wages came under attack, as seen in the trends in average weekly earnings. For more than two decades after the end of World War II, workers experienced increases in real earnings. For example, between 1948 and 1959, both expansionary years in the business cycle, average weekly earnings grew from $197 to $261 (in 1982 dollars). The growth in weekly earnings slowed but nonetheless continued until 1972, when wages were 21 percent higher than in 1959. Since then, the average real wage has fallen. By 1989, the figure stood at $264, compared to $316 in 1972, a drop of 16 percent. Some of the decrease came about through the growth in part-time work, but even among the most privileged group, white males who worked full-time and full-year, annual earnings fell by nearly 10 percent between 1973 (when the average peaked) and 1989 (U.S. President, 1983, 1991).

One aspect of the attack on labor has been the dramatic decline in unionism (Curme, Hirsch, and Macpherson, 1990). The new economic pressures have led firms to pursue strategies that have weakened organized labor. The 1970s saw the growth of managerial opposition to organizing efforts (Freeman and Medoff, 1984, 230–239) and the advent of widespread concessionary bargaining (Mitchell, 1980). Despite the concessions, union members still fared better than their unorganized counterparts. From the early 1970s to the mid-1980s, the gap between union and nonunion wages grew by perhaps as much as 100 percent (Wachter and Carter, 1989; 241, 262). While union wages did not suffer as much as nonunion wages, the impact of restructuring on union membership was devastating. In 1954, one in three private nonagricultural workers was a union member. By the late 1980s, the number had shrunk to one in six. Unionization declined throughout this period, but there was a sharp acceleration in the decline during the 1980s, when the unionization rate fell from 23.8 percent in 1979 to 16.3 percent in 1989. It was due, in part, to the market pressure on durable manufacturing, which in earlier decades had been sheltered from international competition and was the stronghold of U.S. industrial unionism.

The incorporation of immigrant workers from low-wage, Third World nations is another facet of the labor-disciplining strategy. Some jobs, such as the cleaning of hotels and office buildings, cannot be exported, and rather than pay established, union-level wages, employers (including the state) prefer to use immigrants, to whom they can pay lower wages. Another reason for using immigrant labor is to meet the competition from low-wage countries by having one's own low-wage work force. That entails creating a "Third World within," in which immigrant workers from Third World countries are used by employers to compete against producers in the developing countries. Sometimes workers from the same countries are employed in both places; for example, Mexican and Chinese garment workers are employed in Los Angeles to compete with garment imports from Mexico, Hong Kong, Taiwan, and China.

The assault on labor is not limited to the direct actions of private enterprises and the state. Efforts to cut labor costs also occur indirectly through attacks on social spending. Cutbacks in health care expenditures, in parks and recreation, in occupational health and safety standards, in education, and in civil rights programs all represent efforts to reduce the social cost of labor.

Corporate Reorganization and Innovation. The second approach to reversing declining profitability is to enhance competitiveness through innovations in production, technology, organization of production, distribution, and financing. Innovation and change are characteristic features of capitalism, leading to constant, unpredictable movement; during periods of crisis, the pace accelerates.

Capitalists make investment decisions based on the criterion of expected returns. The ideal model, of investment in expanded productive capacity through the development of plants and equipment, is but one way of increasing profit. During the 1980s, profits were pursued in other ways as well, leading to a decline in productive investment (Harrison and Bluestone, 1988, chap. 3; Kolko, 1988, chap. 3).

A prominent form of investment in the 1980s was acquisitions, mergers, and takeovers. Such investments were frequently financed by debt, often borrowed from investment bankers and/or financed by "junk bonds." Takeovers were sometimes hostile, forcing companies to defend themselves. They were compelled to distribute more dividends and take on more debt to cover operating expenses. Some companies were faced with "greenmail" (payoffs to unwanted suitors who threaten a hostile takeover). The result was an increased burden of debt even to pay off interest on debt.

Speculation grew not only in the buying and selling of firms, but also in the buying and selling of securities. As a result, insider trading scandals occurred on Wall Street, and a chaotic stock market responded not to the health of a company but to changes in the value of its stock alone. This large-scale shifting of capital did not enhance productivity. As Joyce Kolko (1988, 67) puts it, "capital circulated among corporations, investment bankers, and lawyers, but not in production."

Corporations sometimes pursued the destruction of productive property. One method was to lower their break-even point by reducing their production and sales while maintaining profits. Firms divested themselves of branches and subsidiaries and sometimes "disinvested," that is, drained capital away from healthy businesses until they collapsed. These strategies obviously had drastic consequences for workers and communities.

Another form of innovation, permitted by the new communications technology, is the locational fragmentation of firms. Not only does this take an international form, with TNCs spreading parts of their operations all over the globe, but it also occurs within a country, region, or city, in the form of contracting out various functions. Decentralization is linked to a shift from Fordist, assembly-line-style mass production, to "flexible specialization," in which smaller plants use skilled workers and flexible, computer-based machinery to produce more varied goods for an ever-changing market (Piore and Sabel, 1984). The rise of "quick response" technologies, linking retailers to producers by computer to speed up reorders on popular items, is a related innovation.

Some authors have dubbed the current period "postindustrial" because of the tremendous rise in services. These include not only consumer services, but more important, producer and business services. The service sector is obviously complex and diverse. It includes financial services (banking, insurance, brokerages), trade, transport, communications, maintenance, law and health, advertising, tourism and leisure, and the like. Some services, such as education and law enforcement, are funded by the state. One huge and costly state service is the military. But many new and elaborate services are emerging in the private sector as well (Kolko, 1988, chaps. 4, 5).

Although services include both poorly paid dishwashers and janitors and highly paid financial advisers and lawyers, the expansion of services is generally accompanied by the growth of a new "class," the professional and managerial class (PMC) (Ehrenreich and Ehrenreich, 1979). Associated with the expansion of higher education, the PMC is composed of all those professionals and managers who help run the private and public sectors even though they are not themselves major owners of capital. It includes the traditional professions, such as law, medicine, education, and the clergy, as well as scientists and engineers. It comprises business managers, such as the managers of global corporations, and a host of professionals who provide business services, such as accountants and advertisers. And it includes the professional and managerial employees of financial institutions. It incorporates the well-paid, educated, white-collar sector of the work force.

In sum, U.S. capitalism is engaged in reorganizing itself, trying to find a way out of the current crisis. Even though many of these developments are not directly aimed at seeking out cheap labor, they have implications, often negative, for the working class.

It is easy to see that the two prongs of restructuring are related to the two major strands of immigration. Latino immigrants generally perform the role of low-wage labor as part of the cheap labor strategy, and Asian immigrants both join whites in the professional and managerial stratum as part of the "investment-in-innovation" strategy and join Latino immigrants in the cheap labor strategy.

The Surge of Conservative Ideology. The economic crisis has led to a political swing to the right that has transformed the role of government and undermined the prior social contract. In response to the political-economic crisis of the Great Depression, the United States built a modern welfare state, which was greatly expanded in the post–World War II period. The government sought both industrial and social peace to gain the stability needed to ensure economic growth. The welfare state fostered social spending and the strengthening of organized labor. It responded to popular movements by workers and people of color for greater economic and social equality, resulting in new entitlement programs for the poor, civil rights legislation for minorities, and greater health and safety protection for labor. These achievements were accomplished by a significant growth in state expenditures.

The gains were transitory, because the welfare state contained contradictions, as we have mentioned. Since this state was developed within capitalism and continued to endorse private ownership of productive property, its major source of revenue was taxation. State spending thus subtracted from profitable production, and business owners (as well as the more advantaged sectors of workers) could complain that they were being sucked dry. Moreover, the welfare state's support for workers, in the form of protecting trade unions and funding social programs that benefited workers and their families, cut into profits. That was acceptable as long as economic growth created an expanding pie that simultaneously provided for higher profits, wages, and social benefits. Increased international competition, which disrupted the U.S. economy and created economic stagnation, eroded this sociopolitical accord. The welfare state had limits, and these limits were revealed by the growing fiscal crisis of the state.

The political response to the crisis has been a shift away from the welfare state, particularly after the election of Ronald Reagan in 1980 and the entrenchment of neoconservatism in the White House. The Reagan administration may have embodied this new conservatism, but there was a broad social base for it. Even the Democrats have embraced elements of the market philosophy. In fact, the policy of deregulation, one of the cornerstones of the right (discussed below), was started by the Carter administration. The new conservatism has shown itself to be a populist movement in other ways. It began with the "tax revolt" against big government (Lo, 1990; Sears and Citrin, 1982). In a period of economic uncertainty and stagnation, an overwhelming majority of the voting public minimized its own losses by paying less into the public coffer. Although people were willing to pay for services from which they benefited directly, there was a strong sentiment to cut transfer programs for the poor. Class position was positively correlated with support for the tax revolt, but even among those in the lowest income bracket, a majority supported lowering taxes. Ironically, the sector that has garnered the lion's share of the benefits of the movement is big business.

The Republican Party capitalized on the shift in public attitude and in the process moved the government agenda to the right. The "Reagan revolution" stood for cuts in social spending and the abolition of state regulation of capital. This trend went beyond letting go of social controls on labor and health and safety standards to include a decline in environmental protection, consumer protection, and a host of other issues. It sought to undo civil rights gains, thereby increasing racial polarization and tensions throughout the nation. Tax measures that transferred the burden from the wealthy to the working class and poor underscored these policies.

A major theme in the restructuring agenda has been to allow the "free market" to run its course. This shift has come about through an attack on the legitimacy of liberal economic policies, that is, Keynesian management of the economy and the regulation of major industries. Under the new macroeconomic policy, the administration was no longer willing to use monetary and fiscal instruments to moderate the effects of recessions. As a result, in the 1981–1982 recession unemployment climbed to nearly 11 percent. The argument was that the recession had to run its course in order to break the back of high inflation and do away with accumulated inefficiencies.

A free market also meant that businesses should not be impeded by government regulation, but instead should be nurtured. Deregulation became a linchpin in the restructuring period. Government, it was advocated, should get out of the business of regulating business. The result has been deregulation of the energy, transportation, communication, and financial sectors.

Neoconservative economic policies have not been limited to unchaining capitalism. The other theme was the creation of a climate favorable to a higher rate of capital investment, which the administration argued "is an important ingredient in raising productivity and economic growth" (U.S. President, 1983, 5). This came in the form of the Economic Recovery Tax Act of 1981, which greatly benefited capital and the rich (U.S. Congress, Joint Economic Committee, 1984).

Another important aspect of the dismantling of the welfare state was increased "privatization," that is, the transfer of public services to the private sector (e.g., Foglesong and Wolfe, 1989).

Sometimes privatization has meant a pursuit of cheap labor, as unionized, public-sector workers are layed off and bypassed by the new private employers.

In order to allow the market to work its magic, the administration sought to rid the economy of institutional rigidities in the labor market. Through promanagement laws and regulations, the administration assisted employers in their attack on labor and accelerated the decline of unionism. The most visible attack against organized labor was the dismissal of PATCO (the air traffic controllers' union) strikers in 1981. The Labor Relations Board, traditionally pro-worker, became more conservative. In this anti-labor climate, firms embraced strategies to decertify existing unions.

The neoconservative agenda was not merely one of restructuring the economy and labor market. A reworking of social policies has been an important part of the ideology. The idea of trimming "big government" has translated into a gutting of social welfare programs and less support for physical and social infrastructures, ranging from highways to education. The official social policy has moved, in the words of one historian, "from the war on poverty to the war on welfare" (Katz, 1986, 249), despite the growth in poverty, including among two-parent families (Ellwood, 1988).

The New Inequality. One social consequence of the economic and political restructuring is heightened income inequality. The distribution of annual wages and salaries narrowed from 1963 to 1975, but after that period the trend reversed, with inequality rising sharply (Harrison and Bluestone, 1988, 119). Much of this distribution was driven by an increase in the absolute and relative number of low-wage workers. This increase is due to several factors, including changes in demographic composition (age, gender, race) and earnings based on skills and education. At the same time, those in industries that experienced significant productivity increases participated in "rent-sharing," which helped push up their wages and contributed to growing wage inequality (Bell and Freeman, 1991).

The new economic inequality has taken old social forms. The tension created by economic uncertainty and policy confusion spilled into the social sphere, as people's anxieties and apprehensions were channeled into collective action that increased group conflicts. In part, this reaction was "rational," since collective action enables some groups to garner the benefits of economic and political restructuring by forcing other groups to absorb a disproportionate share of the costs. Politicians and the political system capitalized on these group tendencies and in the process transformed issues of economic failure into issues of protecting and enhancing social status. In this type of battle for privilege, the groups that were previously the most organized and powerful usually gain the upper hand. Consequently, the process tends to reproduce social inequalities along existing lines.

Racial inequality is one of the fundamental social injustices accentuated by restructuring. People of color have borne a disproportionate share of the cost of restructuring. The wage gap between whites and people of color increased between the early 1970s and mid-1980s (Haberfeld and Shenhav, 1990; Hinojosa-Ojeda, Carnoy, and Daly, 1991). This growing gap was driven, in part, by the fact that people of color were displaced more often by plant closures and downsizing, suffered longer periods of unemployment, and experienced larger losses in earnings than whites (Herz, 1991; Kletzer, 1991; Ong, 1991). The problems of the private sector have been compounded by the government's retreat from civil rights. This era has witnessed the dismantling of many affirmative action programs, the use of subtle racism in political campaigns, and the assertion of "white" rights against reverse discrimination. Economic polarization may not be merely a short-term phenomenon. The dwindling support for public education, for example, has created a stratified educational system that promotes elitism and reproduces intergenerational inequality.

Asian Immigrants and Restructuring

The large-scale immigration from Asia after 1965 not only coincided with economic restructuring, but was affected by and contributed to these structural changes. The immigration of Asians

to the United States is both an economic and political phenomenon. In particular, the new Asian immigration has grown in response to the passage of legislation in 1965 that finally removed
all vestiges of Asian exclusion in U.S. immigration policy. This
shift in policy was at least partially responsive to the changing
role of U.S. capital in the region. With a rise in the activities of
U.S. TNCs in Asia, along with U.S. military activity that supported this expansion, the United States could no longer afford
to maintain a blatantly racist immigration policy with respect to
the region.

The political history of changing U.S. Asian immigration policy is discussed in Chapter 2. Here we focus on the role of Asian
immigration in the economic restructuring of the United States.

Asian immigrants to the United States play a multitude of
roles in the restructuring process. They help supply the labor,
skills, and entrepreneurial energy that facilitate economic restructuring. Some are hired, often through direct recruitment, to
fill critical shortages brought on by the neoconservative policies.
That is especially true for highly skilled occupations requiring
advanced education. The lack of adequate funds for advanced
training, the tendency of some of the best students to pursue
high-salary jobs in the financial and legal sectors, and the inability to alleviate some oppressive working conditions have produced a shortage of personnel in the health, engineering, and
scientific fields. Professionally trained Asian immigrants have
been employed to offset some of these shortages. These professionals work in the innovative and technically developing aspects of restructuring.

As we have observed, there is a tendency for new Asian immigrants to be heavily drawn from the middle class. Many Asian
immigrants are educated, urban individuals who come to the
United States as professionals, technicians, managers, and small
business owners. The U.S. Immigration Act of 1965 encouraged
this stratum to come by giving preference to trained people and
to those with capital to invest. The legislators did not anticipate,
however, that people from *Asia* would fill these slots.

Why did the United States encourage professional and managerial immigration, especially in the mid-1960s? And why did

Asians, in particular, respond to this call? These questions are central to understanding the new Asian immigration.

On the U.S. side, as suggested above, restructuring has two prongs: cheapening labor and pursuing innovation. This duality produces a contradiction in the area of education. On the one hand, the United States wants to cut social spending, including spending on education. On the other, it needs highly trained personnel. This duality leads to efforts to stratify the educational system more, by promoting elitism and differentiation between schools. Nevertheless, there is a strong democratic impulse in the nation that defines equality of opportunity in educational terms. If U.S. capitalism is to be open to all equally, then equal schooling must likewise be universally available. Otherwise, the immense inequalities in the society cannot be justified.

The educational system of the United States is thus a major political battlefield (e.g., Carnoy and Levin, 1985; Shor, 1986). Conservatives push for greater inequality in the schools. Democratic forces push for greater equality. And parents try to get the best for their children to give them an advantage in this competitive system. Such wrenching issues as school desegregation, busing, and public funding for private schools have left the U.S. educational system in a shambles. Meanwhile, there has been an underproduction of certain kinds of trained personnel.

The public schools are not the only locus of this problem. Cutbacks in social spending (as part of the cheapening of labor strategy) affect other spheres, too. The United States has been reluctant to spend money on the training of health personnel, such as nurses, in a general effort at cost containment for health care. The ultimate goal is to reduce health care costs for capitalist employers by lowering the costs of their benefits packages. This policy creates a shortage of nurses in the United States and a demand for immigrant nurses.

In general, the cheap labor approach to restructuring has the impact of curbing the development of local professionals by limiting the opportunities of the local working class. People who work for minimum wage can hardly afford to send their children to college. Attacks on the working class thus have the consequence of undermining the strategy of reorganization and innovation by limiting the growth of the class that can implement it. This contradiction sets the stage for the immigration of professionals and managers.

On the Asian side, as already mentioned, education has been fostered among the NICs and other developing countries. Some of the training (e.g., nurses' education in the Philippines) has been developed for the express purpose of emigration and the remittances it produces. But most educational plans in Asian countries aim at developing their own professional-managerial stratum, in pursuit of development through innovation.

Asian countries also suffer from internal contradictions in terms of being able to absorb their own highly trained personnel. First, cheap labor policies have restricted social spending and, therefore, the demand for certain kinds of social services, such as health care. Trained health care personnel find it difficult to obtain jobs. Second, because the homelands are still developing, opportunities for employment in the private sector are also limited. Third, the training the professionals and managers receive is often under Western aegis, sometimes as part of study-abroad programs, and is more suited to the needs of advanced capitalism than to the individual's own country. Fourth, countries such as the United States offer much higher salaries or possibilities for profitable investment than do the homelands. It thus pays for the individual to relocate. Finally, the professionals and managers share the capitalist ideology of individualism. There is a tendency not to be concerned about national welfare and to put one's own career first. The fact that one is "deserting" the nation that paid for one's education is not brought into consideration. Of course, in some cases individuals have returned, using their accumulated experience and savings in their homelands.

Despite the catastrophic divisions over U.S. educational policy, U.S. schools still offer easier access to higher education than do most Asian schools. Many Asian middle-class families are attracted to the United States because of the educational opportunities it affords their children.

The dualism of restructuring thus creates contradictions in both the sending and the receiving countries. In general, Asian countries are producing more highly trained members than they can absorb, while the United States produces fewer than it needs. These imbalances, it must be stressed, are not "natural"; they are a product of the contradictions of capitalism, the resulting class struggle, and the efforts to restructure the global economy.

The continuing demand for Asian professionals on the U.S. side does not ensure their continued immigration, as shown by changes in U.S. immigration policy in the 1970s that made this immigration more difficult. Interest groups in the United States are divided about professional immigration, and those who feel the effects of competition exercise what political influence they have to make the arrival of Asian professionals more difficult. Actual immigration policy thus reflects not only the economic needs of capital, but also the political fallout of the conflicts that filling these needs engenders.

The contributions of Asian immigrants to economic restructuring are not limited to those made by professionals. Many Asian immigrants rely on small businesses to establish a foothold in the United States. As in the past, they use familial and other collective resources to start their ventures. In doing so, they help establish the contracting shops that are part of vertical fragmentation, provide services such as restaurants for the growing PMC, and run mom-and pop operations in the deteriorating inner city, where fleeing white retailers have left a vacuum of opportunity.

Not all Asian businesspeople fall into the petty capitalist class. Others are owners, executives, and investors of major Asian transnational businesses that are establishing bases in the U.S. economy. In other words, these Asian immigrants are manifestations of a globalizing economy, in which national boundaries no longer confine business activity.

Finally, as mentioned earlier, despite the greater visibility of Asian immigrant members of the middle class and the international business community, a sizable proportion of new Asian immigrants are forced to join Latino immigrants as low-wage workers or to depend on public assistance. Many of these poor immigrants are refugees from Southeast Asia, but substantial numbers of immigrants from other Asian countries also arrive without the educational or financial resources to propel them into professional or business-owning occupations.

Asian immigrants have played a role not only in economic restructuring but also in political restructuring. The cold war has come to an end. The European ex-Communist bloc is making efforts to join the capitalist world economy and its renewed commitment to free markets. Most of the post-1965 Asian immigration to the United States occurred within a cold war context, however. Indeed, U.S. military involvement in Asian countries to try to halt the spread of Communism has been a major theme of the post–World War II period.

Asia has experienced several Communist revolutions, starting with China in 1949. Since then, revolutionary movements in Korea and Vietnam have led to wars in which the United States played the role of defender against the spread of Communism. The United States has also supported anti-insurrectionist governments in such countries as the Philippines.

While these efforts were mainly aimed at curbing Soviet and Chinese influence, they had an economic underpinning. Their purpose was to keep as much of the world open to capitalist investment and markets as possible. Anti-Communist wars were thus a part of the world capitalist political economy.

The new Asian immigration to the United States has obviously been deeply affected by both actual and potential warfare. Many new Asian immigrants have come to the United States as refugees, particularly from Southeast Asia. Others, such as Koreans, and Chinese from Hong Kong and Taiwan, have come from divided countries, where political instability and the threat of war or Communist takeover have made the future uncertain.

Many of the new immigrants have been aligned with the United States and its military in these conflicts, and their political ideology, at least on arrival, is to the right of center. As with Cuban immigration, some of the new Asian immigrants are fiercely anti-Communist and have the potential for pushing the United States to the right. That is especially likely for the refugees from anti-Communist wars. On the other hand, some Asian immigrants from divided countries have lived under right-wing, authoritarian regimes and are more likely to be critical of the ideology of anti-Communism. The internal politics of Asian American communities today can thus be quite complex, with the political struggles of their homelands replicated in their new home. Of course, once these immigrants arrive in the United States, local experiences also come to shape political identification and ideology.

Many Asian immigrants to the United States are helping to renew capitalism, not only through their economic activities, but also by reinforcing its values. In part reflecting developments in their homelands, they embrace capitalism with enthusiasm. This trend poses a challenge to those political forces in the United States that are more critical of capitalism, as well as to older Asian Americans, some of whom have developed a "progressive" politics.

The political leanings of the new Asian immigrants remain to be worked out. The harsh realities of economic inequality and racism fostered by the system may lead some to turn toward the left. And in some cases, such as South Korea, a vibrant leftist movement in their homeland may inspire some new immigrants to question capitalistic values.

As their numbers grow and their influence increases, Asian immigrants are not merely filling the positions that are being created as a result of restructuring. They are actively participating in the restructuring process. They are helping reshape the economic landscape by creating new and alternative ventures. And they have the potential to emerge as an important new political force, influencing legislation and policy on both the local and the international level.

Los Angeles as a Global City

Global restructuring has changed the character of certain cities. Instead of serving to integrate regional and national entities, some cities have emerged as centers of the new global world order. They are called "global cities" (Cohen, 1981; Feagin and Smith, 1987; Friedmann, 1986; Sassen, 1988, chap. 5). Global cities vary in their specific functions, but generally they are focal points of world trade, they house the headquarters of TNCs, and they serve as financial centers. Such cities thus help coordinate the flow of capital, production, and trade on an international level.

Los Angeles has become a global city, with a commanding position in the Pacific Rim area (Davis, 1987; Soja, 1987; Soja, Morales, and Wolff, 1983). It is a major port of entry and exit for the huge growth in U.S. trade with Asia and parts of Latin America. It also serves as a TNC and banking headquarters for U.S. and Asian firms. Coordination of the increasingly complex and interconnected Pacific Rim economy is managed, in part, from Los Angeles.

In addition, Los Angeles is a nucleus for two other important global-oriented activities. It is a media center producing movies, television, music, news broadcasts, and other forms of popular culture and communications. In the process, it helps shape the ideology of global capitalism. Second, Los Angeles is a major center of U.S. military production, especially in the aerospace field. It thus helps lay the foundation for continued U.S. influence in the world order.

As a global city, Los Angeles has become a prime area for PMC growth. Business services have proliferated to support the TNCs, trading companies, and banks. These professionals include lawyers, doctors, engineers, housing developers, personal finance managers, brokers, and accountants. The core of white-collar workers staffing global enterprises attract more white-collar workers who perform services for them. These people are generally affluent, with considerable disposable income. They also tend to be white, although increasing numbers, especially among technically trained personnel, are from Asian countries.

On the other hand, the swollen professional and managerial stratum of the global city has a need for hotels, restaurants, entertainment, and other personal services, such as house cleaning and child care. Corporate offices need to be built and kept clean. This underside of the global city requires a low-wage sector, which in Los Angeles is made up largely of immigrant labor, mainly from Mexico and Central America.

Los Angeles, like the United States as a whole, has also suffered deindustrialization, as many of its heavy manufacturing plants have shut down or moved elsewhere. This development is not inherent to global cities, but rather reflects the overall status of the United States in a restructuring world economy. Nevertheless, the decline in heavy manufacturing has had a significant negative effect on the Los Angeles African American community, which has suffered major job loss and impoverishment.

Paul Ong (1989) has documented that Los Angeles is experiencing a widening divide between rich and poor, a divide that is also marked by racial difference. This polarization reflects both the general consequences of restructuring, including its dual tendencies, and the peculiarities of a global city. As in the United States as a whole, economic inequality in Los Angeles is related to the growing class-and-race polarization. Here, however, the presence of large numbers of immigrants redefines the process into a multiracial phenomenon. Non-Hispanic whites (commonly referred to as Anglos) occupy the top tier, and African Americans the bottom tier, with Latino immigrants generally performing the role of low-wage labor.

Asian immigrants play a multitude of roles in this complex configuration. Some are high-level participants in Pacific Rim trade and production, as owners, executives, and investors of major Asian businesses. Some are professionals who work in the innovative and technically developing aspects of restructuring. Some become small business owners, providing services such as restaurants for the growing professional and managerial stratum. Some run businesses in the deteriorating inner city, filling vacancies left by fleeing white retailers. And some join the Latino immigrants as low-wage workers in light manufacturing and service industries. Los Angeles's Asian immigrant communities contain the full spectrum of classes. Nevertheless, given their tendency to come from PMC backgrounds, they are more likely to congregate in this class, preparing their children to move into it if they themselves have not succeeded in doing so.

The new Asian immigration to Los Angeles is occurring within the context of a rapidly changing global economy. To understand the characteristics of the new immigrants, as well as the role they are playing within the U.S. political economy, one needs to place this immigration in the larger context. Asian immigrants are not only shaped by this context but are themselves shapers of it. They are among the actors who are helping change the face of Los Angeles, the United States, and the world.

References

Aoyama, Yuko. 1989. "Japanese Investment in the United States: The Case of Real Estate Investment in Downtown Los Angeles." Master's thesis, Graduate School of Architecture and Urban Planning, University of California, Los Angeles.

Bell, Linda, and Richard Freeman. 1991. "The Causes of Increasing Interindustry Wage Dispersion in the United States." *Industrial and Labor Relations Review* 44(2):275–287.

Bluestone, Barry, and Bennett Harrison. 1982. *The Deindustrialization of America*. New York: Basic Books.

Bowles, Samuel, David Gordon, and Thomas Weisskopf. 1986. "Power and Profits: The Social Structure of Accumulation and the Profitability of the Postwar U.S. Economy." *Review of Radical Political Economy* 18(1–2):132–167.

Bradshaw, Thornton F., Daniel F. Burton, Jr., Richard N. Cooper, and Robert D. Hormats, eds. 1988. *America's New Competitors: The Challenge of the Newly Industrializing Countries*. Cambridge, Mass.: Ballinger.

Carnoy, Martin, and Henry M. Levin. 1985. *Schooling and Work in the Democratic State*. Stanford: Stanford University Press.

Chan, Sucheng. 1991. *Asian Americans: An Interpretive History*. Boston: Twayne.

Cheng, Lucie, and Edna Bonacich, eds. 1984. *Labor Immigration under Capitalism: Asian Workers in the United States before World War II*. Berkeley: University of California Press.

Cheng, Lucie, and Leslie Evans. 1991. "Transnational Migration and the Formation of an International Professional-Managerial Class." Paper presented at the annual meeting of the American Sociological Association, Cincinnati, August.

Cheng, Lucie, and Ping-chun Hsiung. 1991. "Women, Export-led Growth, and the State: The Case of Taiwan." In *State and Development in the Pacific Rim*, ed. Richard Appelbaum and Jay Henderson, pp. 233–266. Newbury Park, Calif.: Sage.

Cohen, R. B. 1981. "The New International Division of Labor, Multinational Corporations, and Urban Hierarchy." In *Urbanization and Urban Planning in Capitalist Society*, ed. Michael Dear and Allen J. Scott, pp. 287–315. London: Methuen.

Curme, Michael, Barry Hirsch, and David Macpherson. 1990. "Union Membership and Contract Coverage in the United States, 1983–1988." *Industrial and Labor Relations Review* 44(1):5–33.

Davis, Mike. 1987. "Chinatown, Part Two? The 'Internationalization' of Downtown Los Angeles." *New Left Review* 164:65–86.

Deyo, Frederic C. 1989. *Beneath the Miracle: Labor Subordination in the New Asian Industrialism.* Berkeley: University of California Press.

———, ed. 1987. *The Political Economy of the New Asian Industrialism.* Ithaca, N.Y.: Cornell University Press.

Ehrenreich, Barbara, and John Ehrenreich. 1979. "The Professional-Managerial Class." In *Between Labor and Capital*, ed. Pat Walker, pp. 5–45. Boston: South End Press.

Ellwood, David. 1988. *Poor Support: Poverty in the American Family.* New York: Basic Books.

Fawcett, James T., and Benjamin V. Carino, eds. 1987. *Pacific Bridges: The New Immigration from Asia and the Pacific Islands.* Staten Island, N.Y.: Center for Migration Studies.

Feagin, Joe R., and Michael Peter Smith. 1987. "Cities and the New International Division of Labor: An Overview." In *The Capitalist City: Global Restructuring and Community Politics*, ed. Michael Peter Smith and Joe R. Feagin, pp. 3–34. New York: Basil Blackwell.

Foglesong, Richard E., and Joel D. Wolfe, eds. 1989. *The Politics of Economic Adjustment: Pluralism, Corporatism, and Privatization.* New York: Greenwood.

Freeman, Richard, and James Medoff. 1984. *What Do Unions Do?* New York: Basic Books.

Friedmann, John. 1986. "The World City Hypothesis." *Development and Change* 17:69–83.

Fröbel, Folker, Jürgen Heinrichs, and Otto Kreye. 1980. *The New International Division of Labor: Structural Unemployment in Industrialised Countries and Industrialisation in Developing Countries.* Cambridge: Cambridge University Press.

Galenson, Walter, ed. 1985. *Foreign Trade and Investment: Economic Development in the Newly Industrializing Asian Countries.* Madison: University of Wisconsin Press.

Gereffi, Gary, and Donald L. Wyman, eds. 1990. *Manufacturing Miracles: Paths of Industrialization in Latin America and East Asia.* Princeton: Princeton University Press.

Gordon, David, Richard Edwards, and Michael Reich. 1982. *Segmented Work and Divided Workers: The Historical Transformation of Labor in the United States.* Cambridge: Cambridge University Press.

Gordon, Linda W. 1990. "Asian Immigration since World War II." In *Immigration and U.S. Foreign Policy*, ed. Robert W. Tucker, Charles B. Keely, and Linda Wrigley, pp. 169–191. Boulder, Colo.: Westview Press.

Haberfeld, Vitchar, and Yehouda Shenhav. 1990. "Are Women and Blacks Closing the Gap? Salary Discrimination in American Science during the 1970s and 1980s." *Industrial and Labor Relations Review* 44(1):68–82.

Hamilton, Clive. 1983. "Capitalist Industrialization in the Four Little Tigers of East Asia." In *Neo-Marxist Theories of Development*, ed. Peter Limqueco and Bruce McFarlane, pp. 137–180. London: Croom Helm.

Harrison, Bennett, and Barry Bluestone. 1988. *The Great U-Turn: Corporate Restructuring and the Polarizing of America*. New York: Basic Books.

Herz, Diane. 1991. "Worker Displacement Still Common in the Late 1980s." *Monthly Labor Review* (May): 3–9.

Hinojosa-Ojeda, Raul, Martin Carnoy, and Hugh Daly. 1991. "An Even Greater 'U-Turn': Latinos and the New Inequality." In *Hispanics in the Labor Force: Issues and Policies*, ed. Edwin Melendez, Clara Rodriguez, and Janis Barry Figueroa, pp. 25–52. New York: Plenum Press.

Katz, Michael. 1986. *In the Shadow of the Poorhouse: A Social History of Welfare in America*. New York: Basic Books.

Kletzer, Lori. 1991. "Job Displacement, 1979–86: How Blacks Fared Relative to Whites." *Monthly Labor Review* (July): 17–25.

Kolko, Joyce. 1988. *Restructuring the World Economy*. New York: Pantheon.

Kruse, Douglas. 1988. "International Trade and the Labor Market Experience of Displaced Workers." *Industrial and Labor Relations Review* 41(3):402–417.

Light, Ivan, and Edna Bonacich. 1988. *Immigrant Entrepreneurs: Koreans in Los Angeles, 1965–1982*. Berkeley: University of California Press.

Lo, Clarence. 1990. *Small Property versus Big Government: Social Origins of the Property Tax Revolt*. Berkeley: University of California Press.

Lynch, Lisa, and Marcus Sardver. 1987. "Determinants of the Decertification Process: Evidence from Employer-Initiated Elections." *Journal of Labor Research* 8 (Winter) 85–91.

Mangiafico, Luciano. 1988. *Contemporary American Immigrants: Patterns of Filipino, Korean, and Chinese Settlement in the United States*. New York: Praeger.

Mitchell, Daniel. 1980. *Unions, Wages, and Inflation*. Washington, D.C.: Brookings Institution.

Morales, Rebecca, and Paul M. Ong. 1991. "Immigrant Women in Los Angeles." *Economic and Industrial Democracy* 12:65–81.

Morales, Rebecca, Paul M. Ong, and Chris Payne. 1990. "New Entrants into the Los Angeles Economy." In *Transnationale Migranten in der Arbeitswelt*, ed. Jürgen Fijalkowski, pp. 223–250. Berlin: Ed. Sigma Bohn.

Ong, Paul M. 1989. *The Widening Divide: Income Inequality and Poverty in Los Angeles*. Los Angeles: Research Group on the Los Angeles Economy, Graduate School of Architecture and Urban Planning, University of California.

———. 1991. "Race and Post-Displacement Earnings among High-Tech Workers." *Industrial Relations* 30(3):456–468.

Piore, Michael J., and Charles F. Sabel. 1984. *The Second Industrial Divide: Possibilities for Prosperity*. New York: Basic Books.

Portes, Alejandro, and Robert L. Bach. 1985. *Latin Journey: Cuban and Mexican Immigrants in the United States*. Berkeley: University of California Press.

Portes, Alejandro, and Ruben G. Rumbaut. 1990. *Immigrant America: A Portrait*. Berkeley: University of California Press.

Riemers, David M. 1985. "The New Asian Immigrants." In Riemers, *Still the Golden Door: The Third World Comes to America*, pp. 91–121. New York: Columbia University Press.

Sassen, Saskia. 1988. *The Mobility of Labor and Capital: A Study in International Investment and Labor Flow*. Cambridge: Cambridge University Press.

Sears, David, and Jack Citrin. 1982. *Tax Revolt: Something for Nothing in California*. Cambridge: Harvard University Press.

Shor, Ira. 1986. *Culture Wars: School and Society in the Conservative Restoration, 1969–1984*. Boston: Routledge and Kegan Paul.

Soja, Edward W. 1987. "Economic Restructuring and the Internationalization of the Los Angeles Region." In *The Capitalist City: Global Restructuring and Community Politics*, ed. Michael Peter Smith and Joe R. Feagin, pp. 178–198. New York: Basil Blackwell.

Soja, Edward W., Rebecca Morales, and Goetz Wolff. 1983. "Urban Restructuring: An Analysis of Social and Spatial Change in Los Angeles." *Economic Geography* 59:195–230.

Takaki, Ronald T. 1989. *Strangers from a Different Shore: A History of Asian Americans*. Boston: Little, Brown.

U.S. Congress. Joint Economic Committee. 1984. *Fairness and the Reagan Tax Cuts*. Washington, D.C.: Government Printing Office.

U.S. President. 1983, 1991. *Economic Report of the President*. Washington, D.C.: Government Printing Office.

Wachter, Michael, and William H. Carter. 1989. "Norm Shifts in Union Wages: Will 1989 Be a Replay of 1969?" *Brookings Papers on Economic Activities*, no. 2, pp. 233–264.

Weiner, Myron. 1990. "Asian Immigrants and U.S. Foreign Policy." In *Immigration and U.S. Foreign Policy*, ed. Robert W. Tucker, Charles B. Keely, and Linda Wrigley, pp. 192–213. Boulder, Colo.: Westview Press.

Part II
Immigration Patterns

Introduction

Lucie Cheng

Post–World War II immigration from Asia takes place in a period of global restructuring, with the pattern of migration framed by the interaction between the Asian countries and the United States. This interaction is determined by the restructuring and by domestic conditions on both sides of the Pacific Ocean. In this context, large-scale immigration from Asia reemerged after a long period of no or low growth during which racial restrictions thwarted Asians from entering the United States. This new surge of Asian immigration began in the late 1960s and rose sharply throughout the 1970s and 1980s (Figure II.1).

Not only have the numbers increased, but so has the ethnic diversity (Table II.1). The Philippines has replaced China and Japan as the country sending the largest number of immigrants; and Vietnamese, whose presence in the United States was negligible before the 1960s, have become one of the largest Asian immigrant groups. While some older immigrant groups, such as the Japanese, showed very little growth, others, such as Indians and Koreans, increased by leaps and bounds. Chinese, the group with the longest history of immigration, reemerged as the second largest immigrant group during this period. Now they come from various locations on mainland China as well as Taiwan and Hong Kong. This section examines developments in Asia and the United States that have contributed to this flow of people, the pattern of immigration, and the spatial and social distribution of immigrants.

The section begins with a discussion of U.S. immigration policies and their impact on Asian immigration. In Chapter 2, Paul Ong and John Liu consider both global and domestic forces that led to changes in immigration law. Various class and social segments of U.S. society promoted different views on immigration, which were mediated through the larger political economy. The desire to maintain hegemonic status globally against the Soviet

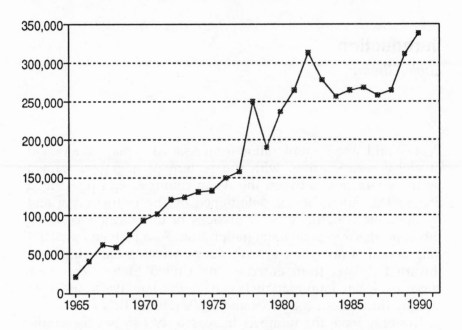

Figure II.1 Asians Admitted to the United States, by Fiscal Year

Union forced the United States to adopt more liberal policies that would bolster its image as leader of the "free world." On the other hand, domestic economic conditions moved the nation to be more restrictive in numbers and more selective in human capital and financial status of potential immigrants. The result was the elimination of racial barriers that had worked against Asian immigration for more than sixty years, the admission of political refugees from civil wars that the United States feared might threaten to tip the balance of power between "communist domination" and the "free world," and an occupational preference system geared to the domestic labor needs of the United States.

Two streams of Asian immigration are evident since 1965: the highly educated professional technical class and unskilled or semiskilled workers. U.S. policies can only partially account for this pattern. The duality is analyzed in Chapter 3 by John Liu and Lucie Cheng. They argue that the same self-interest that led the United States to adopt more liberal immigration policies at

Table II.1. Asian Immigration to the United States,
by Selected Countries

Country	Number of Immigrants[a]		
	1960s	1970s	1980s
China[b]	122,300	250,000	395,400
India	31,200	176,800	231,200
Japan	38,500	47,900	37,500
Korea	35,800	272,000	306,500
Philippines	101,500	360,200	431,500
Vietnam	4,600	179,700	352,600
Total	333,900	1,286,600	1,754,700

Source: U.S. Bureau of the Census, *Statistical Abstract of the United States, 1992* (Washington, D.C.: Government Printing Office, 1992).

[a]Numbers are rounded to the nearest hundred.
[b]China includes People's Republic of China, Taiwan, and Hong Kong.

home moved it to become deeply involved in the affairs of Asian countries. This process was partly responsible for the creation of two pools of potential emigrants.

U.S. military and political involvement in Asia and selected but significant financial aid created a favorable environment for some Asian countries, such as Taiwan, South Korea, and the Philippines, to pursue a development strategy that fully integrated them into the restructuring capitalist world economy. A sizable middle class emerged to serve this expanded economy. Having been trained in a system highly articulated with that of the United States and reared in a rapidly changing culture penetrated by Western values, the middle class, particularly the highly educated, acquired technical knowledge and professional attitudes that defy national boundaries and assimilated a capitalist ideology that emphasizes the pursuit of individualistic goals.

The extended international personal networks that they built in the course of work often provided them with the means to move across the Pacific.

The myriad ties between the United States and Asia also allowed for the renewal of substantial unskilled and semiskilled Asian immigration. Regional wars produced huge numbers of homeless children and caused groups of people such as the Hmong, who fought with U.S.-supported forces, to become refugees. They and women who married U.S. servicemen formed a large potential pool of unskilled and semiskilled immigrants. Domestic political instability in Asia and better economic opportunity in the United States spurred additional emigration and, facilitated by the family unification principle of the U.S. Immigration Act, resulted in chain migration from Asia.

What impact does the new Asian immigration have on U.S. society? How do old residents and new immigrants relate to each other? Chapter 4 attempts to answer these and other questions through a careful analysis of the Asian American population in Los Angeles, where most Asian immigrants are concentrated. Using both published and unpublished quantitative data, Paul Ong and Tania Azores focus on demographic, economic, and settlement patterns.

The new Asian immigration has diversified the existing Asian American population by ethnicity and class, changed its age and sex composition, and reversed the numerical dominance of the native born. Increased cultural diversity, while greatly enriching the Los Angeles metropolis, has created new barriers to the formation of a pan–Asian American identity, a subject that is discussed later in the volume.

The dual streams of Asian immigration noted in Chapter 3 are treated in Chapter 4 in terms of economic diversity and class polarization. Ong and Azores point out that not all professionally trained Asian immigrants have successfully transferred their skills into commensurate employment; even for those who have, their average compensation lags behind that of their Anglo counterparts. Migration often means downward mobility, and the "glass ceiling" keeps the Asian American professional down. At the other end of the economic scale are the still larger number of unskilled and semiskilled immigrants whose choices are limited to unemployment or low-wage jobs. Many Asian immigrants try to forestall the glass ceiling effect and inadequate job compensation by self-employment. But here Ong and Azores reveal a depressing picture. Asian entrepreneurs are concentrated in small business and in the most competitive and volatile niches of the economy. Entrepreneurship has not been a panacea for immigrant employment problems.

Race continues to be a factor in residential settlement patterns of Asian Americans. It is less salient as an external constraint but operates through personal preferences of the new immigrants. Asians are victims of racism, both as perpetrators and as targets. Ong and Azores found that, given the same economic ability, Asians preferred to live in Asian and Anglo neighborhoods, while avoiding African American communities. The authors discuss the political and social implications of this geographic configuration.

As the metropolitan area with the largest number of Asian Americans, Los Angeles faces tremendous challenges and at the same time has the opportunity to be a forefront for positive social change. Ong and Azores provide an analysis to help us explore strategies of economic and political empowerment to bring about that change.

2. U.S. Immigration Policies and Asian Migration

Paul Ong and John M. Liu

In the fifty years preceding the landmark 1965 Immigration Act, Europe was the main origin of people permanently settling in the United States. After 1965, Asia became a major source of immigration. Constituting less than 4 percent of total U.S. immigration between 1921 and 1960, Asians comprised 35 percent of legal immigration from 1971 to 1980 and 42 percent from 1981 to 1989 (Bouvier and Gardner, 1986, 8, 17; Papademetriou, 1991, 48). From 1971 to 1989, more than four million Asians immigrated to the United States, primarily from China (including Hong Kong and Taiwan), India, Korea, the Philippines, and Vietnam.

Understanding the larger societal changes that produced this radical immigration shift is not simple. Disparate forces, opposing ideologies, and conflicting political-economic objectives have prevented the formulation of a logically coherent set of policies. The laws that were enacted were the products of compromise among competing goals articulated by various segments of U.S. society, divided along class and social lines. The United States has never had a consensus regarding immigration. For instance, opinion polls consistently show public opposition to expanding immigration, yet legislation often disregards this sentiment (Morris, 1985). Even when there has been a consensus, the high degree of uncertainty over the consequences of any law or regulation has compounded the difficulty of devising policies that optimally realize any given underlying goal. Often the unanticipated outcomes have differed greatly from the ones intended.

Despite the complexity and uncertainties, it is possible to detect the logic of U.S. immigration policy formation within the larger political economy. U.S. immigration policy objectives have fluctuated because the factors shaping both racial and labor issues have changed continuously. In the post–World War II era, global and domestic forces moved the nation toward liberalizing its immigration laws. Internally, the civil rights movement made state-supported racism less tenable than before. While this movement fought for the extension of political rights and later economic rights, the attack on de jure discrimination logically extended to the immigration arena. It would have been inconsistent and dangerous to allow racism to persist in the immigration laws.

Global forces were perhaps even more important than domestic ones. As the United States became inextricably drawn into the world system, it adopted policies intended to legitimize and protect its hegemony against the Soviet Union in an increasingly integrated but restive world. In terms of immigration, this meant formulating policies that preserved U.S. dominance and promoted its image as leader of the "free world," while maintaining the right to set numerical limits. Eliminating racial barriers, accepting large numbers of political refugees, and encouraging the immigration of highly educated individuals under a preferred occupational category were policies that arose from these strategic concerns.

After 1965, changing economic and political conditions led to several revisions that affected immigration from Asia. Declining job opportunities and lobbying by special interest groups brought about a restriction of occupational immigration in 1976. Economic forces later worked to loosen immigration constraints. In the face of a severe shortage of highly educated labor in the late 1980s, the Immigration Nursing Relief Act of 1989 and the Immigration Act of 1990 again turned to foreign sources to address the country's labor and economic shortfalls by providing special preference to immigrants that met requisite human and financial capital standards.

The Dismantling of Racial Restrictions

In the last one hundred years, U.S. immigration laws have treated Asians equivocally. No group encountered more discriminatory immigration legislation than Asians in the pre–World War II period (Konvitz, 1946). Yet beginning during the war and continuing through the postwar period, a sudden and extraordinary reversal occurred as Asians became a major beneficiary of revised immigration policies.

Congress first levied restrictions against Asians in the Chinese Exclusion Act of 1882. Before the 1880s, the United States loosely regulated the number and types of people permitted to enter the country. Capitalists generally supported the unrestricted migration of able-bodied labor, especially after the Civil War, when the United States began an industrial ascendancy that would make it the leading industrial power by the turn of the century (Calavita, 1984). A newly emerging organized labor movement opposed capitalist support of unfettered immigration and was a major force in obtaining passage of the Exclusion Act, which prohibited the admission of unskilled Chinese workers (Saxton, 1971).

Nearly all subsequent immigration legislation regarding Asians in the pre–World War II period either iterated or extended the racial exclusions first inflicted on the Chinese. The Gentlemen's Agreement of 1907–1908 cast Japanese and Koreans into this exclusionary net, and the 1917 Immigration Act denied entry to Asian Indians. A provision in the 1924 Immigration Act reaffirmed these prohibitions by banning the admission of persons ineligible for citizenship, a category that included all Chinese, Japanese, Koreans, and Asian Indians. The Tydings-McDuffie Act in 1934 added Filipinos to the list of excludables. Although the primary purpose of this legislation was to grant independence to the Philippines by 1946, it also declared Filipinos to be aliens and limited their immigration to fifty persons per year.

Given this history, a waning of racial discrimination in World War II and its aftermath seemed unlikely, but fundamental internal and international changes chipped away at the racial hierarchy. Domestically, wartime exigencies required the hiring of nonwhites in industries previously closed to them. Expanded minority participation in industry and in the military unleashed demands for greater equity, a process encouraged by the federal government. In 1941, President Franklin Roosevelt signed Executive Order 8802, ending employment discrimination in defense industries and federal agencies.

International acceptance of the United States as wartime leader of the free world added pressure to abolish all racially discriminatory policies and to adopt immigration policies congruous with democracy's fight against fascism. President Roosevelt and his administration saw repeal of racially proscriptive laws as a particularly vital step in refuting Japanese propaganda condemning the United States for its anti-Asian immigration policies.

Ironically, the easing of bias against Asian immigration coincided with the United States' most devastating anti-Asian action, the incarceration of nearly one hundred ten thousand U.S. residents and citizens of Japanese descent in 1942. The following year, the discriminatory immigration walls began to crack with the lifting of restrictions against the Chinese, a wartime ally (Riggs, 1950). This time, organized labor no longer uniformly or adamantly fought for continued Chinese exclusion. Though the American Federation of Labor (AFL) favored the status quo, the Congress for Industrial Organization (CIO) advocated strongly for its termination. Roosevelt placated domestic fears by noting that the repeal of exclusion gave China an annual quota of only 105 persons. In exchange, the nation would gain an important symbolic victory in the international arena.

Quotas based on national origins persisted as a problem after the war. Emergence as a global power mandated additional social change if the United States was to preserve its international image and leadership. Decolonization, rising nationalism in Third World nations, and Communist expansion forced the nation to broaden the bases of its legitimacy. Its dominance as a world leader depended on more than possessing the most powerful military. The ability of the United States to enhance its political position hinged also on the eradication of the most blatant forms of racism, which many Asian and African countries regarded as an abominable colonial legacy. The Truman administration maintained, for example, that "the Chinese Communists will continue to exploit the xenophobia latent in most of Southeastern Asia for decades, implanted there in some part by the Oriental exclusion features of past American immigration law" (U.S. Congress, House, President's Commission on Immigration and Naturalization, 1952, 52).

Presidential urging alone was insufficient to eliminate racial inequality. Previous presidents had worried about the international repercussions of exclusionary immigration laws (Coolidge, 1909; Neu, 1967), but domestic racism generally had prevailed over foreign affairs. The anti-Chinese movement had forced President Rutherford Hayes to renegotiate the 1868 Burlingame Treaty with China to create a legal foundation for passage of the Chinese Exclusion Act. Two decades later, the anti-Japanese movement pushed President Theodore Roosevelt to negotiate the Gentlemen's Agreement with Japan. In the post–World War II period, a new global role meant the United States could no longer afford the international cost of domestic racism. Congress soon repealed remaining constraints on immigration from India, the Philippines, Korea, and Japan.

These changes were possible because domestic racism was not as rabid as before. Economic growth in the postwar period allowed minorities to make political and economic gains that did not threaten whites. Employment and income advances translated into political improvements as racial minorities struggled for their civil rights, culminating in the passage of the 1964 Civil Rights Act and the 1965 Voting Rights Act (Burstein, 1985). The drive for racial justice created a sociopolitical context conducive to the obliteration of de jure discrimination in immigration laws.

Another important domestic development was the convergence of interests between capital and labor. Expanding productive activities placed capital in the forefront of promoting U.S. hegemony. Unlike the case in the pre–World War II period, organized labor now shared this national goal. Labor bolstered the status of the United States as a world leader by exporting its own brand of unionism to developing countries. At home the major unions relaxed their insistence on racial exclusion in immigration and later supported the end of racial quotas, a position compatible with their pro–civil rights stance. Nevertheless, labor refused to abandon its position that numerical limits were a necessary safeguard to keep immigration in line with the economy's absorptive capacity.

A coalescence of these diverse forces formed the background for the enactment of the new basic immigration law in 1952. Congress readily discarded the concept of Nordic superiority used to justify the discriminatory elements of the 1924 act. It canceled the general interdiction toward Asian immigration, thus completing the piecemeal repeals of earlier years (U.S. Congress, Senate, Committee on the Judiciary, 1950, 455, 458). Yet it was still unwilling to eliminate completely ethnic and racially biased quotas. Instead of placing Asians on an equal footing with other immigrants, Congress devised the Asia-Pacific Triangle, which roughly comprised all Asian countries from India to Japan and the Pacific Islands north of Australia and New Zealand. Nations falling within this area received an annual quota of only one hundred, with a ceiling of two thousand for the entire region. Any person at least one-half Asian by ancestry would be charged against this Asian quota, even if that individual had been born in a nation outside the triangle. The determination of quota chargeability by blood rather than country of birth applied only to Asians.

Key members of Congress justified retaining the regional limitation because the act was more generous to Asians than was the national-origins formula used in the 1924 Immigration Act (Bennett, 1963). This contention was undeniably true, since there were no quotas for Asian nations in the 1924 act! Congress's argument additionally ignored the racial bias inherent in using the census to calculate the annual national-origin quotas. Because of earlier anti-Asian legislation, the Asian population was minuscule. Use of the census as the basis for national quotas merely perpetuated past discrimination toward Asians.

President Truman vetoed the 1952 Immigration Act, but Congress overrode him. In his veto message, Truman stated tersely that unjust treatment of Asians in the new law would damage foreign policy by hampering "the efforts we are making to rally the men of the east and west alike to the cause of freedom" (U.S. Congress, House, President's Commission on Immigration and Naturalization, 1952, 276). In spite of Truman's concerns, the removal of biased quotas had to wait for more than another decade. As with civil rights legislation, progress was slow.

In the decade following the 1952 enactment, U.S. immigration law became a statutory maze as Congress haphazardly added amendments, primarily in relation to the admission of political refugees. In the early 1960s, both the executive branch and Congress initiated efforts to rationalize the 1952 act.

A concerted effort to abrogate all remaining discriminatory immigration laws and regulations emerged in the 1960 presidential election. The Democratic Party opposed the use of the 1920 national-origin quotas in its national party platform, a position John Kennedy, the Democratic candidate, actively supported throughout the campaign (Bennett, 1963, 265). On assuming power, Kennedy, and later Lyndon Johnson, worked to expunge all extant prejudicial provisions.

In contrast to the case in earlier decades, little organized resistance developed (Reimers, 1985, 67–69). Three factors explain the absence of a strong opposition. One was a favorable economic environment. The United States was in the midst of its longest sustained economic expansion. Unemployment in 1965 stood at 4.5 percent and was reaching the full-employment level. A second factor was the success of the civil rights movement. The struggle for voting and employment equality and the drive to end discriminatory immigration laws were mutually reinforcing. Finally, the perception that abolition of the Asia-Pacific Triangle was unlikely to lead to a huge ingress of Asians eased the fears of many interest groups. This combination of factors led to the 1965 Immigration Act, which overhauled previous immigration legislation, including removal of the national-origins quotas and the Asia-Pacific Triangle concept. The act brought an end to systematic discrimination against Asian immigrants.

The 1965 law reorganized the immigration system to favor family reunification in two ways. First, it instituted a new preference system that eventually allocated 80 percent of available visas to extended family relatives of U.S. citizens and to immediate family members of permanent residents. Second, it extended nonquota status to the parents of U.S. citizens, exempting them from any numerical limitations, a privilege already enjoyed by spouses and children of U.S. citizens.

Initially, the preference system applied only to the Eastern Hemisphere, that is, all countries and colonies other than those in the Caribbean and North and South America. Each nation had a maximum annual quota of 20,000 persons. In 1971, legislation removed all hemispheric distinctions to establish a single world-wide ceiling of 290,000 people. A reduction to 270,000 occurred in 1980 (Levine, Hill, and Warren, 1985, 20). These revisions placed Asians on an equal footing with immigrants from the Americas. Most of the parties concerned with immigration is-sues—the administration, Congress, and organizations favoring or fearing the nullification of racial bias—believed the new pref-erence system would not result in large-scale immigration from Asia (Reimers, 1985, 75–77).

Despite perceptions at the time of passage, Asians gained much from the 1965 Immigration Act. Whereas they accounted for less than 7 percent of total immigration in 1965, their share increased to nearly 25 percent five years later. By the mid-1970s, Asians constituted well over one-third of all immigrants. In the first decade after the 1965 act, Asians entered primarily under the family reunification provisions, with a sizable number also admitted through occupational preferences (discussed in the next section).

The admission of refugees substantially increased the number of Asians during the late 1970s and early 1980s. Growing in-volvement, especially military involvement, by the United States in Third World nations such as Vietnam had produced new po-tential sources of immigration. With the fall of its political allies in the mid-1970s, the United States accepted thousands of Southeast Asian refugees, for both political and humanitarian reasons.[1] Asians, who were only 9 percent of the nearly 213,000 refugees in the 1960s, comprised 39 percent of 539,000 refugees in the 1970s. From 1981 to 1988, 70 percent of the 867,000 refu-gees came from Asia. The combined effect of family reunifica-tion, occupational entries, and refugees was to push the Asian share of total immigration to greater than 43 percent between 1975 and 1984 (U.S. Immigration and Naturalization Service, 1987, vii).

By 1989, however, the Asian share of legal immigration had dipped to 29 percent because of the increase of Latino immigra-tion following passage of the 1986 Immigration Reform and Con-trol Act (IRCA). IRCA attempted to control undocumented immi-gration by imposing sanctions on employers who continued to hire illegal migrant workers. It additionally offered amnesty to undocumented migrants who either had lived in the United States a specified amount of time or had worked as agricultural laborers. Of the nearly three million people applying for amnesty, the overwhelming majority was of Mexican ancestry. Only about 5 percent of the applicants were Asians (Bean, Vernez, and Keely, 1989, 69). Still, Asian immigration in absolute terms remained extremely high, totaling more than a quarter million per fiscal year during the latter half of the 1980s.

The Development of Occupational Preferences

The economic objectives and the political conflicts that arose over them are nowhere more apparent than in the debates surrounding the use of occupational preferences in the immigration laws. Because of the occupational quotas in the 1965 act, a major feature of contemporary migration has been the movement of professionals and other highly trained Asians to the United States. The origin of occupational preferences dates from the 1924 Immigration Act, which allocated the first 50 percent of visas to certain relatives of U.S. citizens, to skilled agricultural workers, and to the dependents of both groups. Inclusion of skilled workers resulted from the shortage of laborers in U.S. agriculture during the early 1920s. Thereafter, the use of occupational preferences was a permanent feature of U.S. immigration law.

After World War II, Congress redefined the occupational preference to favor individuals in technical fields such as engineering, science, and health. The desire for highly skilled labor reflected the growing technological complexity in production. Work became more fragmented and specialized, encouraging the emergence of a large, technologically based and university-trained professional class. Military and industrial considerations also induced a shift in occupational needs.

The United States faced a potential shortage of manpower, a condition the Joint Congressional Committee on Atomic Energy believed would allow the Soviet Union to surpass the United States in military technology (U.S. Congress, Joint Committee on

Atomic Energy, 1956, iii). There was reason for concern. In the mid-1950s, the United States fell behind the USSR in the number of students graduating in scientific and engineering fields (U.S. Congress, Joint Committee on Atomic Energy, 1956, 483). For many, the launching of Sputnik in 1957 was a sign of Soviet scientific superiority. The immediate U.S. response was to focus on improving its educational system. Immigration clearly had a central role in the long-range effort to catch the Soviets. The contributions of foreign scientists to the construction of the atomic bomb and later to the development of rocketry proved that highly educated immigrants were crucial to building a technological lead in military weapons.

Industry shared the need for highly educated labor. Reinforced by the founding of engineering departments at prestigious universities, formally educated engineers gained prominence as an essential component for continued industrial growth (Ahlstrom, 1982). The major problem facing industry in the first two decades of the postwar period was the scarcity of engineering personnel in the face of rising demand. A similar problem existed in the health field. The proliferation of private health insurance and the establishment of public health coverage generated an enormous demand for health practitioners.

An early attempt to fulfill these emerging needs through immigration came with passage of the Displaced Persons Act of 1948. Scientists and people with specialized technical skills were among the groups receiving the first 30 percent of visas allocated under the act (Hutchinson, 1981, 497). When Congress revamped the 1924 Immigration Act in 1952, it again gave first preference to the highly educated. In hearings conducted over the bill, officials from the Immigration and Naturalization Service proposed giving preferential treatment to persons who "would be of most value to the United States," because "industrial expansion would be facilitated if desirable specialists could be obtained from oversubscribed countries" (U.S. Congress, Senate, Committee on the Judiciary, 1950, 450–451). Although President Truman disagreed strongly with other provisions of the bill, he concurred with the request for skilled labor. His commission on immigration stated that the law "should encourage entry in the United States of persons whose skills, aptitudes, knowledge or experience are necessary or desirable for our economy, culture, defense, or security" (U.S. Congress, House, President's Commission on Immigration and Naturalization, 1952, 119–120).

One subcommittee recommended giving 30 percent of the quota and first preferential status to aliens and their families "whose services are urgently needed in the United States" (U.S. Congress, House, President's Commission on Immigration and Naturalization, 1952, 457). The final bill later raised this figure to 50 percent, with skilled workers defined as persons possessing "education, technical training, specialized experience, or exceptional ability" (Bennett, 1963, 141). In practice, scientists, engineers, and health practitioners dominated the list of qualified occupations. The 1952 act also left the door open for the admission of less skilled persons through a lower, nonpreference category, which received any unused quotas. These individuals could enter only when the Department of Labor certified that they were not taking jobs from U.S. workers.

Despite the favorable status accorded professionals and the highly educated, they comprised less than 6 percent of quota immigrants and only 2 percent of total immigration from 1954 to 1964. The United States failed to attract the targeted group of highly educated Europeans, because Europe enjoyed an economic boom in the postwar period, a prosperity ironically underwritten by the U.S. Marshall Plan. Since preferential treatment of the highly skilled and the highly educated continued to be oriented toward Europe and other developed nations, the numerical objectives established in the law represented what the United States desired rather than what was attainable. Continued low utilization of this category by Europeans led the National Commission for Manpower Policy to conclude that the labor certification program was largely ineffective (U.S. National Commission for Manpower Policy, 1978, 33, 56).

Although the 1952 act yielded little in the way of immediate results, it did have a delayed effect on the migration of highly educated labor. The law facilitated the admission of exchange students from developing countries who came here to acquire the technical skills necessary for economic growth in their home nations. When these students returned home, they brought back with them Western technical skills as well as the English language and U.S. values. Acquisition of these skills and cultural attributes created an international pool of highly educated labor that was, and is, highly substitutable. Possession of these qualities underlaid the future migration and integration of highly educated foreign workers into the U.S. economy.

Efforts to rewrite the immigration laws in the early 1960s led again to debates over the treatment of the highly educated. President Kennedy's administration favored retaining, as a first preference, half the quotas for "persons with special skills, training, or education advantageous to the United States." The Johnson administration kept this recommendation when it resumed negotiations around revising the law (Reimers, 1985, 66, 72). Congressional proposals differed from that of the executive. They sought to reserve 30 percent of the quota for occupational immigrants. The final bill retained only 20 percent of the quota for these workers because of the extreme underutilization of the 1952 provisions for qualified professionals and because of efforts to minimize changes in the ethnic composition of future immigration.

The 1965 act downgraded preferential treatment of highly educated persons by equally dividing the 20 percent of visas into a third and sixth preference. More than 20 percent could enter if quotas under the family preferences went unused. The third preference applied to qualified professionals. Individuals eligible for this preference required the sponsorship of neither a relative nor an employer because they held occupations on the Department of Labor's Schedule A, a list of jobs for which qualified U.S. workers were hard to find. Before the mid-1970s, the list included three groups: those with advanced degrees in particular fields, including the scientific fields; those with a bachelor's degree in eighteen academic specializations, primarily in engineering and the health fields; and the clergy. The sixth preference pertained to other skilled and unskilled workers employed in jobs where there was a domestic labor shortage.

Even with the downgrading of occupational preferences, there was an ironical increase in the total flows of the highly educated. The elimination of racial barriers combined with the continuation of occupation preferences, albeit at only 20 percent of the allocated quotas, created a window of opportunity for highly educated Asians and enabled the United States to reach its goal of acquiring needed workers through immigration. The potential for large-scale movement of highly educated Asians was considerable.

A ready pool of labor had already developed through the educational exchange programs discussed earlier. In the decades after World War II, the number of South and East Asian foreign students in U.S. colleges and universities grew impressively, from 10,000 in the mid-1950s to about 142,000 in the mid-1980s, with a disproportionate share studying in the technical fields (Institute of International Education, various years). The potential pool of immigrants expanded with the global spread of academic programs based on Western, primarily U.S., curricula. As foreign graduate students returned to professorships in their home countries, they introduced Western material and technology into their educational systems (Portes and Walton, 1981). Many Asian nations embraced Western-oriented systems of higher education to achieve international prestige and to reinforce internal class distinctions.

A second condition that prompted migration of highly educated Asians was an international disparity in the rewards to labor. Greater availability of high wages and professional opportunities in the United States than in the periphery provided material incentives for Asians to migrate. The discrepancy in rewards between Asia and the United States was not entirely due to happenstance. It was a historical product of the unequal relationship between developed and developing nations within the world system. The willingness of U.S. firms to hire highly educated immigrants provided the "pull." The fact that Asians who found employment as engineers experienced no discernible wage discrimination is one indication of how well the U.S. economy absorbed Asian professionals (Finn, 1985). Even among those unable to practice their profession, the benefits of working in a less prestigious job provided enough incentive for many to relocate in the United States.

The corresponding "push" arose from the inability of Asian countries to absorb their highly educated persons. Many sending Asian countries adopted an economic strategy—export-driven industrialization—that relied on labor-intensive economic development with minimal opportunities for highly educated labor. Even when developing countries pursued technical training as a developmental strategy, human resources often became available before they could be fully used by the economy.

With the relaxation of racial barriers, a significant migration of highly educated Asians began almost immediately after the enactment of the 1965 act. Many Asian physicians, nurses, engineers, and scientists entered without first obtaining individual clearance from the Department of Labor because their occupations were on Schedule A. Not all highly educated Asians came directly as immigrants. Nurses frequently entered the United States first as nonimmigrants on temporary visas, while engineers and scientists were often students. Once in the country, many readjusted their legal status to permanent residency.

The post-1965 entry procedures had a stunning impact on the size and ethnic composition of highly educated workers in the United States. In 1964, out of 5,762 immigrant scientists and engineers, only 14 percent came from Asia (National Science Foundation, 1972, 26). By 1970, the absolute number had increased to 13,337, with Asians comprising 62 percent of the total (National Science Foundation, 1972, 3). The increase among Asian immigrants was more than eightfold, while migration from the rest of the world remained stable. A similar change occurred in medicine. Of the 2,012 foreign medical graduates (FMGs) entering as permanent residents in 1965, 10 percent came from Asia, compared to 28 percent from Europe and 42 percent from North and Central America. FMGs admitted as permanent residents more than tripled to 7,144 by 1972, with Asians accounting for 70 percent of the total FMG population and just under one-quarter of all physicians available to enter the labor market (Interstudy, 1974, 660; Lee, 1975, 408–409). Among nurses, Asians accounted for 327 of the 3,430 immigrants in 1966. Nine years later, 4,183 of the 6,131 immigrant nurses were from Asia (U.S. Immigration and Naturalization Service, 1991).

Although these increases were sharp, the 20 percent allocation reserved for the third and sixth preferences still constrained the movement of highly educated Asians. Unlike their European counterparts, Asians overused the two occupational preferences. From 1965 to 1976, nearly 30 percent of the Asian immigrants, representing more than 185,000 persons, entered as occupational immigrants.

Economic Restructuring and Policy Revisions

The economic restructuring discussed in Chapter 1 had a noticeable though inconsistent impact on immigration policies. Changes that centered on occupational preferences most overtly reflected the shifts in economic trends. Just as broader societal developments engendered interests that moved in diverse directions, immigration policies swung like a pendulum, first toward greater restriction and then toward relative relaxation.

Beginning in the early 1970s, the immigration of highly educated Asians diminished. In part, this downturn was due to greater reliance on family reunification preferences, which cut into the number of unused quotas that could be reassigned to the occupational categories. There was also an economic factor: declining job opportunities and increasing global competition. In the early 1970s, the United States underwent a period of protracted economic stagnation. The annual unemployment rate, which stood at 4.5 percent in 1965, climbed to 8.5 percent in 1975. By the 1982 recession, unemployment peaked at 9.7 percent, the highest level since the Great Depression. Average wages and salaries remained correspondingly stagnant, although some workers suffered more than others (Harrison and Bluestone, 1988).

The economic stagnation of the 1970s combined with the slowdown in military spending after the end of the Vietnam War to affect adversely the industries that employed highly educated workers. The High Technology Recruitment Index, which measures the demand for scientists and engineers, hit two deep troughs in 1971 and 1975 (*Manpower Comments*, 1987, 1). This period saw a noticeable decrease in the number of engineers who immigrated to the United States. Depressed economic conditions undermined the desirability of high levels of immigration and augmented efforts to modify the immigration laws.

Concurrently, efforts were made to rewrite the regulations

governing highly educated persons. Congress amended the 1965 Immigration Act in 1976 to tighten entry requirements for third-preference professionals. The 1976 amendment required professionals to have "prearranged employment in order to acquire third preference status." Moreover, it was now the employer's responsibility to show that U.S. workers were negatively unaffected before a third-preference applicant could receive a labor certificate (Bodin, 1977, 39–41; Yochum and Agarwal, 1988, 266–67). These legislative changes, together with administrative rulings that drastically reduced the occupations receiving blanket certification, considerably slowed the entry of professionals. By the late 1970s, only dieticians with an advanced degree, physical therapists with a bachelor's degree, and those with exceptional abilities in the sciences still received blanket certification.

The Health Professions Educational Assistance Act of 1976 added qualitative barriers to the 1965 act. To gain admission as medical professionals, alien physicians and surgeons first had to pass the National Board of Medical Examiners' Examination or its equivalent, the Visa Qualifying Exam. They needed also to demonstrate a competency in oral and written English. The joint effect of the 1976 amendment and the Health Professions Act was to reduce significantly the total applications for labor certificates, from 24,857 in 1976 to 9,581 two years later. Over the next four years, applications never exceeded 65 percent of the peak year total in 1976 (Yochum and Agarwal, 1988, 270).

Nowhere was the role of interest groups more apparent than in medicine, where the number of FMGs had grown remarkably since the 1965 act. Asian FMGs represented one-fifth of all practicing physicians as well as one-third of the interns and residents in graduate training programs by the mid-1970s (Stevens, Goodman, and Mick, 1978, 1). Their sizable presence inevitably raised the issue of whether the United Stated required any more FMGS.

The U.S. Department of Health, Education, and Welfare (HEW) argued for continued use of FMGs (Fink, 1976, 2261–2265; Weinberger, 1975, 308–325). It contended that any growth in the output capacity of health professional schools ran the danger of producing a glut of physicians. From the government's perspective, FMGs offered more flexible control over the supply of physicians than did the continued expansion of medical schools (Interstudy, 1974).

The medical profession, working through its various associations, publications, and membership in public and quasi-public organizations, strove to convince Congress that there was no longer a doctor shortage. It argued that the supply of U.S. medical graduates (USMGs) more than adequately met the health needs of the U.S. public, especially if the federal government financed the opening of new medical schools (de Vise, 1974; Interstudy, 1974; U.S. Department of Health, Education, and Welfare, 1975, 5467–5468). Physician lobbyists acknowledged that certain geographic areas faced a shortage of doctors. They attributed this fact to the uneven regional distribution of U.S. physicians, not to any absolute scarcity of doctors.

The medical profession buttressed its position with two additional arguments. It contended that contrary to the original intent of the 1965 act, preferential treatment of FMGs contributed to the "brain drain" of developing nations. This position mirrored the accusation of some developing countries that easy entry into the United States robbed those nations of potentially valuable talent and of resources already invested in the training of non-returning doctors. A second tack questioned the care provided by FMGs because of their high failure rates on the Educational Council for Foreign Medical Graduates exam and the Federal Licensure Examination.

The medical profession carried the day when it persuaded Congress to declare in the 1976 Health Professions Educational Act that a shortage of physicians no longer existed. This proclamation disqualified foreign doctors from the Department of Labor's list of needed occupations (Schedule A). Of course, curtailing the inflow of FMGs had its cost. Hospitals lacking the financial ability or prestige to attract large numbers of interns, residents, and staff physicians of U.S. citizenry had been a primary employer of FMGs. Yet the American Hospital Association (AHA) did not oppose efforts to have doctors removed from Schedule A or to stiffen entry requirements. Instead, the AHA worked quietly for the inclusion of waivers that ensured hospitals access to FMGs and foreign-trained nurses (Gehrig, 1975, 487–490).

Efforts to obstruct the migration of the highly educated extended to the engineering field in the early 1980s. In 1982, Congress debated a proposed law requiring foreign students to leave the country after graduation for at least two years before applying for admission to the United States (Scully, 1983). Had this regulation passed, it would have seriously interrupted the flow of Asian scientists and engineers by eliminating the possibility of their adjusting from student to permanent resident status. Employers, such as universities and high-tech firms dependent on foreign-born personnel, successfully lobbied against the proposal. The debates continued within the engineering profession. Some citizens pressed their complaints that the "illegal recruitment of foreign engineers poses a significant threat to the employment of U.S. engineers" (Shulman, 1987, 15). The Institute of Electrical and Electronic Engineers argued that if employers used existing workers more efficiently, the apparent shortage of engineers would disappear (Watanabe, 1989).

The tightening of occupational preferences slowed but did not halt the movement of highly educated Asians. A sizable number found alternate modes of entry by coming to the United States as visitors. Once in the country, they looked for firms willing to sponsor them for employment and permanent residency. Through this means, employers traditionally dependent on highly educated immigrant labor, such as electronic, chemical, and pharmaceutical firms, research and development companies, and other businesses requiring advanced degrees, partially avoided critical labor shortages (National Science Foundation, 1986). The other avenue of entry was through the more available family preferences. Highly educated persons entering during the late 1960s and early 1970s became eligible to sponsor relatives, many of whom were also professionals (Liu, Ong, and Rosenstein, 1991; Stevens et al., 1978). Through these various means of entry, professional and technical workers comprised 30 percent of the Asian immigrants who entered during the 1989 fiscal year and reported a prior occupation; Asian immigrants comprised 52 percent of professional and technical workers from throughout the world.

Whereas the economic stagnation of the 1970s produced greater restrictions on immigration, the economic recovery of the late 1980s had the opposite effect. The necessity for and dependence on foreign-born labor persisted even though the United States had overcome many of the macro restructuring problems that appeared in the 1970s. Alarming projections about the growing skills gap in the current and projected U.S. labor pool accompanied the intractable labor shortages. For example, the Hudson Institute, in a report prepared for the Department of Labor, indicated that the U.S. labor force at the turn of the century would be incapable of meeting the rising need for highly skilled, specially trained personnel in the increasingly sophisticated economy (*U.S. Code Congressional and Administrative News,* 1990, 6721).

Existing labor shortages and projections of continued shortages of skilled workers added momentum for passage of new immigration legislation. Because it was unlikely that sufficient U.S. workers could be trained quickly enough to meet legitimate employment needs, organizations such as the President's Council of Economic Advisors advocated assigning immigration a greater role in closing this gap:

> Immigration policy can also contribute to the smooth operation of the U.S. labor market in the 1990s. While continuing the humanitarian principles that have shaped immigration policies in the past, the Federal Government can encourage the immigration of workers with skills important to the economy, both by increasing the number of visas for workers with a job in hand and by increasing quota levels for potential immigrants with higher levels of basic and specific skills. (*U.S. Code Congressional and Administrative News,* 1990, 6721)

Despite the demand for foreign-born labor, the waiting period for immigrants of exceptional ability (third preference) was eighteen months, and applicants in the other employment category (sixth preference) faced a thirty-month wait (*U.S. Code Congressional and Administrative News,* 1990, 6722).

Responding to this situation, Congress initially resorted to piecemeal measures. It approved legislation in 1989 allowing sixteen thousand foreign nurses holding temporary work visas to become permanent residents (*Interpreter Releases,* 1989, 1318). A majority of those who qualified were Asians, primarily Filipinas.

The law also streamlined the process to recruit new temporary foreign nurses and created a visa category (H-1A) for these workers.

The incessant need for highly educated personnel eventually led to a major revision of the immigration laws in the 1990 Immigration Act. This act instituted a new preference system based on three tracks, one each for family-sponsored, employment-based, and diversity immigrants. Highly educated immigrants benefited in several ways. First, segregating the employment-based preferences meant that the availability of occupational visas was no longer directly dependent on the number of people admitted as family immigrants. Second, the act more than doubled the allocated visas for occupational immigrants and their families, from 54,000 to 120,000, with 80,000 for high-level professionals and their families. Members of professions with advanced degrees or aliens of exceptional ability received 40,000 visas, as did skilled and unskilled workers (with a cap of 10,000 for the latter). Congress intended this new track to increase the percentage of employment-based immigrants within the total immigration (*U.S. Code Congressional and Administrative News*, 1990, 6716).

Highly educated persons also could gain admission through the diversity preference track if they came from countries that had sent fewer than 50,000 immigrants in the five years preceding 1990. Although this new track primarily favors immigrants from Europe (up to 40 percent of the initial 55,000 allocated visas in this category were for Ireland), certain Asian nations such as Indonesia and Malaysia are also potential beneficiaries.

Passage of the 1990 act elated employers that had become dependent on immigrant and temporary foreign labor, particularly hospitals, research universities, and high-tech firms. These few sectors of the U.S. economy cannot solely decide the future trajectory of immigration policy, however, as resistance from other interest groups remains formidable. The employment of Asian and other highly educated immigrants still leaves many unanswered questions about economic development in the United States.

While skilled labor was the primary economic target of the

act, the law also eased the entry for capitalists by allocating 10,000 visas to employment-creating investors. This provision has placed the United States in direct competition with other advanced economies, such as Australia and Canada, for Asian capitalists. One group particularly sought after are persons from Hong Kong who are seeking haven before the 1997 political re-absorption of the colony by the People's Republic of China. Al-though family reunification has remained at the heart of the United States's immigration policy, attracting both human and financial capital has resurfaced as a major economic considera-tion in this period of economic restructuring.

Future Prospects

Countervailing forces make it difficult to project the rate of Asian immigration for the rest of the 1990s. For example, we will not likely witness a new wave of Asian refugees to match that of the late 1970s and early 1980s, because the administration is now more concerned with refugees from eastern Europe and the for-mer Soviet Union. On the other hand, some factors encourage continued large-scale Asian immigration. As argued above, highly educated and capital-rich Asians stand to benefit from the 1990 act. The major effect of the relevant provisions will be to alter the composition of the class background of Asian immi-grants rather than to increase the inflow dramatically.

The most potent source of growth lies in another element of the immigration law. Under both the 1965 and 1990 immigration acts, parents, spouses, and children of citizens are exempt from the quota limits. This exemption could lead to a chain immigra-tion that greatly exceeds the limits established under the 1990 Immigration Act. If individuals admitted through the exempted categories become citizens and then sponsor other family mem-bers through the nonquota provisions of the act, the multiplier effect could be quite large. Asian immigrants have been a major utilizer of the exempt categories. For the 1989 fiscal year, 125,000 immigrated from Asia under the quota provisions while another 86,000 gained admission as exempt immediate relatives (U.S. Immigration and Naturalization Service, 1990). Fourteen thousand of the latter were from the People's Republic of China, 15,000 were from Korea, and 11,000 were from India. The number of exempt immediate relatives from the Philippines (about 27,000) nearly equaled the European total of 29,000.

Over time, the use of the immediate-relative avenue of entry is likely to grow. A study by the U.S. General Accounting Office concluded:

> The Asian countries we studied, especially China, exhibited some of the characteristics anticipated to occur during extensive chain migration (for example, a high percentage of naturalized petitioners and relatively short times before the arrival of exempt-immediate relatives). (1988, 61)

Without new restrictions, it is likely that exempted immediate relative immigrants from Asia will outnumber those admitted through the quotas by the end of the century.

The one factor that may stem future Asian immigration is racism. Asians have not escaped the reemergence of overt racial discrimination in the United States. They have been the scapegoats for widespread anti-Japan sentiment and victims of hate crimes (California Attorney General's Asian/Pacific Advisory Committee, 1988; U.S. Commission on Civil Rights, 1986). Fortunately, race has yet to become a prominent issue in the immigration debates. This is not to deny that the narrowing of occupational preferences and the cap on immediate-relative immigration have had a disproportionately adverse impact on Asians. But the executive branch has enforced these restrictions without retracting its policy of eliminating racial barriers to immigration. Nonetheless, rising racial prejudices and hostilities threaten to contaminate the debate over immigration policies. An opinion poll conducted by the Roper organization indicates that most respondents believed that Europeans have on the balance contributed positively to the United States. Under 50 percent held a similar view toward Asians (Roper, 1982). The decade-long congressional debates leading to the enactment of the 1990 act also evidenced uneasiness with the high levels of Asian immigration and a desire to increase immigration from Europe (Bean, Vernez, and Keely, 1989, 101).

Even in an era when defense spending may decline because of the political reforms and revolutions in the former USSR and eastern Europe, there is an enduring sentiment that dependency on highly educated Asians represents a threat in a world where economic competition between the United States and Asian newly industrialized countries (NICS) is intensifying. With economic growth and better research facilities, many Asian NICS are now in a stronger position to retain their highly educated labor and to recruit their compatriots working in the United States (Gittlesohn, 1989). Although return migration to the countries of origin has been small, the returnees possess technological knowledge that will enable the NICS to develop high-tech industries (Watanabe, 1989). If the United States loses more of its technological lead and its ability to control high-tech markets, there will be greater cries for a closing of its borders both to market competition from Asia and to the movement of Asians, particularly the highly educated.

The disquietude with Asian immigration hardly portends a return to the racist policies that existed before World War II. Two decades of Asian immigration have led to the formation of new advocacy groups among the immigrant population. They have become an important part of the political scene, within both the civil rights movement and mainstream electoral politics as voters, politicians, and sources of campaign funds. Asian American political strength helped counter congressional attempts to curtail drastically the family-sponsored preferences that had revitalized the Asian population in the United States. This political muscle also may prevent a renewal of blatant discrimination against Asians. But whether Asian Americans alone can completely contain those interest groups desiring to make U.S. immigration policy Eurocentric again is questionable.

It is unclear how the United States will weigh its competing domestic economic and political interests. Ambiguity about the U.S. role in the evolving global economy adds to the uncertainty about the direction immigration policy will take. Future changes are likely to be protracted processes, particularly if Asian Americans transfer their economic clout to both the domestic and international political arenas.

Note

1. The 1965 act included provisions for political refugees. Passage of the Refugee Act in 1980 removed refugees from the quota system and brought U.S. policy into conformity with the 1967 United Nations Protocol on Refugees. A refugee is defined as "any person who is outside his or her country of nationality and who is unable or unwilling to return to that country because of persecution or a well-founded fear of persecution." The president, in consultation with Congress, annually establishes the number of refugees that the United States will accept from different regions of the world.

References

Ahlstrom, Goran. 1982. *Engineers and Industrial Growth*. London: Croom Helm.

Awasthi, Shri. 1968. *Migration of Indian Engineers, Scientists, Physicians to the United States*. IAMR Report no. 2/1968. New Delhi: Institute of Applied Manpower Research.

Baker, Lyle, and Paul Miller, eds. 1987. *The Economics of Immigration*. Proceedings of a conference at the Australian National University, 22–23 April 1987. Canberra: Australian Government Publishing Service.

Bean, Frank, Georges Vernez, and Charles Keely. 1989. *Opening and Closing the Doors: Evaluating Immigration Reform and Control*. Lanham, Md.: University Press of America.

Bennett, Marion T. 1963. *American Immigration Policies: A History*. Washington, D.C.: Public Affairs Press.

Bhagwati, Jagdish N. 1976. *The Brain Drain and Taxation II: Theory and Empirical Analysis*. Amsterdam: North Holland; New York: American Elsevier.

Bodin, Aaron. 1977. "Labor Certification Programs." In *Tenth Annual Immigration and Naturalization Institute*, ed. Austin Fragomen, pp. 27–43. New York: Practicing Law Institute.

Bouvier, Leon F., and Robert W. Gardner. 1986. "Immigration to the U.S.: The Unfinished Story." *Population Bulletin* 41(4):1–50.

Briggs, Vernon M., Jr. 1984. *Immigration Policy and the American Labor Force*. Baltimore: Johns Hopkins University Press.

Burstein, Paul. 1985. *Discrimination, Jobs, and Politics: The Struggle for Equal Employment Opportunity in the United States since the New Deal*. Chicago: University of Chicago Press.

Calavita, Kitty. 1984. *U.S. Immigration Law and the Control of Labor, 1820–1924.* London: Academic Press.

California Attorney General's Asian/Pacific Advisory Committee. 1988. *Final Report.* Sacramento: Office of the Attorney General.

Coolidge, Mary R. 1909. *Chinese Immigration.* Reprint. New York: Arno Press, 1969.

de Vise, Pierre. 1974. "The Changing Supply of Physicians in California, Illinois, New York, and Ohio: Redistribution of Physicians since 1960 and Projections to 1990." In U.S. Congress, Senate, Committee on Labor and Public Welfare, *Health Manpower, 1974,* Part 2, Hearings before the Senate Committee on Labor and Public Welfare, 93d Cong., 2d sess., pp. 421–448. Washington, D.C.: Government Printing Office.

Engineers Joint Council. 1969. *Foreign-Born and Educated Engineering Manpower in the United States.* New York.

Fink, Paul. 1976. "Memo from E. Fuller Torrey, Presented to the Subcommittee on Health, November 18, 1975." In *Health Manpower Legislation, 1975,* Part 4, Hearings before the Senate Committee on Labor and Public Welfare, 94th Cong., 1st sess., pp. 2261–2265. Washington, D.C.: Government Printing Office.

Finn, Michael. 1985. *Foreign-National Scientists and Engineers in the U.S. Labor Force, 1972–1982.* Oak Ridge, Tenn.: Oak Ridge Associated Universities.

Gehrig, Leo J. 1975. "Statement before the Subcommittee on Health and the Environment, February 21, 1975." In *Health Manpower Programs,* Hearings before the House Committee on Interstate and Foreign Commerce, 94th Cong., 1st sess., pp. 487–499. Washington, D.C.: Government Printing Office.

Ghosh, B. N., and Roma Ghosh. 1982. *Economics of Brain Migration.* New Delhi: Deep and Deep Publications.

Gillette, Robert. 1989. "Threat to Security Cited in Rise of Foreign Engineers." *Los Angeles Times,* 20 January, pp. 8, 14.

Gittlesohn, John. 1989. "Surging Economy Spurs Many Asians to Return Home." *Chronicle of Higher Education,* 15 November, pp. A45–46.

Harper, Elizabeth J. 1979. *Immigration Laws of the United States.* 1978 Supplement. Indianapolis: Bobbs-Merrill.

Harrison, Bennett, and Barry Bluestone. 1988. *The Great U-Turn: Corporate Restructuring and the Polarizing of America.* New York: Basic Books.

Hutchinson, Edward P. 1981. *Legislative History of American Immigration Policy, 1798–1965.* Philadelphia: University of Pennsylvania Press.

Institute for International Education. Various years. *Open Doors: Report on International Exchange.* New York: Institute for International Education.

Interpreter Releases: Report and Analysis of Immigration and Nationality Law. 1989. 66 (4 December): 1316.

Interstudy. 1974. "Information Regarding Foreign Medical Graduates in the United States." In *Health Manpower, 1974,* Part 2, Hearings before the Senate Committee on Labor and Public Welfare, 93d Cong., 2d sess., pp. 648–730. Washington, D.C.: Government Printing Office.

Jasso, Guillermina, and Mark R. Rosenzweig. 1982. "Family Reunification and the Immigration Multiplier: U.S. Immigration Law, Origin-Country Conditions, and the Reproduction of Immigrants." *Demography* 23(3):291–312.

Konvitz, Milton. 1946. *The Alien and the Asiatic in American Law.* Ithaca, N.Y.: Cornell University Press.

Lee, Philip R. 1975. "Statement before the Subcommittee on Health and the Environment, February 20, 1975." In *Health Manpower Programs,* Hearings before the House Committee on Interstate and Foreign Commerce, 94th Cong., 1st sess., pp. 387–430. Washington, D.C.: Government Printing Office.

LeMay, Michael C. 1987. *From Open Door to Dutch Door: An Analysis of U.S. Immigration Policy since 1820.* New York: Praeger.

Levine, Daniel B., Kenneth Hill, and Robert Warren, eds. 1985. *Immigration Statistics: A Story of Neglect.* Washington, D.C.: National Academy Press.

Liu, John M., Paul M. Ong, and Carolyn Rosenstein. 1991. "Dual Chain Migration: Post-1965 Filipino Immigration to the United States." *International Migration Review* 25(3):487–513.

Mann, Arthur. 1979. *The One and the Many: Reflections on the American Identity.* Chicago: University of Chicago Press.

Manpower Comments. April 1987. Washington, D.C.: Scientific Manpower Commission.

Mink, Gwendolyn Rachel. 1982. "The Alien Nation of American Labor: Immigration, Nativism, and the Logic of Labor Politics in the United States, 1870–1925." Ph.D. dissertation, Cornell University, Ithaca, N.Y.

Morris, Milton D. 1985. *Immigration: The Beleaguered Bureaucracy.* Washington, D.C.: Brookings Institution.

National Research Council. 1988. *Foreign and Foreign-Born Engineers in the United States: Infusing Talent, Raising Issues.* Washington, D.C.: National Academy Press.

National Science Foundation. 1972. *Scientists, Engineers, and Physicians from Abroad: Trends through Fiscal Year 1970.* Washington, D.C.: Government Printing Office.

————. 1985. *Immigrant Scientists and Engineers, 1982–84.* Washington, D.C.: Government Printing Office.

————. 1986. "Survey of 300 U.S. Firms Finds One-Half Employ Foreign Scientists and Engineers." *Highlights, Science Resource Studies,* 28 February, pp. 1–4.

Neu, Charles. 1967. *An Uncertain Friendship: Theodore Roosevelt and Japan, 1906–1909.* Cambridge: Harvard University Press.

Niland, John. 1970. *The Asian Engineering Brain Drain.* Lexington, Mass.: Heath Lexington Books.

Papademetriou, Demetrios G. 1991. "Temporary Migration to the United States: Composition, Issues, Policies." Paper presented at the Joint East-West Center and University Research Center of Nihon University Conference, "International Manpower Flows and Foreign Investment in the Asia/Pacific Region," Tokyo, 8–13 September.

Papademetriou, Demetrios G., and Mark J. Miller, eds. 1983. *The Unavoidable Issue: U.S. Immigration Policy in the 1980s.* Philadelphia: Institute for the Study of Human Issues.

Portes, Alejandro, and John Walton. 1981. *Labor, Class, and the International System.* New York: Academic Press.

Reimers, David M. 1985. *Still the Golden Door: The Third World Comes to America.* New York: Columbia University Press.

Riggs, Fred W. 1950. *Pressures on Congress: A Study of the Repeal of Chinese Exclusion.* Reprint. Westport, Conn.: Greenwood Press, 1972.

Roper Public Opinion Research Center. 1982. *A Guide to Roper Center Resources for the Study of American Race Relations.* Storrs, Conn.: The Center.

Rosenberg, Nathan. 1972. *Technology and American Economic Growth.* New York: Harper and Row.

Saxton, Alexander. 1971. *The Indispensable Enemy: Labor and the Anti-Chinese Movement in California.* Berkeley: University of California Press.

Scully, Malcolm G. 1983. "Senate Eases '2 Year' Rule on Foreigners at U.S. Colleges." *Chronicle of Higher Education* 26 (May 25):18.

Shulman, Seth. 1987. "Engineers and Immigration." *Technology Review* 90 (January):15.

Smith, James, and Finis Welch. 1986. *Closing the Gap: Forty Years of Economic Progress for Blacks.* Santa Monica, Calif.: Rand Corporation.

Stevens, Rosemary, Louis W. Goodman, and Stephen S. Mick. 1978. *The Alien Doctors: Foreign Medical Graduates in American Hospitals.* New York: John Wiley and Sons.

U.S. Code Congressional and Administrative News. 1990. "Legislative History of the Immigration Act of 1990." 8:6710–6801.

U.S. Commission on Civil Rights. 1986. *Recent Activities against Citizens and Residents of Asian Descent.* Clearinghouse Publication no. 88. Washington, D.C.: Government Printing Office.

U.S. Congress. House. Committee on Foreign Affairs. 1974. *Brain Drain: A Study of the Persistent Issue of International Scientific Mobility.* Prepared for the Subcommittee on National Security Policy and Scientific Developments. Washington, D.C.: Government Printing Office.

———. Committee on Government Operations. 1968. *The Brain Drain of Scientists, Engineers, and Physicians from the Developing Countries in the United States.* Hearing before a Subcommittee. 90th Cong., 2d sess. Washington, D.C.: Government Printing Office.

———. Committee on the Judiciary. 1977. *Foreign Medical Graduates.* Hearings before the Subcommittee on Immigration, Citizenship, and International Law. 95th Cong., 1st sess. Washington, D.C.: Government Printing Office.

———. President's Commission on Immigration and Naturalization. 1952. Hearings. Washington, D.C.: Government Printing Office.

U.S. Congress. Joint Committee on Atomic Energy. 1956. *Engineering and Scientific Manpower in the United States, Western Europe, and Soviet Russia.* Washington, D.C.: Government Printing Office.

U.S. Congress. Senate. Committee on the Judiciary. 1950. *The Immigration and Naturalization Systems of the United States.* Senate Report 1515. 80th Cong., 1st sess. Washington, D.C.: Government Printing Office.

U.S. Department of Health, Education, and Welfare. 1975. "'H' Manpower Legislative Proposal." *Congressional Record* 121 (March 6): 5467–5468.

U.S. General Accounting Office. 1988. *Immigration: The Future Flow of Legal Immigration to the United States.* Report to the Chairman, Subcommittee on Immigration and Refugee Affairs, Committee on the Judiciary, U.S. Senate. Washington, D.C.: Government Printing Office.

U.S. Immigration and Naturalization Service. 1987, 1989. *Statistical Yearbook of the Immigration and Naturalization Service.* Washington, D.C.: Government Printing Office.

———. 1990. *Immigration Statistics: FY89, Advance Report.* Washington, D.C.: Government Printing Office.

———. 1991. *Immigrants Admitted to the U.S., 1972–1991* [Computer file]. Washington, D.C.: Immigration and Naturalization Service [producer].

U.S. National Commission for Manpower Policy. 1978. *Manpower and Immigration Policies in the United States.* Special Report no. 20. Washington, D.C.

U.S. President. 1989. *The President's Comprehensive Triennial Report on Immigration, 1989.* Washington, D.C.: Government Printing Office.

Watanabe, Teresa. 1989. "Taiwanese 'Brains' Leave U.S.," *Los Angeles Times,* 29 December, pp. A1, A26–27.

Weinberger, Caspar. 1975. "Statement before the Subcommittee on Health and the Environment, February 20, 1975." In *Health Manpower Programs,* Hearings before the House Committee on Interstate and Foreign Commerce, 94th Cong., 1st sess., pp. 308–326. Washington, D.C.: Government Printing Office.

Yochum, Gilbert, and Vinod Agarwal. 1988. "Permanent Labor Certifications for Alien Professionals, 1975–1982." *International Migration Review* 22(2):265–281.

3. Pacific Rim Development and the Duality of Post-1965 Asian Immigration to the United States

John M. Liu and Lucie Cheng

Immigrants to the United States are typically imagined as people with limited education and skills who are fleeing from poverty or civil war. When the immigrants are from Asia, the "boat people" come immediately to mind. While many Asians do indeed fit this image, there is another group of Asian immigrants who are highly educated and possess professional or skilled occupational backgrounds. This second group has given Asian immigration to the United States a dual character and is one of the profound transformations wrought by the policy changes discussed in the previous chapter.

The changes in U.S. policy, however, tell only half the story. Global developments during this period have also had a far-reaching impact on the sending countries. How both the semi-skilled/unskilled and professional immigration streams arose from the seven major Asian sources is the subject of this chapter. We argue that the particular development process of the Pacific Rim after World War II created the conditions for the duality of Asian immigration.

Geopolitical Restructuring in the Post–World War II Period

Before the 1940s, the only region in Asia where the United States had undisputed hegemony was in the Philippines, a U.S. colony since 1898. Japan had rapidly emerged as the preeminent economic and military power in East Asia. Great Britain and France, in the meanwhile, clung precariously to their colonial possessions in South and Southeast Asia. The outbreak of World War II changed this political and economic configuration as U.S. interests extended into areas where they previously had had limited access. India, long regarded by the British as one of the empire's "crown jewels," became increasingly exposed to U.S. influence. In China, the United States assumed a dominant role by intervening in the struggle between the Nationalists and Communists during their shaky united front against the invading Japanese armies. Wartime involvement, in turn, affected the economic and political alignments that took place in the immediate post-war period.

At the conclusion of the war, the United States and the Soviet Union became locked in a contest for political hegemony. This competition led to a series of wars involving both countries but fought in territories that belonged to neither: China (1945–1949), Korea (1950–1953), and Vietnam (1962–1975). The wars ended with a divided China, mostly Communist; a divided Korea, half Communist and half non-Communist; and a first divided then totally Communist Vietnam. The political and economic elites, along with ordinary people, fleeing from this turmoil formed a significant pool of Asian immigrants to the United States. Given its dominant role in the region, the United States was a logical destination in the postwar period.

To safeguard its interests and to prevent the Soviet Union from gaining the upper hand, the United States began laying the foundations for the economic relations that would channel the flow of capital, technology, and people between Asia and itself. It did this by underwriting the reconstruction of selected parts of war-torn Asia. U.S. aid was less extensive and coordinated than it was under the Marshall Plan for Western Europe, but it sufficed to promote recovery in much of non-Communist East Asia.

Japan received significant U.S. financial support during its occupation (1946–1951). Though the governance of occupied Japan was formally the joint responsibility of the Allied powers, in practice the reconstruction was strictly a U.S. affair. The United States assumed a similar responsibility in Korea. U.S. aid to China, a third major recipient, was more narrowly confined to supporting the Nationalists against the Communists.

Two major political events—the establishment of the People's Republic of China in 1949 and the outbreak of the Korean War less than a year later—altered the pattern of U.S. foreign aid. The new pattern more clearly defined the economic connections underlying subsequent Asian immigration to the United States. Communist victory in mainland China deepened U.S. involvement in the affairs of the Chinese Nationalist government on Taiwan. Between 1953 and 1964, the United States injected an average of US$100 million a year into the Taiwanese economy. This sum represented one-third of the Republic of China's capital investments and more than 90 percent of the nation's international balance of payments deficit (Li, 1988, 162). By 1978, Taiwan–United States trade was US$7.39 billion, making the Republic of China the second largest trading partner behind Japan in the Asia-Pacific region and the seventh largest trading partner with the United States worldwide (Li, 1988, 177).

Similarly, the Korean War led the United States to provide greater aid to South Korea. Militarily, the United States expended nearly US$3.5 billion, a sum three times greater than the amount given to any other East Asian nation except Vietnam. In addition, South Korea received 6 percent of all U.S. nonmilitary foreign aid since 1945 (Nemeth and Smith, 1985, 203).

The increases in aid to Taiwan and South Korea coincided with diminishing assistance to Japan. Formation of the People's Republic of China (PRC) and a Communist regime in North Korea led the United States to discard its plans for the radical reform of Japanese policy and society. Instead, the United States concentrated on restoring the Japanese economy as quickly as possible so that Japan would be less susceptible to the appeal of Communism. Full revival of the Japanese economy came with the Korean War, when Japan served as the principal staging area for United Nations activities. The return to economic health meant that the Japanese no longer needed large amounts of U.S. aid and placed Japan in a situation analogous to that of Western Europe. In both regions, relatively quick recoveries resulted in dynamic economies that absorbed the labor capacities of their populations, including those in professional, technical, and kindred (PTK) occupations. That removed a critical structural incentive for highly educated and skilled people to emigrate. As a result, PTK immigration to the United States from Western Europe and Japan has been negligible.

Diversion of U.S. assistance to Taiwan, South Korea, and the Philippines made it possible for their governments to stifle internal dissent and maintain totalitarian rule. It also allowed these nations to pursue an economic development policy that required substantial sacrifice from the populace. The United States strongly supported these actions because, from its perspective, a strong state vis-à-vis domestic groups was imperative to economic development and political stability in the Asian countries. It perceived sustained economic growth and continued political equanimity as the best insurance of continued U.S. supremacy in the region.

Taiwan and South Korea used their tight control over labor to build their manufacturing industries. Both nations effectively employed foreign capital, including economic and military aid, loans, and private investments, to turn their trade deficits into surpluses. U.S. capital was available for foreign ventures because rising domestic labor costs pushed business interests to search for more profitable outlets abroad. To attract these investors, Taiwan and South Korea offered favorable terms of return and facilitated the local recruitment of professionals to work in the transnational corporations. The hiring of locally recruited personnel integrated these professionals into an economic network that required a mobile labor force not bound by national boundaries.

The Philippines was unable to emulate the successes of Taiwan and South Korea, despite its having the firmest political and economic relationship with the United States. Largely because of its colonial relationship with the Philippines, the United States had long-term responsibilities to fulfill. Having long justified its colonization as safeguarding the welfare of the Filipino people, the United States was under both legal and moral obligation to maintain its economic assistance to the country. This special relationship may be one reason for the failure of the Philippines to become a Pacific Basin economic success story.

During the 1960s, when the Marcos regime devised an economic strategy that depended solely on the U.S. war effort in Vietnam, the Philippines enjoyed a high growth rate. The shortsightedness of this approach became apparent when the United States abruptly left Vietnam. Withdrawal of U.S. forces left the

Philippines with an economic infrastructure ill-suited to the needs of the local populace. One example was the development of medical and nursing programs to provide personnel to care for the military and civilian casualties in Vietnam. This health professional educational infrastructure remained unimpaired after the Vietnam conflict and has continued to produce a surplus of physicians and nurses, many of whom seek admission to the United States.

The war in Vietnam also directly and indirectly created new sources of Asian immigration to the United States. Direct migration from Vietnam occurred with the sudden collapse of Thieu's regime in 1975 and involved two different groups. One consisted mainly of professionals and their dependents, many of whom had worked for the U.S. government in Vietnam. The other group comprised the so-called boat people, who fled Vietnam during the early years of Communist consolidation of the country. Many of the latter eventually immigrated to the United States via a third country.

Vietnam indirectly contributed to renewed immigration from mainland China as well. Before the United States could extricate itself from Vietnam, it needed to curb growing Soviet influence there. This factor was one reason behind the reestablishment of relations with the People's Republic of China. After 1972, renewed political contacts enabled China to make adjustments in its economic policy, including a relaxation of its control over migration. Large numbers of the coastal population went to Hong Kong, whence many later proceeded to the United States. Another group of actual or potential emigrants was the thin stratum of college-educated people. Factors influencing their possible exodus included the change in ideology from "politics in command" to "money in command," political uncertainty in China, and the formation of an international professional class with its own ideology, material standards, and networks.

Those college-educated Chinese who leave add to the growing U.S.-supported pool of immigrants/refugees from the politically displaced elite families of Taiwan, South Korea, Vietnam, and the Philippines. It is not coincidental that many first- or second-generation Asian Americans are children of prominent figures in their home countries. The recent flight of Hong Kong elites fearful of the colony's fate after 1997 is a repetition of this pattern.

Before World War II, Hong Kong functioned mainly as an entrepôt for trade between China and the West. Its economic role weakened with the disrupted flow of Chinese goods to the West because of the civil war and the founding of the PRC. Hong Kong (and Taiwan), however, did benefit from the inflow of human and capital resources as young entrepreneurs and capitalists sought refuge in the British colony. Its position as an entrepôt became wholly untenable when the United Nations placed an embargo on China after its entry into the Korean War.

Hong Kong took advantage of the massive inflow of low-cost unskilled Chinese labor from nearby Guangdong Province and reconfigured itself into a manufacturing economy (Chen, 1984, 3). The United States benefited from this reorientation as it became Hong Kong's major export trade partner. By 1964, the British colony was exporting 28 percent of its domestic production to the United States, compared to 22 percent to the United Kingdom, the second largest export market. The United Kingdom retained the second spot in 1982 but received only 9 percent of Hong Kong's exports, whereas the U.S. proportion rose to 38 percent (Hung, 1984, 29).

Economic support, with the trade relations that it engendered between the United States and particular regions of Asia, created the context for general Asian migration to the United States. Recognition of the economic relations binding these nations to the United States was a crucial factor in the easing of U.S. restrictions on Asian immigration in 1954 (Reimers, 1985). But the aid was equally instrumental in paving the way for a second linkage that directly affected both semiskilled and PTK immigration from South Korea, the Philippines, and Taiwan.

Asian Highly Skilled and Talented Immigration

The totalitarian regimes of Taiwan, South Korea, and the Philippines transformed traditional class relations through land reform and state development. Although the specific class restructuring differed in each nation, the emergence of a sizable middle class that increasingly congregated in major metropolises, such as Taipei, Seoul, and Manila, was a common outcome. Rapid industrial growth in many East Asian nations during the 1960s intensified the urbanization process, creating overpopulation and environmental menaces. Amid the economic growth, the foundation for later discontent was also taking shape.

Professionals in the middle class played a major role in fashioning the emergent dissent. Trained in an educational system highly articulated with that of the United States, they possessed a capitalist ideology that emphasized the pursuit of individualistic goals. Overpopulation and deteriorating environmental conditions frustrated the ability of many professionals to realize their goals and often left them unemployed or underemployed. Their dissatisfaction created political conflicts with the ruling class. The dissident professionals, unless they became opposition leaders, sought a more liberal environment in which to practice their professions. When the opportunity to leave came with the relaxation of U.S. immigration laws in 1965, they seized it. Others in the middle class followed their lead.

The development of a capitalist ideology, particularly among professionals, reflected the central role of the United States in reorganizing Asian educational infrastructures at the primary and secondary levels. U.S. involvement stemmed from a belief that teaching about democracy and modernization would immunize Asia to both the fascist tendencies of the past and the communist overtures of the future. Assimilation of these values also would hasten Asia's entry into the ranks of the developed world.

To reach children during their formative years, the United States concentrated its educational aid at the primary and secondary levels. U.S. academics assisted in the pursuit of these objectives at the higher educational level by espousing convergence theory and its later embodiment as classical modernization theory (Novack and Lekach, 1964; Portes and Walton, 1981; So, 1990). This theoretical orientation asserted that underdeveloped nations could enjoy the same standards of living as the developed world by emulating the developmental paths taken by the West.

Many Asian nations readily accepted the U.S. Westernization message, particularly concerning the development of high-level talent. A program statement by the Education and World Affairs Committee, a private research organization, elucidates the major reasons why Asian nations embraced this message. The committee argued that educated talent was indispensable to the developmental process, because such individuals:

1. Constituted the intellectual bridge to the developed world by assessing and adapting relevant ideas and technologies originating elsewhere,
2. Possessed the abilities to develop and manage the productive processes, the resources, and the complex structures of modern society,
3. Were in a position as the intellectual elite to make the structural and institutional changes necessary for a nation to become a modern state,
4. Represented the future in their influence on the educational and other molding institutions that would shape succeeding cohorts of educated persons (Clark, 1970, 192–193).

The committee might have added that these individuals expanded the international labor pool. Common technical knowledge, shared professional values and attitudes, and participation in international personal networks enabled well-educated persons to use their training beyond the confines of any single national economy. Increasing interchangeability of educated workers paralleled the wider use of unskilled workers across national boundaries. The use of both types of labor gave greater coherence to the international division of labor (Portes and Walton, 1981).

Convergence of educational objectives helps account for the pervasive influence of the United States in creating the rationale and means for Asian skilled and talented immigration. U.S. influence occurred in two areas: the revamping of educational institutions and curricula, and the training of educators in the home country or in the United States. Involvement in these areas formed the networks connecting highly educated Asians with the United States and the incentives to use these networks. Examination of the Filipino experience illustrates the establishment of these networks and their operation.

As a colony, the Philippines recreated the U.S. educational structure and curriculum in their entirety during the early part of the century, including the use of English as the medium of instruction. Many students of this period "went to school when special textbooks had not yet been introduced in the Philippine Islands, when George Washington and Abraham Lincoln were made childhood's heroes and even the less interesting events of American history and its succession of Presidents were taught with the same insistence as in Kalamazoo or Podunk" (Lasker, 1931, 221–222).

U.S. volunteers served as the first instructors and mentored many of the next generation of Filipino teachers. Although the curriculum later incorporated Philippine characteristics, and educational institutions primarily employed indigenous personnel, Filipinos continued to idealize U.S. models, values, and norms (Pido, 1986, 49). Colonization predisposed Filipinos to emigrate to the United States. For Filipinos desiring to further their learning, the scarcity of higher educational institutions and the growing demand for limited spaces at the college level provided the actual push.

The Philippine territorial government attempted to regulate this movement by sponsoring students (*pensionados*) to study in colleges and universities throughout the United States. Ensured of leadership positions in the educational, business, civic, and governmental arenas, most pensionados returned to the Philippines on completion of their studies. Only about five hundred persons qualified for the pensionado program, yet the demand for higher education was far greater. Nearly fourteen thousand self-supporting students followed the lead of the pensionados by emigrating to the United States between 1910 and 1938 (Melendy, 1981, 32).

Continuing demand for higher education and the opportunities to realize it remained in disequilibrium after World War II. Widespread wartime destruction in the Philippines caused the bulk of U.S. aid to be directed toward the reconstruction of basic physical plants. For reasons mentioned earlier, educational facilities were among the first to be rebuilt. But rapid reestablishment of the educational system again reproduced the structural imbalances of the prewar period. Advocacy of universal education by the U.S. and Philippine governments meant concentrating resources on the construction of elementary schools, followed by secondary schools. High startup and maintenance costs limited state expenditures to all but a few publicly supported colleges and universities. Sporadic economic development also dampened the immediate need for additional highly educated persons.

Reaching more children unavoidably raised the demand for institutions of higher learning in the Philippines. Entrepreneurs filled this gap by opening private colleges and universities. As profit-driven businesses, these institutions encouraged even larger enrollments. They graduated far more people than could be absorbed by the domestic labor market, thus adding to the surplus already created by the public universities (Thurston, 1970, 15). Estimates in the late 1960s indicate that jobs were available for only half the college graduates (Ruth, 1970b, 55).

Educated Filipinos caught in this situation faced two alternatives. One was to participate in a domestic labor market characterized by both "credential" inflation (i.e., raising the qualifications for available jobs) and underemployment (i.e., the hiring of overqualified people for a position). The other was to go abroad as students (exchange or self-supporting) or as emigrants (Ruth, 1970b, 52), an option Filipinos frequently began to exercise in the late 1960s by moving to the United States.

The United States made comparable attempts to Americanize the Korean educational system, though its involvement there was less extensive than in the Philippines. Nonetheless, U.S. participation contributed directly to the development of similar structural bottlenecks. The U.S. military government (1946–1949) originally intended to use education as the major vehicle for the democratization of Korean society. Many elements of the military government program, such as compulsory primary education and the creation of local school boards, became provisions of the First Republic's constitution. U.S. efforts to reform the curriculum ended with the Korean War, because the conflict destroyed 90 percent of the libraries and laboratories and 50 percent of the classrooms (Ruth, 1970a, 124). Just as in the Philippines, physical devastation forced the United States to spend the $100 million it had earmarked for education on replacing elementary and secondary schools rather than on curricular reform (McGinn et al., 1980, 86–89).

The U.S. imprint on South Korea's higher education was more enduring. In 1946, the military government formed Seoul National University (SNU) by combining Kyungsong Imperial University with nine public and private junior colleges. It was organized along the lines of a U.S. university, and its first president and several key staff members were U.S. citizens, while most of the faculty were Korean nationals. A shortage of qualified personnel led most colleges and universities to recruit more U.S. or U.S.-trained faculty (Ruth, 1970a, 126).

Introducing U.S. curriculum and technology, these instructors swayed those South Koreans seeking continuation of their studies toward the United States. The return of these students raised the percentage of foreign-trained faculty. At SNU, the faculty educated abroad more than doubled, from 21 percent in 1966 to 46 percent in 1988, with 72 percent receiving their degrees from U.S. institutions (Population and Development Studies Center, 1988, 2–8).

The cost of establishing and maintaining an institution such as SNU hindered the opening of new spaces at a rate commensurate with the demand generated from below. This demand had steadily grown even while current graduates were having difficulty finding jobs or pursuing graduate studies. An estimated 60 percent of the fifteen thousand students graduating in 1960 were unable to find employment within three months after leaving school. To maintain a better balance between graduation rates and labor needs, the South Korean government encouraged students to enter vocational schools, fixed promotion rates to public higher education, and tried to limit the establishment of new higher-education institutions.

These measures were unsuccessful. By 1966, high school and college enrollments exceeded predictions by 30 and 38 percent, respectively, and the number of new colleges nearly doubled (McGinn et al., 1980, 37–39). That same year, Heather Low Ruth (1970a, 133) reported, only half the students found employment within one month after graduation. Faced with these structural obstacles, many students and professionals left for the United States. Of the estimated seven thousand educated South Koreans departing for the United States from 1953 to 1968, fewer than one thousand returned. The American-Korean Foundation estimated that about 20 percent of the latter group permanently resettled in the United States after being home less than a year because of their failure to obtain satisfactory employment (Ruth, 1970a, 135).

Compared to the Philippines and South Korea, Taiwan was only minimally affected by the United States in its primary and secondary schools, with one important exception—the widespread adoption of English as a second language. The Japanese colonial legacy was of much greater importance in the organization of the lower educational levels, because only limited wartime damage occurred to the system. Survival of the infrastructure plus the government's policy of increasing the supply of highly educated people resulted in an average annual growth of 13 percent for college and university graduates from 1959 to 1966.

This spectacular growth intensified the competition for places in higher education and produced a surfeit of graduates. In 1966, only 13,575 out of 49,000 applicants passed the exam qualifying them for admission into an institution of higher education. The number actually admitted was smaller, as many students failed to be accepted into the curriculum or institution of their choice. That same year, unemployment among college and university graduates was 3 percent, but graduates not immediately participating in the labor force constituted about 38 percent (Ruth, 1970c, 29–33).

Thus, Taiwan too faced a situation in which demand for higher education, availability of spaces, and employment after graduation were out of alignment with one another. Ruth (1970c, 13) attributes this discrepancy in part to the Confucian ethic's emphasis on acquiring an education. A small but proportionally significant population of mainland families also contributed to the heavy demand for higher education. They expected and depended on university education for their children to maintain the family's status in Taiwanese society. McGinn and colleagues (1980, 66) make similar assertions for South Koreans. Although Confucianism cannot be dismissed as a factor in higher educational achievement, it is difficult to gainsay the primacy of Western models of development in stimulating higher educational demand. As seen earlier with the Philippines and later for India, similar rapid educational growth occurred in countries outside the influence of Confucianism.

Even without major U.S. input in the organization of primary and secondary education in Taiwan, the United States still affected educational objectives and the training of personnel. The widespread study of English and the growing presence at the university/college level of faculty trained in the United States are indicators of this impact. As at SNU, the portion of U.S.-trained faculty, particularly at the doctoral level, at the National Taiwan University (NTU) has risen since the 1960s. By 1987, more than one-third of NTU's faculty members had received their highest degree from U.S. institutions, a number likely to grow, with more than 90 percent of recent Taiwanese graduates studying in the United States (Tsai, 1988, 15, 5).

Exchange and joint educational programs also have had considerable impact in the transmission of U.S. influence. Precisely because the United States had so little input into Taiwan's lower education, exchange and joint opportunities have assumed a more prominent role in implementing a U.S. weltanschauung. In the 1950s and 1960s, organizations such as the Asia Foundation, the Agency for International Development, and the Sino-American Cultural Exchange Foundation enabled Taiwanese faculty to study in the United States. Conversely, the National Science Council and the Education Ministry of the Republic of China (ROC) sponsored more than two thousand five hundred long- and short-term visitors to Taiwan between 1967 and 1978. Most of the invitees were Chinese living in the United States. Joint ventures such as the one between the ROC National Science Council and the U.S. National Science Foundation arranged for exchanges spanning from three months to two years. In 1978, this joint program was the second largest of the forty bilateral scientific programs in which the United States participated (Li, 1988, 172). Exchange and joint programs shaped the curriculum in Taiwanese colleges and universities as well as channeled the continuous flow of persons between the ROC and the United States.

The United States had minimal involvement with the educational systems of Hong Kong and India. Former colonial ties to the British empire tightly wove their educational structures to that of Great Britain. Absence of this precursor suggests that the linkage of these two regions with the United States would be weaker than the United States' relationship with the Philippines, South Korea, and Taiwan. In terms of overall immigration patterns, this is true (Liu, 1990). But the economic linkage forged with Hong Kong and India after World War II placed the United States in a position to take advantage of any weakening of the ties between either region with Great Britain. The United States was particularly well situated to exploit possible rifts between India and Great Britain. Many of the structural inducements leading to emigration from the East Asian nations under the overt influence of the United States were similarly present in India.

In the 1950s, India pursued an aggressive development program by expanding educational facilities at nearly 11 percent per year. This growth rate doubled the annual enrollment about every six and one-half years. Trilok Dhar and colleagues (1976, 5) contend that "next to the United States, India probably has more students in universities than any other country, though the proportion of university students per 1,000 population is among the lowest." The ensuing mismatch between highly educated persons and actual labor needs prevented India from absorbing all its university graduates. By 1967, one out of every ten university graduates went abroad. The emigration of scientists was 11 percent; of doctors, 10 percent; and of engineers, 23 percent (Domrese, 1970, 221–236). Of those who remained, the proportion of unemployed within the total stock of educated labor rose from 14 to 15.7 percent between 1955 and 1961 (Dhar et al., 1976, 10). In absolute numbers, this percentage translated to about one hundred thousand unemployed and three hundred thousand underemployed university graduates in 1967 (Domrese, 1970, 232).

Robert Clark (1970, 191, 197) offers an important caveat about the surplus of Indian PTKs that is also applicable to the ready availability of highly educated persons in East Asia. He notes that the oversupply of highly trained Indians existed in relation to *current demand*. The number of highly educated workers did

88   John M. Liu and Lucie Cheng

not exceed *actual* social and economic needs or the developmental potential of the nation. If this observation is extended to East Asia, out-migration clearly represented a brain overflow given the immediate absorptive capacity of domestic institutions of higher education and the internal labor market. Whether this migration was simultaneously a brain drain is a contentious issue that involves varying assumptions about the *possible* role of highly educated emigrants in the rate of future development.

Irrespective of the brain-drain issue, India's inability to absorb all its highly educated citizens led to migration abroad. About three-quarters of Indian emigrants left for the United Kingdom, followed by the United States. U.S. technical assistance to India in the 1950s made migration to the United States viable. Indians sent to the United States to acquire skills through short-term training or graduate study laid the groundwork for subsequent migrations (Minocha, 1987, 361). After 1965, the flow of Indian PTKS toward the United States rose dramatically as migration to the United Kingdom tapered off (Domrese, 1970, 218–219). The limiting of immigration to the United Kingdom after 1962 caused Asian Indians to settle in other Commonwealth nations, mainly Australia and Canada, or in the United States.

The United Kingdom's limited ability to absorb Hong Kong's exports in the postwar period likewise pushed the colony into closer association with the United States. Hong Kong's rapprochement with the United States points to another possible precursor—an export-oriented economy—leading skilled and talented Asians to immigrate to the United States. Hong Kong, South Korea, and Taiwan all developed such economies very early in the postwar period.

Export-oriented economies require constant infusions of foreign capital, technology, and highly educated persons. All three factors are evident when foreign investments are direct rather than indirect. The latter type of investment usually occurs through portfolio holdings, that is, the owning of stocks or shares, and does not generally entail any management control. Since stock transactions result only in the transference of existing proprietorship, they do not inject new capital, technology, or know-how into the host country economy.

In contrast, direct investments are in business assets that the foreign investor manages either fully or to a large extent. Hence, there is a real exchange of capital, a diffusion of technology, and a shifting of management personnel as well as the availability of ready overseas markets. Direct investment may occur through the establishment of branch offices, subsidiary companies, associate companies, or joint ventures. Regardless of form, movement of foreign personnel is necessary to provide management and to train the local supervisory labor force. Training, the use of equipment, the actual production of goods, and the sharing of proprietary/nonproprietary information effectuate the transference of technology and skills (Hung, 1984, 180–181, 197; Wu, 1985, 12). This process further contributes to the substitutability of highly educated labor. For these reasons, then, an export-oriented economy may help channel the movement of persons with high levels of education and skills.

Direct U.S. investment is readily apparent in Hong Kong. Despite the fact that Hong Kong is a British colony, the United States has been the largest foreign investor there, accounting for almost 54 percent of the foreign investment in Hong Kong's manufacturing sector by 1971, whereas the United Kingdom's share was only 11.3 percent. During the next decade, both nations lost ground to Japan. Still, the United States remained the largest investor, contributing 43.6 percent of total foreign investment (Hung, 1984, 190).

Export-oriented economies and the infusion of Asian educational systems with United States/Western modes of thought, patterns of action, and ideals predisposed the Asian middle class and professionals to emigrate. Both factors depended on the a priori existence of a more general economic linkage. For the United States, its connection to the Philippines, the three Chinese-speaking regions, India, Vietnam, and South Korea emanated from its emergence as a hegemonic power after World War II.

From the preceding discussion, it might appear that the Asian sending nations are irrevocably in a subordinate position to the United States. There is no doubt that this was so during the first three decades after the conclusion of World War II. But the dynamic growth of the Asian export-oriented economies has enabled these nations to challenge U.S. economic hegemony in the region. One indicator of this development is the mounting trade deficits between the United States and Asia's newly industrialized countries (NICs). A similar trend is evident in education. U.S. technological superiority faces competition from improvements in Asian higher education, and Asian graduates are becoming a significant portion of the skilled occupational force in the United States.

Semi-skilled and Unskilled Asian Labor

Extensive and prolonged economic involvement of the United States in Asia not only created the basis for the immigration of professionals and other skilled middle-class people, but also allowed for the renewal of substantial unskilled and semiskilled Asian immigration. Semiskilled Asians from the Philippines, the three Chinese-speaking regions, South Korea, Vietnam, and India were 13.3 percent of total Asian immigration from 1965 to 1989. The potential pool of unskilled workers among all entering Asians in this period was roughly 46.5 percent (Table 3.1).[1] In relation to total U.S. immigration, Asian semiskilled and unskilled represent a possible two out of every ten immigrants.

Some of the same factors influencing middle-class emigration also encourage working-class Asians to leave. U.S. ideological penetration of Asia and myriad economic, political, and military ties with the region fostered a common belief among working-class Asians that the United States was a land of opportunity. The success stories of earlier Asian immigrants who attained status and wealth despite their working-class origins gave substance to the belief and further stimulated the desire to emigrate. Regional wars, domestic political instability, and the favorable economic opportunities in the United States served both to spur additional emigration and to create the potential pool of working-class emigrants. The family reunification principle of the 1965 Immigration Act facilitated their exit from Asia.

Wars in Korea (1950–1953) and Vietnam (1962–1975) were major direct and indirect contributors to the supply of working-class Asian immigrants. The carnage of both conflicts produced a huge number of orphans and abandoned children, usually from the liaisons between local women and the U.S. military. Many of these children found homes in the United States, which organized large-scale adoption schemes. From 1953 to 1965, 16 percent of Koreans migrating abroad were adoptees (Repetto et al., 1981, 115). Similarly, beginning in 1988, the United States allotted twelve thousand visas for Amerasians, that is, the children of United States–Vietnamese parents (U.S. Immigration and Naturalization Service, 1990, xxvi). How many of these children will join the ranks of the unskilled and semiskilled labor force is to a large extent determined by the class status of their U.S. sponsors.

The Korean and Vietnamese conflicts were also directly responsible for the migration of entire groups of people who fought against the Communists. In the Vietnam War, whole ethnic groups, such as the Hmong, who fought with U.S.-supported forces in Laos, were relocated to the United States (Hendricks, Downing, and Deinard, 1986). The collapse of the non-Communist regimes in Vietnam, Laos, and Kampuchea led to the forced evacuation of entire villages of anti-Communist soldiers and their families. Many of these people were illiterate and had few occupational skills beyond farming and making war. They were prepared at best for unskilled work on their arrival in the United States. There they joined the hundred of thousands of other refugees who found themselves in a similar economic position (Arax, 1987).

These conflicts also had an indirect effect in creating and stimulating the migration of working-class Asians. Waging war, or limiting its scope, led to the proliferation of military bases throughout the Asian Pacific Rim. These bases exposed the local populace to U.S. money, culture, and standards of living, instilling people with an inclination to emigrate. In the Philippines, local residents could be found in long queues outside Subic Naval Station. They hoped for an opportunity to enlist in the U.S. navy and thereby gain a chance to enter the United States.

Military bases offered another opportunity, mainly for women, to gain admission into the United States through marriage. From 1947 to 1975, almost 166,000 Asian women entered the United States as the wives of U.S. servicemen. The military brides came mainly from Japan (67,000), the Philippines (57,000),

South Korea (28,000), and South Vietnam (8,000) (Reimers, 1985, 24–25). These women were among the first of the post–World War II Asian immigrants and had two significant effects on future Asian immigration. First, their marriages served as a major artery through which many working-class Asians gained entry to the United States. Bok-Lim C. Kim (1977) notes that most military brides came from peasant or laboring backgrounds and that most of the U.S. soldiers they married shared this working-class

Table 3.1. Immigration of Semi- and Unskilled Workers from Selected Asian Nations

Year	(A) Total Immigrants	(B) Total No. of Persons Reporting an Occupation	(C) Total Semi- and Unskilled Workers	(C)/(A) (%)	(C)/(B) (%)
1965	10,872	3,120	1,774	16.3	56.9
1966	28,926	10,935	6,117	21.1	55.9
1967	45,049	19,458	7,833	17.4	40.3
1968	42,248	18,578	6,606	15.6	35.6
1969	54,628	23,213	7,976	14.6	34.4
1970	70,037	30,450	9,185	13.1	30.2
1971	76,738	33,441	7,982	10.4	23.9
1972	90,320	37,606	10,704	11.9	28.5
1973	93,078	33,417	11,089	11.9	33.2
1974	99,541	35,011	14,397	14.5	41.1
1975	102,352	38,568	15,460	15.1	40.1
1976	113,222	41,941	17,406	15.4	41.5
1977	118,690	44,729	20,480	17.3	45.8
1978	202,308	75,890	47,595	23.5	62.7
1979	141,202	48,297	27,507	19.5	57.0
1980	172,237	—	—	—	—
1981	183,446	—	—	—	—

Continued on next page

Table 3.1 (*Continued*)

Year	(A) Total Immigrants	(B) Total No. of Persons Reporting an Occupation	(C) Total Semi- and Unskilled Workers	(C)/(A) (%)	(C)/(B) (%)
1982	213,072	63,566	36,960	17.3	58.1
1983	186,319	58,985	35,094	18.8	59.5
1984	179,316	57,373	32,789	18.3	57.2
1985	186,005	59,704	35,584	19.1	59.6
1986	188,105	60,039	36,733	19.5	61.2
1987	180,421	61,179	36,911	20.5	60.3
1988	184,390	63,785	39,284	21.3	61.6
1989	216,156	84,663	53,235	24.6	62.9
Total	3,178,678	1,003,948	518,701	16.3	51.7

Sources: U.S. Immigration and Naturalization Service, *Annual Reports, 1965–1977*, and *Statistical Yearbooks, 1978–1989* (Washington, D.C.: Government Printing Office).

Note: Semi- and unskilled workers include the following categories: sales; administrative support; precision production, craft, and repair; operator, fabricator, and laborer; farming, forestry, and fishing; service. The number of major occupational categories used by the INS varies over time. The selected countries are India, Korea, Philippines, Vietnam, People's Republic of China, Republic of China (Taiwan), and Hong Kong. Data for 1980 and 1981 are unavailable from the U.S. Immigration and Naturalization Service.

origin. Once in this country, these women became beacons for other family members wishing to emigrate.

Second, military brides helped change the gender composition of Asian immigration. Whereas earlier immigrants were predominantly young, unattached males, women at present comprise the majority. Brides formed the vanguard of this transformation, but the primary component of the change was made up of women who accompanied their husbands and fathers at the time of immigration or joined them soon after. Many of these women work as second wage earners, often in unskilled or semiskilled jobs or as unpaid labor in family enterprises (Arax, 1987; Young, 1983). Of course, not all Asian women lack professional or skilled occupational backgrounds. Many Filipinas, for instance, have professional training (see Chapter 6).

Beyond the consequences that flowed from U.S. military involvement, the underdevelopment of the domestic economy in poor Asian countries is yet another reason for people to emigrate. Although the nations from which many Asians originated enjoyed economic prosperity from the 1960s onward, other countries, such as China and Vietnam, have experienced continuing underdevelopment. A constant threat of internal war and violence has compounded their economic difficulties. These conditions created a pool of potential immigrants: unskilled and semiskilled workers, both rural and urban, who could take advantage of family and other personal networks to gain entry to the United States.

This stream of semi- and unskilled workers involves a continuation of pre-1945 migration. Halted because of anti-Asian U.S. immigration policy and political turmoil within many Asian societies, the migration of family members to join husbands and sons resumed after 1965. For example, the coastal province of Guangdong on mainland China, whence many Chinese Americans departed more than a century and a half ago, has again become a large source of immigration with the relaxation of both China's and the United States's migration policies. These immigrants typically have little education and rely on the established Chinese American community for their livelihood. The low cost of their labor has helped revive declining Chinatowns in major U.S. cities. Labor-intensive industries in the United States benefiting from this inexpensive labor have fostered the immigration of these groups of Asians. The active recruitment of Chinese and Thai garment workers is a notable example.

These Chinese and other low-skilled Asians fuel further working-class immigration through the money they send back to their countries of origin. While remittances boost the living standard of families back home, they serve as convincing testimony to others that there is an abundance of opportunities in the

United States. Belief in these opportunities keeps the disposition to emigrate strong. People choosing to leave have faced less resistance from their home governments than before, because remittances have also built up foreign currency reserves that are essential for acquiring foreign goods and technology. It is with good reason that Asian nations such as the PRC and Vietnam have either loosened their emigration policies or turned a blind eye to violations of existing emigration policy.

Pervasive U.S. involvement in the post–World War II restructuring of the Asian Pacific regional political economy established the conditions for both professional/skilled and semiskilled/unskilled worker immigration. The rise of capitalist ideology and the articulation of U.S. and Asian educational systems provided the basic motivation and opportunities for emigration. Highly publicized success stories of Asian immigrants helped sustain the motivation of other potential emigrants.

Persistence of both streams is likely, given the internal dynamics of various Asian societies. On the one hand, export-led economies such as Taiwan and South Korea must continuously encourage the migration of professional and other skilled persons, because such a flow helps promote trade, technological transfer, and foreign investments. Although developing countries often worry about the brain drain, recent studies question its applicability to Asia. Only a small portion, as little as 10 percent, of expatriate professionals need return to their country of origin for them to have a considerable impact on domestic economic growth. Asian countries are now less concerned about stopping the flow abroad and instead are focusing on how to attract back those who would be most useful to their economic development.

On the other hand, nations such as the People's Republic of China and Vietnam benefit from the mass migration of unskilled and semiskilled labor. The remittances provided by these immigrants are crucial in securing desperately needed foreign currency to maintain future economic development. Besides bringing in capital, this type of immigration helps act as an escape valve for internal dissatisfaction and reduces population pressures on limited economic resources.

Present Asian immigration to the United States represents the contemporary consequences of past U.S. participation in the Asian Pacific region after 1945. The institutionalization of the various relationships underlying U.S. ties to Asia suggests that the dual patterns of immigration will continue into the near future. Whether these connections will stay strong depends on how the United States deals with the challenges posed by the more robust of the Asian newly industrializing economies. Whether the United States will have a bearing on future Asian immigration patterns remains to be seen.

Note

1. An estimate of semi-skilled and unskilled workers can be obtained from published U.S. Immigration and Naturalization Service data. If we group all Asian immigrants who declared an occupation and subtract those who stated that they were professional, technical, and kindred workers (PTKS) or administrative, executive, and managerial personnel, the remainder approximates the size of semi-skilled and unskilled immigration. It is difficult to determine whether this measure under- or overestimates the pool of semi- and unskilled labor, since little is known about the educational and occupational status of those individuals who declared themselves to be nonworking spouses. Moreover, no accurate measure exists of the prevalence and duration of underemployment among Asian immigrants.

References

Arax, Mark. 1987. "Many Refugees Work While Getting Welfare." *Los Angeles Times*, 9 February, pp. 1, 8, 16.

Chen, Edward K. Y. 1984. "The Economic Setting." In *The Business Environment in Hong Kong*, 2d ed., ed. David G. Lethbridge, pp. 1–51. Hong Kong: Oxford University Press.

Cheng, Lucie, and Leslie Evans. 1988. "Brain Flow: The International Migration of the Highly Skilled—A Theoretical Introduction." Paper presented at the University of California at Los Angeles International Workshop on the Movement of Highly Educated Labor in the Pacific Rim, Los Angeles, 29 August–2 September.

Clark, Robert. 1970. "The Asian Subcontinent: The Migration of Talent in Perspective." In *The International Migration of High-Level Manpower: Its Impact on the Development Process*, ed. Committee on the International Migration of Talent, pp. 179–214. New York: Praeger.

Dhar, Trilok N., Alice Stone Ilchman, and Warren F. Ilchman. 1976. *Education and Employment in India: The Policy Nexus*. Columbia, Mo.: South Asia Books.

Domrese, Robert J. 1970. "The Migration of Talent from India." In *The International Migration of High-Level Manpower: Its Impact on the Development Process*, ed. Committee on the International Migration of Talent, pp. 215–257. New York: Praeger.

Hendricks, Glenn L., Bruce T. Downing, and Amos S. Deinard, eds. 1986. *The Hmong in Transition*. Staten Island, N.Y.: Center for Migration Studies; Minneapolis: Southeast Asian Refugee Studies of the University of Minnesota.

Hung, C. L. 1984. "Foreign Investments." In *The Business Environment in Hong Kong*, 2d ed., ed. David G. Lethbridge, pp. 180–211. Hong Kong: Oxford University Press.

Kim, Bok-Lim C. 1977. "Asian Wives of U.S. Servicemen: Women in Shadows." *Amerasia Journal* 4(1):91–115.

Lasker, Bruno. 1931. *Filipino Immigration to Continental United States and to Hawaii*. Reprint. New York: Arno Press, 1969.

Li, Kwoh-ting. 1988. *Economic Transformation of Taiwan, ROC*. London: Shepheard Walwyn.

Liu John M. 1990. "A Comparative Historical Perspective of Post–World War II Asian Immigration to North America and Australia." Paper presented at the annual meeting of the American Sociological Association, Washington, D.C., 11–15 August.

Liu, John M., Paul M. Ong, and Carolyn Rosenstein. 1991. "Dual Chain Migration: Post-1965 Filipino Immigration to the United States." *International Migration Review* 25(3):487–513.

McGinn, Noel F., Donald R. Snodgrass, Yung Bong Kim, Shin-Bok Kim, and Quee-Young Kim. 1980. *Education and Economic Development in Korea*. Cambridge: Council on East Asian Studies, Harvard University.

Melendy, H. Brett. 1981. *Asians in America: Filipinos, Koreans, and East Indians*. New York: Hippocrene Books.

Minocha, Urmil. 1987. "South Asian Immigrants: Trends and Impacts on the Sending and Receiving Societies." In *Pacific Bridges: The New Immigration from Asia and the Pacific Island*, ed. James T. Fawcett and Benjamin Carino, pp. 347–373. Staten Island, N.Y.: Center for Migration Studies.

Nemeth, Roger J., and David A. Smith. 1985. "The Political Economy of Contrasting Urban Hierarchies in South Korea and the Philippines." In *Urbanization in the World Economy*, ed. Michael Timberlake, pp. 183–206. New York: Academic Press.
Novack, David E., and Robert Lekach, eds. 1968. *Development and Society: The Dynamics of Economic Change*. New York: St. Martin's Press.
Pido, Antonio J. A. 1986. *The Pilipinos in America: Micro/Macro Dimensions of Immigration and Integration*. Staten Island, N.Y.: Center for Migration Studies.
Population and Development Studies Center, 1988. "The Seoul National University: History, Organization, and Activities." Paper presented at the University of California at Los Angeles International Workshop on the Movement of Highly Educated Labor in the Pacific Rim, Los Angeles, 29 August–2 September.
Portes, Alejandro, and John Walton. 1981. *Labor, Class, and the International System*. New York: Academic Press.
Reimers, David M. 1985. *Still the Golden Door: The Third World Comes to America*. New York: Columbia University Press.
Repetto, Robert, Tai Hwan Kwon, Son-Ung Kim, Dae Young Kim, John E. Sloboda, and Peter J. Donaldson. 1981. *Economic Development, Population Policy, and Demographic Transition in the Republic of Korea*. Cambridge: Council on East Asian Studies, Harvard University.
Ruth, Heather Low. 1970a. "Korea." In *The International Migration of High-Level Manpower: Its Impact on the Development Process*, ed. Committee on the International Migration of Talent, pp. 121–151. New York: Praeger.
———. 1970b. "Philippines." In *International Migration of High-Level Manpower*, pp. 46–80.
———. 1970c. "Taiwan." In *International Migration of High-Level Manpower*, pp. 19–45.
So, Alvin Y. 1990. *Social Change and Development: Modernization, Dependency, and World-System Theories*. Newbury Park, Calif.: Sage.
Thurston, John L. 1970. "East and Southeast Asia: An Overview." In *The International Migration of High-Level Manpower: Its Impact on the Development Process*, ed. Committee on the International Migration of Talent, pp. 3–18. New York: Praeger.
Tsai, Hong-chin. 1988. "The Return of Students and Scholars from the United States to Taiwan and Its Impact: A Case Study of National Taiwan University." Paper presented at the University of California at Los Angeles International Workshop on the Movement of Highly Educated Labor in the Pacific Rim, Los Angeles, 29 August–2 September.

U.S. Immigration and Naturalization Service. 1966–1977. *Annual Reports*. Washington, D.C.: Government Printing Office.

———. 1978–1990. *Statistical Yearbook of the Immigration and Naturalization Service*. Washington, D.C.: Government Printing Office.

Wu, Yuan-li. 1985. *Becoming an Industrialized Nation*. New York: Praeger.

Young, Philip K. Y. 1983. "Family Labor, Sacrifice, and Competition: Korean Greengrocers in New York City." *Amerasia Journal* 10(2):53–71.

4. Asian Immigrants in Los Angeles: Diversity and Divisions

Paul Ong and Tania Azores

Since the 1960s, Asian Americans[1] have been the fastest growing minority group in the United States, more than doubling their size between the 1960s and 1970s and again during the 1980s, with much of this growth driven by immigration. By 1990, Asian Americans numbered 6.9 million nationwide, nearly two-thirds of whom were foreign born.[2] This trend is not just quantitative but also qualitative. Significant social, economic, and political changes have accompanied a rapid ethnic and class diversification of the Asian American population. The phenomenal growth over the last quarter-century has raised serious issues regarding political representation, access to public resources, and the meaning of civil rights. The emergent heterogeneity is redefining the concept of race and the nature of interracial relationships. With diverse immigrant populations that do not have a common cultural, historical, or economic base, it is questionable whether Asian Americans have a solid foundation for a collective group identity. At the same time, new lines of conflict are being drawn along racial lines: clashes between Koreans and blacks are the most visible but certainly not the only element in a complex web of intergroup relationships (see Chapter 9).

It is possible to derive insights into this transformation by examining Asian immigrants in Los Angeles.[3] The Asian American population in Los Angeles, whose growth parallels the national trend, increased nearly fivefold between 1970 and 1990, from roughly 190,000 to approximately 926,000.[4] With this phenomenal growth, Los Angeles has emerged as the home of the single largest Asian population in the United States, easily outnumbering the populations in other major metropolitan areas, including San Francisco–Oakland, Honolulu, and New York.[5] Los Angeles is a prototype of the dramatic impact of Asian immigration since 1970. The experiences of this community reflect and contribute to the larger social and economic transformations in the United States, such as growing cultural diversity, reemergence of ethnicity in the form of enclaves, and increasing economic disparity.

Waning and Waxing of Immigration

The first wave of Asian immigrants began with the arrival of the Chinese in 1848. The Chinese community in Los Angeles developed not long after the establishment of its counterpart in northern California. As opportunities in the gold field waned and racial hostilities grew in that region of the state, an increasing number of Chinese settled in Los Angeles. By 1890, the population stood at 4,424, according to the census. As in the rest of the state, the 1882 Chinese Exclusion Act had an adverse impact in Los Angeles. The population fell by nearly half, to 2,602, by 1910 and remained stagnant for the next few decades.

The Japanese filled the vacuum left by the exclusion of the Chinese. Numbering only 36 in 1890, the county's Japanese population grew to 8,461 by 1910. Like the Chinese, however, the Japanese, in Los Angeles and throughout the state, were seen by many whites as a threat to society. The anti-Asian movement led to the Gentlemen's Agreement of 1907–1908 and the 1917 Immigration Act, which severely restricted Japanese immigration. Unlike the Chinese, however, the Japanese in Los Angeles were able to form a family-based society, allowing for a slow population increase through both natural growth and internal migration. By 1930, the population stood at 35,390.

With the doors closed on China and Japan, the Philippines became the source of cheap agricultural labor for California, because, as a colony of the United States, it was not included in the prohibitions of the Immigration Act. The U.S. census reports that the state's Filipino population grew more than tenfold between 1920 and 1930, from under 3,000 to more than 30,000. The Philippine Independence Act of 1934 terminated large-scale immigration of Filipinos, however. Although no Los Angeles County population figures for Filipinos are available before 1950, when they numbered 7,117, the census reports that there were 4,498 in the city of Los Angeles in 1940.

The relaxation of racial restrictions after World War II enabled some new Asian immigrants to settle in Los Angeles, but immigration did not resume on a large scale until after the passage of the Immigration and Naturalization Act of 1965. The resulting influx from Asia and the Pacific helped swell Los Angeles's Asian American population from some 120,000 in 1960 to more than a million today.[6] The importance of immigration, particularly in recent years, can be seen in the 1990 census, which shows that approximately 403,000 Asians immigrated to Los Angeles in the 1980s.

The new immigrants entered through various channels. Most Chinese, Koreans, South Asians, and Filipinos came under the quotas and family reunification provisions of the immigration law. Southeast Asians came as political refugees, often having lived for years in refugee camps in Asia. Many Japanese came as a part of the growth of Japanese national (transnational) corporations in the United States, either as employees of these firms and their family members or as employees in the large number of restaurants and other stores that service the former group. While many immigrants came directly from abroad to Los Angeles, others came through secondary migration after first settling in other parts of the country.

With this growth, Asian Americans have dramatically increased their share of the total population, reversing a historical decline that began in the early 1900s. In the second half of the nineteenth century, the Asian presence in the county of Los Angeles grew from less than 1 percent in 1860 to over 4 percent in 1890. The imposition of various legislative restrictions on Asian immigration, starting in 1882, began to have an effect by the turn of the century. In 1900, the proportion of Asians in Los Angeles was reduced to less than half its size in 1890. Although it seemed to rebound slightly in the following two decades, 1930 again saw a sharp decline in proportional representation of Asians, a trend that continued until 1950. A steady increase in the size of the Asian American population began in 1960 and accelerated in the 1970s and 1980s. By 1990, the proportion of Asian Americans in the county was over 10 percent; by the end of the century, it could be 14 percent, depending on the growth patterns of other groups.

The resurgence of the Asian American population is part of the broad racial recomposition of Los Angeles. Recent immigration has led to a phenomenal increase of the Latino population, which grew from 15 percent to 36 percent of the total population between 1970 and 1990. Although the African American population has remained stable, at about a tenth of the total population, the Anglo (non-Hispanic white) population has declined in absolute and relative terms. In 1970, Anglos comprised 71 percent of the population, but two decades later, they constituted only 41 percent. The reemergence of the Asian American population, then, has taken place in the context of a racial transformation of the total population, amid changes that have added to the complexity of race relations in this urban area.

Demographic Diversity

Renewed large-scale immigration has transformed the Asian American population in terms of ethnicity and nativity. Before 1980, there was always a single dominant ethnic group. From 1860 to 1900, the Asian population of the county was almost exclusively Chinese, most of whom came from the same region of China. Beginning in 1910, the Japanese emerged as the dominant group, peaking in 1930 at 91 percent of all Asians. Although the predominance of the Japanese declined in the post–World War II period, they still constituted 72 percent of all Asians in 1960 and continued to be a majority into the early 1970s. But as immigration climbed, other groups eventually surpassed the Japanese. By the 1980 census, Asian Americans were a culturally pluralistic population: 27 percent Japanese, 23 percent Filipino, 22 percent Chinese, 14 percent Korean, 6 percent Vietnamese, and 4 percent Asian Indian.

Ethnic diversification continued in the 1980s (Table 4.1). The Chinese experienced the largest absolute increase, from 94,000 at the beginning of the decade to 245,000 by 1990. Filipinos increased by approximately 119,000 during the 1980s. Besides Chinese and Filipinos, the groups that experienced the highest

Table 4.1. Ethnic Composition of the Asian American Population, Los Angeles County, 1970–1990

Ethnic Group	1970	1980	1990	1980–90	Increase, 1980–90 (%)
Chinese	40,798	94,521	245,033	150,512	159.2
Filipino	33,459	100,894	219,653	118,759	117.7
Korean	8,650	60,339	145,431	85,092	141.0
Japanese	104,078	117,190	129,736	12,546	10.7
Vietnamese		27,252	62,594	35,342	129.7
Asian Indian		18,770	43,829	25,059	133.5
Thai		9,449[a]	19,016	9,567	101.2
Other Southeast Asian[b]			31,920		
Other Asian	3,300[c]		28,349		

Sources: U.S. Bureau of the Census, *Census of Population and Housing, 1970, 1980, 1990* (Washington, D.C.: Government Printing Office, 1973, 1983, 1993); and *Census of Population and Housing, 1970, 1980, 1990 Public Use Sample: 5% County Level Sample* [Computer file] (Washington, D.C.: U.S. Bureau of the Census [producer]).

[a]Based on number of immigrants born in Thailand.
[b]Approximately 28,000 Cambodians, 3,700 Laotians, and 300 Hmong.
[c]Estimated from Public Use Micro Dataset.

growth rates were Koreans (141%), Asian Indians (134%), and Vietnamese (130%). The diversity is even more complex than indicated by the racial data from the census. For example, Asian Indians and Filipinos represent a multitude of language groups. The Chinese immigrant population exhibits another form of heterogeneity, differences in country of origin. Thirty-five percent were born in China, 26 percent in Taiwan, 14 percent in Vietnam, 11 percent in Hong Kong, 14 percent in other countries throughout the greater Southeast Asian region, and the rest in several dozen other nations.

Along with ethnic recomposition, there has been a shift to a more foreign-born population. This trend is not unexpected, given the influx of immigrants, but what is surprising is the magnitude of the change. During the period between the Great Depression and the civil rights movement of the 1960s, when there was a general curtailment of immigration, the size of the native-born population grew as a proportion of all Asian Americans. Since then, the growth of the Asian American community has largely been driven by immigration. The consequences are clearly evident in the statistics: the foreign-born proportion of the population increased from 34 percent in 1970 to 72 percent in 1990.[7] The shift in nativity composition, of course, was due to differences in growth rates. The U.S.-born population more than doubled over the two decades, but this growth was minuscule compared to the elevenfold increase for the foreign-born population.

The relative size of the foreign-born population differs markedly among ethnic groups, a product of distinctive immigration patterns. For Japanese, a group that has not experienced a renewal of large-scale immigration, less than one-third are immigrants (Table 4.2). For the other two groups that experienced earlier waves of immigration, the Chinese and Filipinos, the post-1965 influx has increased the proportion that is foreign-born. In 1990, over three-quarters of each group were foreign-born. The groups with the highest proportion of foreign-born are the newly established populations: the Koreans, South Asians, and Southeast Asians. In each of these groups, over eight-tenths are foreign-born.

While the foreign-born segment dominates the overall Asian

Table 4.2. Characteristics of Asian Immigrants, Los Angeles County, 1990

Group	Foreign-Born as % of Total	Foreign-Born as % of Those Aged 24–64 yr	Entered U.S. 1980–90 (%)	Naturalization Rate (%)	High-Skill[a] (%)	Low-Skill[a] (%)
Chinese	77	90	62	40	35	39
Filipinos	76	92	57	49	54	9
Japanese	33	38	49	24	31	33
South Asians	79	98	60	35	53	18
Koreans	83	98	61	33	28	46
Southeast Asians	82	99	72	33	12	60
All Asians	72	85	60	38	37	32

Source: Tabulations from 1990 PUMS.

[a]Working-age immigrants.

American population, the composition by nativity varies by age categories. Among those twenty-four years or younger, about half are born in the United States. The highest rate is among young Japanese Americans, three-quarters of whom are native Americans. On the other hand, an overwhelming majority of the working-age adults are foreign-born. Excluding Japanese Americans, well over nine-tenths of this age cohort are immigrants.

The immigrant populations also differ in terms of educational achievement and English-language ability. We classify over a third of the working-age immigrants (aged twenty-four to sixty-four) as having low skill levels—that is, they have poor English-language abilities (do not speak English well or at all), less than a high school education, or both. Interestingly, a third also have high skill levels—that is, they have both reasonable English-language abilities (speak English exclusively, very well, or well) and at least a bachelor's degree. There are important variations in the skill levels by ethnicity. Among Filipinos and South Asians, a majority falls in the high-skill category. On the other hand, among Koreans and Southeast Asians, those in the low-skill category greatly outnumber those in the high-skill category.

Another important distinction among immigrants is the length of time in the United States, which is associated with differences in the level of acculturation into U.S. society. In general, English-language abilities and naturalization rates increase with years in the United States. For example, while only 36 percent of those who entered between 1985 and 1990 spoke English very well or exclusively, the corresponding rate is 66 percent for those who entered between 1965 and 1969. The naturalization rate for those who entered between 1980 and 1984 is only 30 percent, considerably lower than the 78 percent for those who entered between 1965 and 1969.[8] These contrasts translate into differences in how well immigrants can participate in the larger social, political, and economic institutions in Los Angeles, creating disparate sets of life experiences.

Interethnic variations show that the process of acculturation cannot simply be reduced to a linear, time-dependent process. In general, we expect the indices of acculturation to vary systematically with the composition by year of entry. For Southeast Asians and Koreans, whose recent immigrants greatly outnumber long-time immigrants, the outcomes are as expected—English-language abilities and naturalization rates are low. But the impact of years in the United States on the English-language abilities of Filipinos is less dramatic. Of recent Filipino immigrants, 63 percent speak English very well or exclusively. Although this proportion is lower than the 80 percent for Filipinos who entered between 1965 and 1975, it is clear that a large majority of Filipino immigrants came to the United States with a functional command of English. This fact is not surprising, given the lingering influence of the United States on the education system in the Philippines, where English has been the major language used in teaching. The Japanese also break with the overall acculturation patterns. This group has the lowest percentage of recent immigrants (49% in the United States for a decade or less) and the highest percentage of long-time immigrants (31% in the United States for more than two decades), but they have the lowest naturalization rate and a high percentage with limited English-language abilities. That may be due in large part to the high numbers of employees of Japanese national corporations located in Los Angeles and their families, most of whom are not eligible for citizenship and have little intention of settling permanently in the United States.

The divergent orientation of these Japanese immigrants compared with other Asian immigrants is perhaps the most extreme example of the contemporary social divisions within the Asian American population, but it certainly is not the only or the most important one. There is no question that ethnic heterogeneity produces a new and rich mix of cultures reflected in the foods, arts, entertainment, and other activities of daily life. At the same time, the ethnic diversity makes Asian American unity exceedingly difficult to achieve. Since the early 1970s, there has not been a single dominant group to set the political agenda. First-generation immigrants often see themselves as separate nationality groups with cultural differences and at times even harbor historical antagonisms. The other side of ethnic diversity is ethnic fragmentation.

Economic Diversity

Ethnicity is not the only factor that divides Asian immigrants. There are also economic divisions, a product of the diverse class backgrounds of this population and the multiple modes of incorporation into the Los Angeles economy. Although most Asian immigrants entered the United States through family sponsorship, they are also very much economic immigrants—people who migrate to the United States for an opportunity to work. The broadest measure of the level of economic activity is the employment ratio, or the employed and self-employed as a percentage of the base population. This immigrant population is economically active, with an employment ratio of 83 percent for prime working-age (twenty-four–sixty-four) males and 63 percent for prime working-age females (Table 4.3). These rates are equal to or higher than the corresponding rates for African Americans and Latinos, and slightly lower than those for Anglos. Three Asian ethnic-gender groups (Filipino and Japanese males, and Filipino females) have employment ratios higher than those of their Anglo counterparts. With the exception of Filipino females, however, Asian immigrants are less likely to work full-time (thirty-five hours or more per week) and full-year (fifty or more weeks per year) than Anglos, indicating that employment tends to be less stable for Asian immigrants.

There are two major exceptions to the high level of economic activity. Joblessness among Southeast Asian males (33%) is two to three times higher than for other Asian immigrant groups. There is also a wide gap among females, with Southeast Asians showing the highest rate of joblessness (58%). These high joblessness rates are the product of these immigrants' status of political refugees, the physical and psychological damages caused by war, and extremely low skills. The other group that exhibits a low employment ratio is Japanese women (49%). This figure is due in part to the presence of a large number of wives of employees of Japanese national corporations. Because of cultural norms and visa restrictions, these women are limited to the role of housewife.

Relative to earlier historical periods, employment of today's Asian immigrants is considerably more varied, a direct and indi-

Table 4.3. Economic Activity of Asian Immigrants Aged 24–64 Years, Los Angeles County, 1989

Group	Males			Females		
	Employment Ratio[a] of Total (%)	% Employed Full-Time/ Full-Year[b]	% Self-Employed[c]	Employment Ratio[a] of Total (%)	% Employed Full-Time/ Full-Year[b]	% Self-Employed[c]
Chinese	79	65	19	61	57	12
Filipinos	89	64	6	83	63	4
Japanese	89	71	19	49	54	11
South Asians	86	69	17	56	57	10
Koreans	85	58	39	57	52	30
Southeast Asians	67	62	11	42	53	15
All Asian Immigrants	83	64	18	63	58	12
Anglos	85	74	18	69	58	11
African Americans	68	66	8	63	61	3
Latinos	83	59	8	55	51	6

Source: Tabulations from 1990 PUMS.

[a]Percentage of working-age population employed in 1990.
[b]Must have worked at least 50 weeks and 35 hours per week in 1989.
[c]Includes unpaid family members.

rect result of the 1965 Immigration Act. During the first half of the century, Asians were concentrated at the bottom of the economic ladder, restricted to retailing, food-service, menial service, and agricultural occupations. After World War II, economic opportunities improved but not enough for Asian Americans to achieve parity. In 1959, Japanese males had the highest average annual earnings among Asian American males but nonetheless lagged behind whites.[9] Over a fifth of Japanese Americans still worked in the agricultural sector, primarily as gardeners. The situation was worse for Filipinos, whose average annual earnings were lower than those of blacks. In the post-1965 era, the economic status of Asian Americans has changed, showing improvements but also persistent problems.

The improvement takes the form of a sizable professional-managerial class. The preference given by the 1965 Immigration Act to the highly skilled and the resulting family-chain migration tied to the first wave of occupational immigrants have produced an Asian immigrant working-age population in which 40 percent have at least a bachelor's degree and 11 percent have an additional graduate or professional degree. Many of these highly skilled immigrants were directly incorporated into the U.S. labor force as workers in jobs related to their chosen field. Managerial and professional Asians with temporary work permits often retain their posts when converting to permanent residency status. Immigrants who entered under the occupational quotas, particularly after the mid-1970s, had fulfilled licensing requirements before being sponsored by employers and thus were in a position to continue their careers.

Not all highly educated persons have translated their training into commensurate employment. Limited English-language proficiency and stringent requirements for credentials for various professional occupations prevent many people from passing or even taking licensing examinations. As a consequence, many immigrant professionals suffer downward occupational mobility in their adopted country. One indicator of downward mobility comes from the 1990 census, which shows that 43 percent of Asian immigrants with a graduate or professional degree do not work in a managerial or professional category. Additional evidence of the prevalence of downward mobility comes from a comparison of Immigration and Naturalization Service (INS) data and census data. Of those who came to Los Angeles between 1983 to 1986, 22 percent had previously worked in a professional or technical occupation in their native country (U.S. Immigration and Naturalization Service, 1991). According to 1990 census data for those who entered the country between 1982 and 1986, only 16 percent were working in one of these occupations (U.S. Bureau of the Census, 1990a). This disparity does not reveal the whole picture, because many professionals are forced to accept lower positions in the technical occupations.

Despite the problem of downward mobility, roughly a quarter of all wage and salaried workers fall into the professional and managerial class (PMC, which constitutes the top end of the economic spectrum (Table 4.4). Not all groups are equally able to go into the PMC. Japanese and South Asian males have the highest rates (40% each), while Southeast Asians of both genders have the lowest rates (16% for males and 11% for females). Females generally have lower rates than their male counterparts, with the exception of Filipinos. Filipinas are more likely to be in this class because many were recruited to the United States as nurses (see Chapter 6).

Being a part of the PMC is desirable, but Asian immigrants are concentrated in the less prestigious and lower-paid PMC occupations. Among managers and administrators, who comprise about a third of the Asian immigrant PMC, few (0.2%) are chief executives. A "glass ceiling" limits upward mobility, so Asians are rarely able to reach the pinnacles of the economic hierarchy. Instead, they tend to occupy more technical or ethnically based positions. For example, 12 percent are financial managers and another 11 percent are managers in food-service and lodging establishments. Among professionals, 31 percent are engineers or computer specialists and 30 percent are health practitioners. Registered nursing is the single largest occupation, accounting for eight out of every ten health practitioners, revealing that Asians are concentrated in the subordinate positions in the medical field.

Along with the large number of Asian immigrant workers in the PMC (71,000) are a slightly larger number (78,000) at the other end of the occupational scale, in low-skill clerical, blue-collar,

Table 4.4. Occupational Distribution of Employed Asian Immigrants, Aged 24–64 Years, Los Angeles County, 1989 (in Percent)

Group	Males			Females		
	Managerial Class[a]	Professional-Low-Skill Occupations[b]	All Others	Managerial Class[a]	Professional-Low-Skill Occupations[b]	All Others
Chinese	32	25	43	20	33	47
Filipinos	17	21	62	27	27	46
Japanese	40	18	42	20	38	42
South Asians	40	17	43	31	29	41
Koreans	26	22	52	22	44	34
Southeast Asians	16	24	60	11	42	47
All Asians	26	22	52	23	33	44
Anglos	36	11	53	34	21	44
African Americans	16	22	62	22	27	50
Latinos	8	32	60	12	50	38

Source: Tabulations from 1990 PUMS.

Note: Does not include those self-employed.
[a]Includes executives, administrators, managers (excluding management-related occupations), and all professional specialty occupations.
[b]Includes sales workers, clerks, records processors, service occupations except those in protective services, textile/apparel workers, assemblers, helpers, and handlers.

and service occupations. Seventeen percent of those in low-skill positions are in sales, with over half working as cashiers. Twelve percent work in "financial records processing" occupations, such as bookkeeping, accounting, and accounting clerk positions, including many with some college education who have difficulty becoming full accountants in the United States. Seventeen percent work in restaurant occupations, primarily as waiters, waitresses, and cooks. Among blue-collar workers, there are nearly seven thousand sewing machine operators, who account for 9 percent of all Asian low-skill workers.

Rather than being crammed against the glass ceiling or working in low-skilled jobs, some Asian immigrants, including many highly educated immigrants unable to practice their professions, have turned to operating their own businesses. Approximately one in six was either self-employed or an unpaid worker in a family business (see Table 4.3). The actual number of family workers is probably higher than that reported by the census because some may work both in the family business and for pay in another firm. Entrepreneurship varies considerably by ethnicity. Self-employment is lowest among Filipinos and highest among Koreans. We suspect that the huge difference between Koreans and Filipinos in this area is not due just to capital resources and culturally defined predilection. It is likely that the greater English-language abilities of Filipinos offer them more opportunities in the labor market than Koreans.

Despite the extensive and favorable attention given to entrepreneurship among Asian immigrants, the statistics paint a more pessimistic picture. Although substantially higher than those for blacks and Latinos, the self-employment rates for Asian immigrants are only marginally higher than those for Anglos. Moreover, Asian entrepreneurs are more likely to be concentrated in less desirable and highly competitive niches. Of self-employed Asian immigrants, 42 percent are in the wholesale and retailing sector, compared to only 16 percent of self-employed Anglos. Although the two groups have nearly identical percentages in manufacturing (9%), four-tenths of Asian manufacturers are in apparel compared to only one-tenth of Anglo manufacturers. As a consequence of this maldistribution, average self-employment income for Asians is about only four-fifths that for Anglos. Self-

employment may be a better option than the limited opportunities in the labor market, but it is not a guarantee of economic
success on a par with Anglos.

The 1987 Survey of Minority-owned Business Enterprises
(U.S. Bureau of the Census, 1991) provides additional insights
into the problems faced by Asian entrepreneurs. Although this
source does not distinguish between immigrant and nonimmigrant owners, it is likely that immigrants owned a vast majority of the sixty-two thousand Asian American businesses reported for metropolitan Los Angeles.[10] These businesses are
concentrated in the small business sector. Three-quarters had no
paid employees, and among those that did, the average was
only four employees, considerably less than the average of more
than seventeen for all firms in Los Angeles. Annual receipts for
Asian firms averaged only $321,000, which can hardly be consid-
ered a large volume.

The limitations encountered by self-employed Asian immigrants and by those working for paid labor have kept average
remuneration relatively low. Nevertheless, Asian immigrant
workers tend to earn significantly more than Latinos, who are at
the bottom of the economic ladder, with averages that are only
about half those for Anglos (Table 4.5). Latino workers, like
Asians, are largely immigrants, but the overwhelming majority
of Latinos, unlike Asians, have little education. Yet despite the
high levels of educational achievement, Asians earn considerably less than their Anglo counterparts. The median for Asian
male immigrants is only 70 percent of the median for Anglo
males, and the comparable figure of 80 percent for females is
only slightly better. What is surprising is that the average for
Asian immigrant workers is lower than that for African Americans.

Accompanying the relatively low earnings for Asian immigrants is a polarized distribution of earnings. Although the earnings distribution among Asian immigrants does not show a simple bimodal pattern, it does have many of the characteristics of
economic polarization that have plagued Los Angeles. A substantial number of workers are at the bottom end. Among those
who work the equivalent of half-time for a full year, approximately one in six Asian immigrant workers is a low-earner (less

Table 4.5. Annual Earnings of Employed Asian Immigrants, Aged 24–64 Years, Los Angeles County, 1989

Group	Males			Females		
	Median Value ($)	% below $12,000	% $48,000 or more	Median Value ($)	% below $12,000	% $48,000 or more
Chinese	26,000	17	20	18,600	25	9
Filipinos	24,600	11	9	21,800	13	8
Japanese	40,000	3	42	20,000	18	7
South Asians	30,100	13	28	19,000	20	9
Koreans	25,000	16	20	18,500	26	9
Southeast Asians	24,000	16	9	18,000	25	4
All Asian Immigrants	26,000	14	18	20,000	20	8
Anglos	37,500	6	35	25,000	12	11
African Americans	26,400	11	11	22,000	15	5
Latinos	18,000	25	6	13,000	42	2

Source: Tabulations from 1990 PUMS.

Note: Earnings include wages and self-employment (farm and nonfarm) income. Sample includes those who worked at least 1,040 hours (half the total of 52 weeks times 40 hours).

than $12,000), which is proportionately higher than the figure for Anglos and African Americans. A recent survey indicates that many of these Asian low-earners are trapped in jobs that offer little opportunity for upward mobility.[11] The proportion at the bottom end is not completely offset by workers at the top end, but nonetheless many Asian immigrants do earn at least an upper-middle-class income. Approximately one in eight Asian immigrant workers is at the top end of the earnings ($48,000), which is proportionately lower than the figure for Anglos but higher than the figure for African Americans. It is possible that other Asian immigrants will move into this category as they become more economically assimilated, but progress is likely to be slow, given the glass ceiling and the limitations of entrepreneurship.

Asian immigrants compensate for limited earnings by pooling income in large households, and the benefits of this strategy can be seen by comparing this group to Anglos. Of Asian immigrant households, 26 percent have five or more persons, compared to only 6 percent for Anglo households. Moreover, 32 percent of Asian immigrant households have three or more in the labor force, compared to only 8 percent for Anglos. This strategy produced a median household income of $37,200 in 1989 for Asian immigrants, close to but still less than the $40,500 for Anglos; consequently, the discrepancy in household incomes between Asian immigrants and Anglos is smaller than the discrepancy in annual earnings. There is, however, a limitation to the pooling of earnings: many Asian immigrants are still unable to escape poverty. The poverty rate among Asian immigrants is 15 percent, compared to 7 percent for Anglos.

The divisions between the haves and the have-nots work along with ethnic differences to fragment further Asian immigrants. In some cases, class disparities reinforce ethnic lines. For example, the economic distance between Japanese and Cambodian is as great as the cultural distance. Within an ethnic population, class and economic position create horizontal cleavages. There is interaction, but exchanges are along lines of employer and employee, merchant and customer, provider and client, and landlord and tenant. Interclass alliance, when it exists, is tenuous and based on necessity. Class solidarity is a theoretical possibility as an alternative to unequal ethnic solidarity, but a common economic position rarely becomes the basis for group cohesion (see Chapter 10). It is not an understatement to say that Asian Americans, and Asian immigrants in particular, are highly segmented.

Old and New Communities

The demographic and economic diversity of Asian immigrants has redefined the residential patterns of the Asian American population as a whole from highly integrated to highly complex and kaleidoscopic. After a century of racial segregation sanctioned by the state and local government, Asian Americans began enjoying freedom in choosing where to live after World War II. What emerged was a high degree of residential assimilation that mirrored the acculturation of the predominantly U.S.-born Asians of this period. Ethnic communities such as Chinatown in Los Angeles City and the Japanese American settlement in Gardena continued to exist, but Asian Americans in general were no longer an isolated racial group by the late 1960s. According to the 1970 census, two-thirds of this population lived in predominantly non-Asian neighborhoods (census tracts) where they constituted 10 percent or less of the population. But this trend toward full residential integration soon came to an end. By 1990, less than one-third lived in predominantly non-Asian neighborhoods.

Immigration played the major role in reversing the trend in residential settlement. Like other immigrants, Asian Americans gravitate to locations where they have friends or relatives. Some have followed a pattern of initially settling in inner-city enclaves that serve as "staging areas" and then moving out to better employment and housing situations. Many others have settled directly into suburban neighborhoods, where they now form a highly visible group, although not necessarily a majority. Although the proportion of Asian Americans living in areas where they comprised a majority increased nearly tenfold, this group accounted for only 6 percent of the Asian American community in 1990 (Table 4.6). The real growth has been in areas where

Table 4.6. Distribution of Asian Americans, by Neighborhood Types, 1970–1990

Neighborhood Type	1970		1990		Increase (%)
	No.	%	No.	%	
0–9% Asian American	107,315	58.9	251,989	27.8	135
10–19 Asian American	39,189	21.0	243,296	26.8	521
20–29 Asian American	17,068	9.1	163,660	18.1	775
30–49 Asian American	18,702	10.0	196,327	21.7	950
Majority Asian American	4,711	2.5	51,273	5.7	988

Source: Tabulations from 1970 and 1990 Census Summary Tape Files.

Asian Americans form a large minority, from 20 to 49 percent of the residents. In this category, the number of Asian Americans increased by over 900 percent, from 36,000 to 360,000 between 1970 and 1990. What has emerged is not a single contiguous Asian ghetto, but rather a collection of Asian clusters that are geographically dispersed throughout much of the highly urbanized portions of Los Angeles.

Some clusters are in inner-city neighborhoods, The central parts of Los Angeles City are home to more than eighty thousand Asian Americans, two-fifths of whom are Koreans, a quarter Filipinos, a fifth Chinese, and the remainder divided between the Japanese and Southeast Asians. These Asian Americans share the inner city with Latinos, who comprise the majority of the population. The three major Asian ethnic groups have identifiable centers: Chinatown, north of City Hall; Koreatown, southwest of downtown along Olympic Boulevard and Western

Avenue; and Filipino Town, in the Westlake area just west of downtown. Chinatown and Koreatown are particularly visible because of the large number of ethnic businesses.

Despite the existence of identifiable ethnic centers, the Asian populations are not concentrated in monolithic areas. Instead, there are many disconnected pockets and a high degree of intermingling. For example, the Chinese population has jumped west, north, and east of the old Chinatown, and the service basin for community groups such as the Chinatown Service Center now comprises several discontiguous areas. Although the largest concentration of Koreans is located in Koreatown, a sizable population resides north of Wilshire Boulevard, around which is a non-Asian commercial district. Finally, Filipinos are as likely to reside in blocks with large number of Koreans as in Filipino Town. Inner-city Asian enclaves in Los Angeles City are communities without sharply defined boundaries.

This pattern also holds for nearly fifteen thousand Cambodians in the inner-city area of Long Beach, the second largest city in Los Angeles County. This community has emerged as the largest Cambodian community in the United States. Like Koreatown, the Cambodian community is an enclave created by modern immigration. The Long Beach community is unique, however, in being a product of the flight of political refugees. While this community has a visible commercial sector, it is also the poorest Asian enclave, as we see later.

Most of the Asian populations residing in the inner city are highly disadvantaged. Many residents are recent immigrants, having been in the United States five or fewer years (Table 4.7). More important, a high percentage have limited education and English-language abilities, which translate into low-wage jobs or joblessness. One consequence is that per capita income is low, about two-thirds or less of the per capita income for all Asian immigrants in the county. The income level for Cambodians is particularly low, in large part because many are jobless and dependent on public welfare. Over half this population (51%) lives in families with income below the poverty level, compared to only 26 percent each of the inner-city Koreans and Chinese. With limited income, inner-city Asians are unable to be homeowners and often live in overcrowded and poorly maintained apartments. Inner-city Filipinos are the exception to this pattern. Central Los Angeles City is the home to a sizable middle-class Filipino population whose members have a fair amount of education and are able to speak English well or very well. Their per capita income is close to that of all Asian immigrants in the county, and their poverty level is only 6 percent.

The growth of inner-city enclaves is only one part of the emerging residential pattern for Asian Americans. Most of the growth of Asian American communities has occurred in suburban enclaves. That is especially true in West San Gabriel Valley, where the cities of Alhambra, Monterey Park, Rosemead, and San Gabriel are at least 32 percent Asian. Monterey Park has the unique status of the only city on the U.S. mainland with a majority (58%) Asian American population (see Chapter 8). Some suburban communities have a dominant ethnic group while others do not. For example, Filipinos comprise 67 percent of all Asians in Carson, the Japanese comprise 56 percent of all Asians in Gardena, and the Chinese comprise 63 percent of all Asians in Monterey Park. Other communities are more pluralistic. The Asian American population in West Covina is 44 percent Filipino and 27 percent Chinese, for example. Cerritos, a city on the southeastern edge of the county, has a balanced Asian American population, with roughly equal Chinese, Filipino, and Korean components (22%, 24%, and 27%, respectively) and with a smaller South Asian population (9%) that is nonetheless highly visible.

Compared to their inner-city counterparts, suburban Asian communities are less disadvantaged (see Table 4.7). The relative number of recent immigrants is lower, although approximately one-fifth to one-quarter still fall in this category. A more important distinction is the higher educational and English skill levels in the suburban areas, which not surprisingly translate into higher income levels and higher rates of homeownership. The Japanese in the South Bay have a particularly high per capita income, due to the combination of a high percentage of U.S.-born residents and well-paid employees of Japanese national corporations. Not all suburban Asian neighborhoods are well

Table 4.7. Neighborhood Characteristics of Asian Immigrants, Selected Areas, 1990

Neighborhood	Recent Immigrants[a] (%)	Recent Movers[b] (%)	Renters (%)	Without High School Degree[c] (%)	Limited English[d] (%)	Median Per Capita Income[e] ($)
Inner City						
Chinese	24	24	70	47	51	5,900
Filipino	33	30	71	9	3	11,800
Korean	39	42	85	24	56	6,700
Cambodian	25	43	92	68	69	3,000
Suburban						
Chinese	26	30	42	33	39	7,900
Filipino	21	26	24	9	4	12,200
Korean	28	37	43	8	38	10,600
Japanese	20	20	38	5	14	20,000
All Asian Americans	22	28	42	17	22	11,300

Source: Tabulations from 1990 PUMS.

Note: The statistics are for all Asian Americans, foreign and U.S. born, and are based on the PUMS areas (PUMAS), which are geographic units below the county level. Inner-city Chinese, Filipinos, and Koreans are those who reside in PUMA 6508, 6502, and 6506, an area that includes Chinatown, Filipino Town, Koreatown, and adjacent neighborhoods. The statistics for suburban Asian groups are based on the following: for the Chinese, the PUMA that includes Monterey Park and Rosemead, which are located in West San Gabriel Valley; for Filipinos, the PUMA that includes Carson; for Koreans, the PUMA that includes Glendale; and for Japanese, the PUMAS that include parts of the South Bay.

Continued on next page

Table 4.7 (Continued)

a Those who entered between 1985 and 1990.
b Those who moved into their home between 1989 and 1990.
c Pertains to those between the ages of 24 and 64.
d Includes those between the ages of 24 and 64 who speak English poorly or not at all.
e Average of per capita income calculated by household.

Table 4.8. Residential Pattern of Asian Immigrants, Los Angeles County, 1989

Group	Dissimilarity Index[a]				In Tracts with at least 30% Asian Americans (%)	Affinity Group[b]
	Anglos	Blacks	Latinos	Other Asians		
Chinese	60	80	64	48	40	Vietnamese (44)
Filipinos	52	70	50	45	18	South Asian (47)
Japanese	49	73	64	45	27	Chinese (49)
South Asians	39	70	59	40	12	Korean (46)
Koreans	54	78	65	45	27	South Asian (46)
Vietnamese	60	71	53	41	26	Chinese (44)
Other Southeast Asians	88	84	75	57	32	Vietnamese (69)

Source: Tabulations from 1990 PUMS.

a Indicates the percentage of the Asian population that would have to move into a non-Asian neighborhood in order to achieve full residential integration.
b The group with the lowest dissimilarity index.

off, however. Asians in communities such as Rosemead have a per capita income comparable to those in the inner city—about $8,900 in 1989.[12]

Although the revitalization of old and the establishment of new Asian enclaves are important phenomena, an equally significant reality is that most Asian Americans have numerous non-Asian neighbors. Despite increased ethnic concentration,[13] Asian Americans continue to be the least segregated among the races. Only 1 percent live in census tracts where they comprise at least 80 percent of the residents. In contrast, roughly one-third of whites, one-fourth of Latinos, and over one-fifth of African Americans live in areas where they constitute such a dominant majority of the residents.

Residential contact with other groups varies by race, as indicated by Table 4.8. Asian Americans have more contact with Anglos than with any other racial group. That may be due to overlapping economic positions for a large proportion of both populations. Moreover, "white flight" is not a strong reaction when Asian Americans move into non-Hispanic neighborhoods (Ong and Lawrence, 1992). Asian American contact with Latinos is more limited but nonetheless not uncommon. Both groups look for similar residential and locational characteristics that facilitate their entry to the social and economic activities of a place. Thus, it is no accident that Asian Americans and Latinos are frequently found in the same neighborhoods, particularly in the inner city. Nevertheless, the choice of which inner-city areas is not random. Residential contact with African Americans is minimal, even in inner-city areas such as South Central. This avoidance by Asian immigrants of African American areas is partly attributable to racial prejudice.

The residential patterns described above are the results of social and economic structures, but the spatial configuration also reinforces these structures and defines many important arenas of intergroup interaction and conflict. As with demographic and economic diversity, the heterogeneity in residential choice and variation in the characteristics of enclaves among Asian immigrants do not easily fit into a simple conceptual model based on race. Race has become less salient for Asians as an external constraint but has continued to shape personal preferences. To the degree that this is true, Asians have shown a greater affinity for other Asians and for Anglos than for other minorities. Clearly, ethnicity and class have an influence at least equal to that of race on the construction of the urban landscape. They define individual taste and financial ability. In some cases, these factors have brought Asians together, but rarely enough to form exclusive ethnic enclaves. Of course, these types of communities may be the final product of the dynamic process that is still under way. Whatever the future holds, the pressing problem today is for Asians to coexist with other racial populations with whom they share geographic space.

The numbers reported above reveal much, but they certainly do not reveal all, particularly the qualitative aspects of the experiences of the new Asian immigrants. For example, while residential contact with African Americans is quite limited, the conflict between Korean merchants and African American residents is a major source of racial tension in Los Angeles. And the numbers do not reveal the daily economic struggles and sacrifices of Asian Americans. Nonetheless, the demographic, economic, and geographic patterns cannot be ignored.

The patterns discussed in this chapter set broad parameters that define the Asian immigrant experience. The pre-migration class composition of new immigrants, for example, explains why a significant share of this population has achieved at least middle-class status. Of course, that does not negate the fact that many highly educated immigrants suffer from downward mobility. Any validity in the notion of Asian Americans as an economic "model minority" rests as much on selective class migration as on cultural factors. It is this very selectivity that has made Asian immigrants a potentially powerful force in Los Angeles's economy.

Asian immigrants' political potential is considerably weaker. Asian immigration has produced an urgent need for programs that address the educational, training, housing, and other needs of this growing population. Asians should receive a fair share of the public resources, and public policies should reflect the unique problems and contributions of the immigrants. The increased population size and greater residential concentration provide a territorial base for Asian Americans to develop the same political institutions present in other minority communities and to elect responsive politicians. This is more of a dream than a reality, however, for Asian Americans have little representation in the political power structure, whether in Los Angeles, the state of California, or the nation. As the largest concentration of Asian Americans in the country, the Los Angeles community has the opportunity to be in the forefront of the difficult struggle for political empowerment.

Notes

1. Since 1980, the U.S. Census Bureau has used the category *Asian and Pacific Islander American* to designate persons who trace their ancestry to the Far East and to East, South, and Southeast Asia, as well as to Pacific Island countries of origin. Some of our tabulations of Asian Americans include Pacific Islanders, who comprise 3 percent of the total Asian and Pacific Islander population of Los Angeles County. As with the rest of the book, however, our discussion focuses only on Asian Americans.
2. The number of Asian and Pacific Islander Americans was 7.3 million.
3. Our study is based on published and unpublished sources. The most important data sources on the population come from census and Immigration and Naturalization Service (INS) reports: the Summary Tape Files (STF) and Public Use Microdata Sample (PUMS) from the census, and INS immigration tapes. The race variable from the census is used to classify the Asian American population. Because the PUMS contains only a 5 percent sample of the population, at times it is necessary to combine some of the smaller ethnic groups. Unless otherwise noted, the category *South Asian* includes Asian Indian, Bangladeshi, Pakistani, and Sri Lankan; and the category *Southeast Asian* includes Vietnamese, Cambodian, Hmong, and Laotian. Although the census undercounts the number of Asian Americans, we do not make any correction, which in itself is a formidable task. For convenience, the terms *Asian Americans* and *Asians*, and parallel terms for ethnic specific groups, are used interchangeably. Los Angeles is defined as the Los Angeles metropolitan area, which is coterminous Los Angeles County and has a population of about nine million persons, about four-tenths of whom reside in Los Angeles City.

4. There were also about 29,000 Pacific Islanders in Los Angeles in 1990.
5. In 1970, the total number of Japanese, Chinese, and Filipinos living in the Honolulu metropolitan area was approximately 234,000, more than twice the 115,000 living in Los Angeles. San Francisco–Oakland was not far behind, with nearly 100,000. By 1990, Los Angeles had 954,000 Asians and Pacific Islanders, while San Francisco–Oakland had 599,000, and Honolulu had 526,000. Growth rates in the New York metropolitan area were even higher, enabling the city to climb from a distant fourth in 1970, with 49,000, to a close third in 1990, with 556,000.
6. According to the 1960 census, there were approximately 115,000 Japanese, Chinese, and Filipinos in Los Angeles. We estimate that there were at most 5,000 other Asians.
7. The 1970 figure is based on the Japanese, Chinese, and Filipino populations, which together accounted for about 93 percent of the total Asian population.
8. The low overall naturalization rate for all Asian immigrants, 38 percent in 1990, has translated into a disproportionately low number of Asian voters. While Asian Americans comprise over 9 percent of the total population in Los Angeles City, they accounted for only 4 percent of those who voted in the April 1993 primary election for mayor, which included an Asian American as one of the two leading candidates.
9. These earnings and other 1959 earnings numbers are taken from *U.S. Census of Population: 1960, Subject Report, Nonwhite Population by Race* (Washington, D.C.: Government Printing Office, 1963). Average annual earnings were $5,308 for all males, $4,761 for Japanese males, $4,034 for Chinese males, $3,649 for Filipino males, and $3,740 for black males. Given the fact that minorities earned less than the average for all males, the average for white males was higher than $5,308.
10. According to the 1987 survey, Asian Americans owned more enterprises than any other major minority group. Although the African American population was slightly larger than the Asian American population, there were only twenty-four thousand African American firms. The Latino population was more than three times larger than the Asian American population, but there were only fifty-seven thousand Latino businesses.
11. This 1994 survey was conducted by a team of graduate and undergraduate students at University of California at Los Angeles under the direction of Paul Ong. More than three face-to-face interviews were conducted in four inner-city Asian neighborhoods.

12. It is impossible to develop ethnic-specific statistics for Rosemead because the city is in the same PUMS area as Monterey Park and because the Summary Tape File contains data only for all Asians.
13. This increase is evident in the exposure index, which measures the racial composition of the neighborhood of a typical Asian American. Between 1970 and 1990, the exposure index of Asian Americans with respect to other Asian Americans grew from 13 percent to 23 percent.

References

Ong, Paul, and Janette Lawrence. 1992. *Pluralism and Residential Patterns in Los Angeles*. Discussion Papers, D9202. Los Angeles: Graduate School of Architecture and Urban Planning, University of California.

U.S. Bureau of the Census. 1932. *Fifteenth Census of the United States: 1930, Population, Vol. 3, Part 1. Reports by States, Showing the Composition and Characteristics of the Population for Counties, Cities, and Townships. Alabama–Missouri*. Washington, D.C.: Government Printing Office.

———. 1943. *Sixteenth Census of the United States: 1940, Population, Vol. 2, Characteristics of the Population. Part 1. U.S. Summary and Alabama–Washington, D.C.* Washington, D.C.: Government Printing Office.

———. 1953. *United States Census of Population: 1950, Special Reports, Nonwhite Population by Race*. 1950 Population Census Report P-E No. 3B. Reprint of Vol. 4, Part 3, Chapter B. Washington, D.C.: Government Printing Office.

———. 1983a. *1980 Census of Population, Vol. 1, Characteristics of the Population. Chapter C, General Social and Economic Characteristics, California*. PC80-1-C6. Washington, D.C.: Government Printing Office.

———. 1983b. *1980 Census of Population, Vol. 1, Characteristics of the Population. Chapter D, Detailed Population Characteristics, Part 6, California*. PC80-1-D6. Washington, D.C.: Government Printing Office.

———. 1983c. *1980 Census of Population, Subject Reports, Asian and Pacific Islander Population in the United States: 1980*. PC80-2-1E, Washington, D.C.: Government Printing Office.

———. 1990a. *Census of Population and Housing, 1990: PUMS A Sample* [Computer File]. Washington, D.C.: U.S. Bureau of the Census [producer].

———. 1990b. *Statistical Abstract of the United States, 1990.* Washington, D.C.: Government Printing Office.

———. 1991. *1987 Economic Censuses, Survey by Minority-owned Business Enterprises, Asian Americans, American Indians, and Other Minorities.* MB87-3. Washington, D.C.: Government Printing Office.

U.S. Immigration and Naturalization Service. 1989. *Statistical Yearbook of the Immigration and Naturalization Service.* Washington, D.C.: Government Printing Office.

Part III
Economic Incorporation

Introduction

Paul Ong

The economic incorporation of new Asian immigrants is not a singular process but a rich, diverse mix of modes of entry into the economy, reflecting the ethnic and class heterogeneity of the population. Some immigrants, such as Filipino nurses and Chinese engineers, are directly recruited by U.S. employers. For them, initial employment is integral to the process of temporary migration and permanent immigration. A small number of immigrants, but a growing group under the entrepreneurial provision of the 1990 Immigration Act, come with substantial capital, which enables them to secure a firm foothold in their adopted country. Most, however, are less fortunate. They must search for employment after arriving in the United States and are often hindered by a lack of transferable skills, an inadequate command of the English language, and racial discrimination.

Outcomes depend on the structure of opportunity defined by the changing economy as well as on individual drives, social and familial resources, and the whims of a market economy. Some immigrants fulfill their dreams of making a fortune, frequently by becoming members of the professional, managerial, and capitalist classes. For others, the drive for financial success turns into a struggle for economic survival.

The chapters in this section illustrate the diverse modes of economic incorporation of new Asian immigrants. Many aspects of the processes discussed here are unique to the post-1965 period, shaped by recent immigration policies and economic factors, but there are also elements mirroring the experience of earlier waves of Asian and non-Asian immigrants. There is both historical continuity and discontinuity.

An example of the repetition of past historical patterns can be seen in the case of new Asian immigrants in the Los Angeles garment industry. Since the turn of the century, this industry has been a major source of employment and self-employment for newcomers. Los Angeles today is similar to New York City at the beginning of the century, when the garment industry absorbed thousands of southern European and Jewish women workers through a subcontracting system dominated by Jewish petits bourgeois. The garment industry in modern Los Angeles plays this same role of absorbing immigrants, but with a new set of ethnic actors. As Edna Bonacich points out in Chapter 5, Asian immigrants have been a source of cheap labor, and more important, they have emerged as the dominant group among subcontractors. As the new petits bourgeois, Asians have come into contact with Latino immigrants, who make up over three-quarters of the work force, producing a new ethnic-class configuration and a new potential source of intergroup conflict.

Despite the parallels between old and new, there are differences. The most important one is the larger structure within which Asians and the Los Angeles garment industry are situated. Today's garment industry is global rather than national. The old exploitative contracting system is still with us, but the organization of the primary manufacturers, retailing outlets, and financial institutions has been reshaped by current realities, particularly mergers funded by junk bonds. These international and domestic conditions have increased the competitive pressure on the garment industry, undercutting wages for workers and profits for subcontractors.

Labor recruitment, which was so prevalent during earlier immigration periods, is still alive, but it has shifted its focus from unskilled to skilled workers. The sizable labor force of foreign-trained nurses working in the United States is a product of contemporary immigration policy, which has periodically given preference to those with technical and medical skills in response to recurring labor shortages in these professional occupations. As Paul Ong and Tania Azores note in Chapter 6, this policy has biased the occupational choice of Filipinas, who pursue nursing to increase their odds of migrating to the United States, and has subverted the educational and health systems in the Philippines. Once in the United States, Filipino nurses face a major hurdle in the form of the licensing test. The many who fail are forced either to return home or to become exploitable labor in the United States. Those who do pass are readily hired by hospitals and earn salaries comparable to those of U.S.-trained nurses. They are far from being fully assimilated into the health system, however. Filipino nurses are heavily concentrated in a few regions, in a few hospitals, and in a few wards, and the sense of alienation is reinforced by a clash of cultures and languages at work.

Many of the Chinese-Vietnamese studied by Steve Gold in Chapter 7 have followed a more traditional economic activity: entrepreneurship. Southeast Asians are considered distinct in that they are political refugees rather than economic immigrants. Although this status gives them access to programs specifically targeted to this population, Southeast Asians nonetheless face many of the same economic struggles as other Asian immigrants. The Vietnamese of Chinese descent, many of whom are "boat people," comprise a particularly disadvantaged group, but they are not without resources. Like pre–World War II Chinese and Japanese immigrants, Chinese-Vietnamese in southern California draw on ethnic resources to develop an ethnically defined subeconomy. The ethnic linkages today are more international than in historical times, however. The Chinese-Vietnamese rely on overseas contacts for both capital and merchandise. Although the ethnic economy is a mode of incorporation, it is far from ideal. The limits of managerial skills and ethnic institutions, along with fierce market competition, hinder the growth, firm size, and viability of the Chinese-Vietnamese businesses. Consequently, firms depend on family and low-wage labor, profits are problematic, and establishments frequently fail.

The case studies in this section not only reveal the diversity in the patterns of economic incorporation but also shed light on the U.S. economy. The United States has a remarkable ability to absorb a heterogeneous wave of immigrants, but capitalism does not offer fairness or equality. It is a system that depends on people willing to exploit themselves and others, to take risks, and to accept failure as a temporary setback. Despite the many hardships documented in this section, most new Asian immigrants have a resilience that enables them to sustain their economic struggles within the confines of capitalism. This persistence is testimony to the spirit of the people, but also to the nature of capitalism. There are enough successes and examples of mobility that immigrants keep their faith in the United States. Consequently, Asians play a key role in supporting and renewing capitalism as an economic and ideological system. At the same time, their actions are helping reshape the economy locally and globally.

5. Asians in the Los Angeles Garment Industry

Edna Bonacich

The garment industry is being restructured on a global scale. It is one of the major international industries, with almost every country, rich and poor, participating in it. Apparel production is often one of the first manufacturing industries to be developed by a country that is trying to industrialize. All over the world new garment producers are arising, changing the relations in the global industry.

The manufacture of clothing demonstrates vividly the new international division of labor (Fröbel, Heinrichs, and Kreye, 1980). Developing countries are becoming major producers, often exporting their wares to the developed countries of the West. As a result, the U.S. industry has had to face rising competition from apparel imports and has suffered some decline and loss of employment. Garment jobs appear to be moving overseas to countries where labor costs are a fraction of the U.S. level.

Capitalists have essentially two ways to deal with intense competition: enhance the productivity of the industry through organizational and technical improvements or squeeze the workers harder. Efforts are under way to introduce new technology, and garment production may see some major changes in the next few decades (Hoffman and Rush, 1988; U.S. Congress, Office of Technology Assessment, 1987). Nevertheless, sewing, which is the primary work activity of the industry, remains highly labor-intensive, showing little impact of technological change. Consequently, the chief competitive strategy of the industry is to keep labor as cheap and exploited as possible.

Immigrants and women are among the cheapest and most exploitable of workers. The garment industry in the United States is thus a prime employer of immigrant women (with immigrant men making up a substantial minority of the labor force). Often the immigrants come from the very countries that are the United

States's most serious competitors. These countries also depend heavily on cheap, exploitable, often female, labor. U.S. manufacturers meet the competitive threat either by shipping some of their production to Third World countries or by employing their own Third World immigrant workers to do the work in the United States. Apparel manufacture, regardless of the locus of production, depends on a fairly homogeneous group of workers, namely, oppressed people, mainly women of color (e.g., Fernandez-Kelly, 1983; Fuentes and Ehrenreich, 1984; Mitter, 1986; Safa, 1981).

Asian immigrant women are an important component of the U.S. garment labor force, along with immigrant workers from Mexico and the Caribbean area. Chinese and Koreans have been especially significant in this industry, and Vietnamese and other Southeast Asian involvement is rising rapidly. It is noteworthy that Taiwan, Hong Kong, the People's Republic of China, and South Korea are the major sources of garment imports to the United States and that immigrants from these countries provide an important labor force for the U.S. industry.

Asian immigrants are not only workers in the industry; they are also contractors, that is, small business owners who contract from manufacturers to do the cutting and sewing of garments from the manufacturers' designs and textiles. Contractors directly employ labor, whereas many manufacturers do not. Garment contractors are thus, in a sense, labor contractors, who mobilize, employ, and control labor for the rest of the industry.

Contracting is the most important role of Asian immigrants in the Los Angeles garment industry. Asians, especially Chinese, are more important as garment workers in other U.S. cities, notably New York and San Francisco.[1] In Los Angeles, the majority of garment workers are Latino immigrants, with Asians making up a significant minority. Asians are the majority of contractors in Los Angeles County, by a small margin.

Asian immigrants are also scattered throughout the industry in other roles. They serve as employees of large corporations and banks that participate in the industry. Some Asian immigrants are moving into designing, importing, and manufacturing. Asians own and operate small apparel retail stores and swap meets. These various activities deserve close study, but this chapter focuses on the roles of contractor and worker, where the Asian immigrant presence is most keenly felt.[2]

The obvious emergence of Asian immigrants as contractors has attracted some research attention, with a focus on "immigrant entrepreneurship" (e.g., Waldinger, 1986; Wong, 1987). The interest lies in how Asian immigrants are able to make a successful leap into the business world. It is generally seen as a positive development and a possible model for other ethnic minorities to follow.

That is not my approach. I see the garment industry as an example of the social decay of capitalism. I see Asian immigrant contractors as embedded in a much larger, hierarchically organized structure. Like most others in it, they are both victimizers and victimized. Since they are fairly near the bottom of the hierarchy, they are more hurt than those higher up, though not as hurt as the workers they employ.

Structure of Relationships in the Garment Industry

Figure 5.1 presents the major institutional actors in the Los Angeles garment industry and signifies the relationships among them.[3] An understanding of the system of relationships provides a context for examining the role of Asian immigrants in the industry.

Manufacturers are the kingpins of the garment industry. They are the individuals and business organizations that initiate the production process, and the designing of fashion and purchase of textiles occur under their auspices. Manufacturers vary considerably in size and are engaged in intense competition with one another.

Manufacturers must market their wares, generally through retailers. There are various types of apparel retailers, including department stores, mass merchandisers, specialty stores, and discount stores. The big retailers are probably the most powerful force in the industry. They compete vigorously with one another, promoting a rapid changing of "seasons," as the old sea-

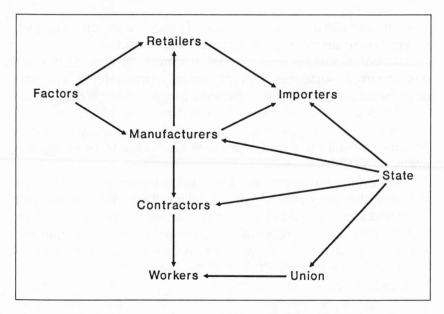

Figure 5.1 Relations of Forces in the Los Angeles Garment Industry

son's garments are swept from the racks and replaced by the next season's offerings.

Retail department stores have been undergoing a major merger movement since the mid-1980s, a phenomenon that sends reverberations throughout the industry. Ownership of some of these chains is now international, so that events occurring in London or Canada send ripples all over the world. These leveraged buyouts have several ramifications for the industry. First, because of restrictions on cash flow, retailers are ordering shorter runs of specialized goods as late as possible, putting new strains on the production process. Second, the excessive debt of the retailers affects their credit-worthiness and hence the financing that their manufacturers can obtain. And third, consolidation of retailing leads to consolidation of buyers and a consequent diminution of selling options for manufacturers.

Manufacturers and retailers in the apparel industry depend on each other. Generally, however, the large retailers are in a better bargaining position than the manufacturers and can squeeze them harder than the other way around.

Garment manufacturing is partially financed through a process known as factoring. Factors typically purchase trade debts from manufacturers. The retailer becomes a debtor of the factor, instead of the manufacturer, who is relieved of the risk of nonpayment by the retailer. The factor conducts a credit check of the retailer and limits the amount of credit he extends to the manufacturers. For these services, he receives a commission of 1 to 1.75 percent (Forman and Gilbert, 1976; Moskowitz, 1977). Factors can also make advances to their clients for an interest charge. Leveraged buyouts in retailing have affected manufacturers by limiting the willingness of factors to declare certain retailers credit-worthy. Thus the manufacturer must assume all the risk of selling to a retailer that might not survive.

Manufacturers, retailers, and factors (and banks in general) are the big players in the garment industry. It is here that large sums of money are made and lost. All three operate in an intensely competitive world and feel that they must cut costs to the bone. As a result, there is plenty of hard dealing. As a banker remarked in an interview, "This industry is not for the fainthearted." These three players wield the power and make the big money and, in the process, control the fate of the immigrants who work for them.

The garment industry is undergoing profound international restructuring, as mentioned earlier. It has increasingly moved from developed to developing countries, with the latter manufacturing clothing primarily for export to developed countries. Over half the apparel bought by U.S. consumers is produced abroad (Rothstein, 1989, 115).

U.S. capitalists are responsible for much of the flight of the U.S. garment industry abroad. They have pursued lower-wage labor in the developing countries through establishing a variety of linkages there. Manufacturers subcontract all or part of the production process abroad. Meanwhile, U.S. retailers produce their own garments in Asia, selling them under their private labels (Waldinger, 1986, 75–76).

The U.S. government has actively encouraged the movement

abroad of apparel manufacturing. The most obvious example is Tariff Item 807 and various elaborations of it such as the Caribbean Basin Initiative (Jacobs, 1988). Item 807 allows goods assembled abroad to be brought back into the United States with a tariff levied only on the value-added. It benefits companies that have their sewing done in maquiladoras in Mexico and the Caribbean.

These tariff policies are not based solely on economic factors. They are part of U.S. foreign policy (Rothstein, 1989). The United States seeks the loyalty of the countries in the Western Hemisphere, providing them with development aid, jobs, and privileged access to the U.S. market, thereby countering incipient revolutionary movements.

These policies also serve as a mechanism for ensuring that Third World debt is repaid to U.S. banks. The U.S. government and international development agencies actively promote wage-lowering austerity programs and a manufacturing-for-export development strategy in Latin America and the Caribbean. Thus the United States not only encourages the production aspect of the flight of the industry, but also fosters the low wages that give Third World countries a competitive advantage.

Although some manufacturers have all their production done "in-house," it is common practice to contract out the sewing, and often the cutting, of garments. In Los Angeles, the process of contracting out is so well established that industry members no longer have a special word to describe manufacturers who use this procedure.

Becoming a contractor does not require much capital. All one needs is a space and a few sewing machines, both of which can be rented. Ease of entry means that there is a proliferation of contractors who are in intense competition with one another; consequently, the turnover rate is as high as one-third per year.

The Los Angeles Garment Industry

Los Angeles is emerging as a major center of garment design, production, and distribution in the United States, second only to New York City. Although the U.S. apparel industry as a whole has been severely affected by imports and has suffered major job loss, the Los Angeles industry has grown. Between 1972 and 1988, employment in the U.S. industry dropped 23 percent, but it grew by 56 percent in Los Angeles. According to the California Economic Development Department (EDD), there were about 95,900 apparel workers in Los Angeles in 1990, making the garment industry the second largest manufacturing employer in the county. Given a large underground economy in the industry, probably a more accurate estimate is 120,000 workers (Olney, 1989, 28).

Although all forms of clothing are produced, the Los Angeles industry focuses on women's wear and the "California look," namely, casual wear, sportswear, and swimsuits. This segment is highly responsive to fashion swings and is not easily exportable because of the need for quick response to changes in demand.

The state of California requires that all garment manufacturers and contractors be registered. The California Division of Labor Standards Enforcement listed 4,586 contractors as of 18 April 1989. The list is not perfect, in that it includes some manufacturers as well as contractors, and an estimated 20 percent of contractors do not register. Still, it provides the best portrait available of the character of contractors, as of 1989.

In 73 percent (3,356) of the cases, the ethnicity of the owners was clear.[4] Latinos made up the biggest group, with 28.5 percent. Vietnamese, Chinese, and Koreans accounted for 16.6, 16.0, and 15.4 percent, respectively. Other Asians (with unidentifiable names or from other countries) made up 10.4 percent, for an Asian total of 58.4 percent, or the majority of owners. "Others," that is, Anglos, Jews, Armenians, Iranians, and others, made up only 13.1 percent. Obviously, garment contracting is an immigrant business.

Of the registered garment firms, 84 percent were located in southern California, 76 percent in Los Angeles. Table 5.1 shows the ethnic distribution of firm owners for the northern and southern halves of the state and for the two centers, San Francisco and Los Angeles. Asians, especially Chinese, predominated in northern California, particularly in San Francisco. In contrast, ownership in the south was more ethnically diverse.

Table 5.1. Ethnicity of California Garment Factory Registrants, by Location, April 1989

					Counties			
	North		*South*		*San Francisco*		*Los Angeles*	
Ethnic Group	*No.*	*%*	*No.*	*%*	*No.*	*%*	*No.*	*%*
Chinese	318	56.1	220	7.9	227	65.6	217	8.7
Korean	26	4.6	492	17.6	18	5.2	480	19.2
Vietnamese	86	15.2	470	16.9	29	8.4	333	13.3
Other Asian	71	12.5	278	10.0	39	11.3	243	9.7
Total Asian	501	88.4	1,460	52.3	313	90.5	1,273	51.0
Latino	16	2.8	939	33.7	9	2.6	887	35.5
Other	50	8.8	390	14.0	24	6.9	337	13.5
Total Ethnic	567	100.0	2,789	100.0	346	100.0	2,497	100.0
Unknown	179	24.0	1,051	27.4	116	25.1	973	28.0
Total	746		3,840		462		3,470	

Source: Drawn from California Department of Industrial Relations, Division of Labor Standards Enforcement, List of Registrants in the Garment Manufacturing Industry, 18 April 1989.

Latinos owned over one-third of the shops; among Asians, the Koreans emerged as the dominant group, followed closely by the Vietnamese.

Asian contractors were not evenly spaced over the Southland. In Table 5.2, the region is divided into areas: the garment district, the remainder of the city of Los Angeles, the remainder of Los Angeles County, Orange County, and the rest of southern California. Koreans were the predominant contractors in the garment district, followed closely by Latinos. In contrast, both Chinese and Vietnamese (as well as Latinos) were more dispersed over the city and county. The Vietnamese were the most spread out and had so far established a predominance in Orange County.

The Chinese in Los Angeles County showed some tendency to congregate in Chinatown. But 29 percent were found in the garment district, and 26 percent were elsewhere in the county, confirming impressions from interviews that Chinatown was declining as a desirable location because of traffic congestion, parking problems, and high rents.

In contrast, Koreans showed no tendency to locate their garment shops in Koreatown. Of Korean garment factories in Los Angeles County, 88 percent were located in the downtown garment district. The Vietnamese were the least concentrated, both in Los Angeles and in the state as a whole. This fact may account for a widespread underestimation of their presence in the industry among the people we interviewed.

Garment contracting is a highly competitive business, and there is considerable ethnic rivalry as each new group tries to get a foothold in the industry by undercutting established ones. Jewish contractors complain about the Asians, Koreans and Chinese complain about the Vietnamese, and so on.

The degree to which competition among contractors is ethnically structured is probably exaggerated. No doubt undercutting is found among contractors of all ethnicities. The problem is not ethnic but inherent in the organization of the industry. The ethnic diversity of owners, coupled with the tendency for ethnicity to correspond somewhat to time of entry, tends to lead participants to focus on ethnic "traits" as a source of the problem. But the fundamental issue is the intense competition

Table 5.2. Ethnicity of Garment Factory Registrants in Southern California, by Area, April 1989

Ethnic Group	Garment District		Other Los Angeles City		Other Los Angeles County		Orange County		Other Southern California Counties	
	No.	%	No.	%	No.	%	No.	%	No.	%
Chinese	62	6.0	99	12.7	56	8.2	1	0.5	2	1.6
Korean	381	37.0	51	6.5	48	7.0	10	6.0	2	1.6
Vietnamese	66	6.4	111	14.2	156	22.7	102	61.1	35	28.0
Other Asian	86	8.3	94	12.0	63	9.2	25	15.0	10	8.0
Total Asian	595	57.8	355	45.4	323	47.1	138	82.6	49	39.2
Latino	312	30.3	317	40.5	258	37.6	11	6.6	41	32.8
Other	122	11.9	110	14.1	105	15.3	18	10.8	35	28.0
Total	1,029	100.0	782	100.0	686	100.0	167	100.0	125	100.0

Source: Drawn from California Department of Industrial Relations, Division of Labor Standards Enforcement, List of Registrants in the Garment Manufacturing Industry, 18 April 1989.

among contractors and the ability of manufacturers to manipulate it to their advantage.

There was some ethnic structuring in the industry as of 1989. Los Angeles had three contractors' associations, one general, one Korean, and one Chinese. A Latino contractors' organization was no longer active, and the Vietnamese had yet to form an organization of their own. These associations tried to improve the situation of their members, but not, as far as we could ascertain, in the form of price cutting. Rather, they helped members deal with disputes with manufacturers, negotiate state regulations, and develop business skills (Emshwiller, 1989).

Most contractors had a difficult time surviving. One Korean woman told me she comes to work at 6:30 A.M. and leaves at 6:30 P.M. each weekday and works on Saturdays until 3:00 P.M., for a sixty-eight-hour week. As she put it, "I look at the stars when I come to work, and I look at the stars when I go home." In seven years as a contractor, she had taken one vacation, and her only desire for that time was to get plenty of sleep. Now she has a bad back. "You work very hard only to get sick," she said. She knew several other contractors who had succumbed to cancer after a life of hard work. This woman would love to get out of the contracting business but believes she would lose too much in taxes if she sold the business. She feels stuck.

The contracting system obviously has tremendous advantages for manufacturers. They do not need to maintain a stable work force, and they can pass on to the contractors the problems of recruiting and laying off workers in response to seasonal fluctuations and style changes. The contracting system increases manufacturers' flexibility. Moreover, contractors have to deal with the problems and anger of the labor force, which the manufacturer can ignore. Even though contractors and their workers are, in every meaningful sense, "employees" of the manufacturer, the contracting system creates a legal fiction that they are not, thereby alleviating the manufacturer of any responsibility for his employees. "It's none of my business," he can say. "The contractor runs his own business, and conditions there are his concern."

In practice, manufacturers have all the power of an employer in an employer-employee relationship. The contractors I spoke with complained that the prices paid to them by manufacturers had decreased in recent years. For instance, in 1984 a Korean contractor received $4.50 for sewing a pair of jeans. In 1989 she received $4.10. A Chinese contractor told us that in 1989 he was paid only $2.80 for a skirt that had brought him $3.50 in 1983. Meanwhile, contractors' expenses had increased, including the price of thread and workers' compensation insurance. The state minimum wage rose to $4.25 per hour on 1 July 1989, but manufacturers were not required to adjust their prices.

The estimated 120,000 workers in the Los Angeles garment industry were predominantly Latino immigrants, most of whom were from Mexico. Smaller proportions came from Central America and Asia. In a survey conducted in 1979, Sheldon Maram (1980) found that 81 percent of Latino workers in the industry were undocumented immigrants. The Los Angeles garment industry thus relies heavily on "illegal" workers.

Wages and working conditions were notoriously bad. The situation has been described as a reemergence of sweatshops (U.S. General Accounting Office, 1988). Poor working conditions in the industry were brought to the public's attention in a three-part story in the Los Angeles Times (Efron, 1989). Although it focused on Orange County, the series reported widespread labor abuses. Some workers stated that they earned only $50 per week for working eleven hours a day, five or six days a week. One case involved a Latina homeworker and her three children, ranging in age from seven to fourteen, who were averaging about $1.45 per hour for their labor. Forty people were injured in a fire in a seventy-six-year-old building in the garment district on 5 December 1989, affirming the dangerous conditions and leading to a crackdown by city safety inspectors (Malnic and Tobar, 1989; Sahagun, 1990).

Most workers were paid on a piecework basis. This practice served as an incentive to work quickly, and experienced workers could build up their pay. One Korean contractor told us that skilled Koreans were able to make up to $20 per hour. But piecework also meant that inexperienced workers had a hard time coming up to minimum wage. Record-keeping to ensure payment of minimum wage was sketchy or even falsified in many firms. Needless to say, benefits or paid vacation time were almost nonexistent. Rampant illegal homework required women and children to work at home in unsafe conditions (Fernandez-Kelly and Garcia, 1989).

A community center in the garment district, Las Familias del Pueblo, reflected the harsh conditions faced by Latino garment workers. The center provided informal child care, among other services, for hardworking mothers. In sum, the garment industry in southern California was the locus of serious labor exploitation and consequent suffering.

Asian Workers

In New York and San Francisco, Asian workers, especially Chinese employed in Chinatown sewing shops, made up an important segment of the garment industry labor force. In Los Angeles, in contrast, Asians were only a minority, perhaps 10 percent, of the garment work force.[5] That was because the Los Angeles industry had access to low-wage, undocumented Latino immigrant workers.

Although not all Asian workers were employed by Asian contractors, there was a tendency for Asian contractors to hire workers from their own ethnic group. Asian contractors also relied on Latino workers, however, sometimes employing them exclusively and sometimes employing an ethnic mix.

Hyung-ki Jin (1981, 20–23) interviewed 204 Korean contractors who employed a total of 5,939 workers, of whom 2,592 were Korean. He estimated that there were three hundred Korean-owned shops in Los Angeles in 1979 employing about 5,400 Korean workers. In 1989, based on a private survey, Jin estimated that the number of Korean contractors in Los Angeles had doubled, to about six hundred (compared to the 480 registered firms I was able to identify). But he believed the number of Korean workers had remained stable at about 5,400.

In August 1989, Darrel Hess (1990) surveyed the 440 members of the Korean Garment Industry Association, receiving completed questionnaires from 60 of them. He found that wives, using their previous knowledge of sewing, played an important role in the establishment of Korean contracting firms. These firms tended to use family labor, and 40 percent of them acknowledged subcontracting to homeworkers. Hess found that 48 percent of the workers were Latina women, 38 percent were Latino men, and 9 percent were Korean women. These figures confirm Jin's impression that Korean contractors were relying less on a Korean labor force.

Korean workers tried to rise above the role of employee as quickly as possible. As the general manager of the Korean Association put it: "Koreans are hardworking and business-oriented. They want to run their own business. As soon as they have saved some money, they leave." This attitude is consistent with the findings from interviews conducted with two Korean women who had briefly been employed as garment workers.[6] One was thirty years old and had a college degree from Korea. She worked for three months as a garment worker because her English skills were poor. But she was unhappy doing labor that was "beneath" her and quit as soon as a white-collar job became available in a Korean-owned firm. The second woman was fifty-nine years old. She had graduated from a seminary college in Korea and had arrived in the United States with twenty thousand dollars. After working for fifteen days as a garment worker, she opened her own garment factory, using the capital she had brought, and employed twenty-three Koreans, four Mexicans, and three blacks, all women. Although these stories may not be typical, they indicate one route out of sewing jobs. This strategy, which is more available to Asian than to Latino immigrants, depends on higher education in their homelands and/or availability of capital to invest in their own businesses.

A study of Chinese garment workers in Los Angeles's Chinatown was conducted in the early 1970s by Peggy Li, Buck Wong, and Fong Kwan (1974). They estimated that Chinatown employed about fifteen hundred Chinese garment workers. Wages and working conditions appeared to be typical for the industry, including the common practice of homework. Contractors often worked alongside their employees and sometimes had paternalistic relations with them.

In her series on sweatshops in Orange County, Sonni Efron (1989) interviewed a Vietnamese woman who had worked in several jobs for below-minimum wage and was now working for $4.25 per hour. Labor Department officials estimated that most of the seamstresses working in the sweatshops of Orange County were Vietnamese refugees (Dinh, 1989), sometimes illegally supplementing their welfare checks (Arax, 1987a and b; Efron, 1989). Like Koreans, Vietnamese try to save money to get out of garment work and become contractors as quickly as possible.

In 1990, I accompanied members of the state Bureau of Field Enforcement (BOFE) of the Division of Labor Standards Enforcement on an investigation of a Thai-owned factory. They had heard that the owner had confiscated the workers' passports and that workers were living on the premises. The factory employed more than fifty workers, all of whom were Thai immigrants, including both men and women, and there was evidence of residence on the premises. The manager claimed that the owner could not be located, so no charges could be filed. According to a Thai policeman who accompanied the investigators to aid with translation, the workers had paid substantial sums to come into the United States and were remitting their earnings to their families in Thailand. An official of the BOFE said he was seeing more and more of this kind of arrangement with new Asian immigrants.

Studies of Chinese garment workers in other U.S. cities, including Kwong 1987 and Nee and Nee 1974, suggest that when the conditions are right, Asian immigrant workers are willing to express their grievances and engage in militant action. The possibility of escape from the working class obviously serves as a damper on militance, but these workers' aspirations to establish themselves economically may also fuel demands for higher pay and benefits. The most reasonable assessment is that Asian immigrant garment workers are no different from any other group of workers: they are both dissatisfied with exploitative working conditions and afraid of losing their jobs. If a unified movement were available that would protect them and improve their working conditions, they would probably support it.

Relations between Workers and Contractors

The contractor is the immediate exploiter of the workers. The workers do not experience the hierarchy of exploitative relations above the contractor, only the contractor as the immediate oppressor. Relative to the life the workers lead, the contractor seems like the affluent beneficiary of their hard labor.

There is an inherent antagonism in the contractor-worker relationship. Contractors must cut labor costs to the bone. That is the nature of their occupation. A nonexploiting contractor is a contradiction that will not survive in the system.

In Los Angeles, the antagonism between contractor and workers took on an ethnic dimension. Although, as we have seen, there were Latino contractors and Asian workers, as well as non-Asians and non-Latinos in both positions, the most common configuration was Asian contractors employing Latino workers. In the heart of the garment district, Latino workers saw Korean contractors as the predominant employer. Thus their antagonism toward contractors took on the character of antagonism toward Koreans.

Racial stereotypes infiltrated the class antagonism. One Korean contractor described Latino workers as follows: "They work two days and leave for five. They are freelancers. They take off and buy beer and marijuana and come back when they run out of money." Latino workers complained that Asian contractors supervised them more closely than others and were more likely to cheat them. A potentially volatile ethnic situation is developing in the Los Angeles garment industry.

It is important to note that Asian contractors were not the main exploiters of the workers. They were just the immediate ones. Thus they became the direct recipients of the (justified) wrath of the workers. Such an arrangement, of course, removed the manufacturers and retailers from the realities of the sweatshops. Nevertheless, these actors' profits and salaries depended on this exploitation and set the terms within which the shops had to function. In summary, in the Los Angeles garment industry, Asians play the role of controlling immigrant labor, keeping it cheap for the manufacturers and retailers and bearing the brunt of the inevitable hostility that arises from oppressing a group of workers.[7]

The Role of the State

The state, both federal and local, regulates the relations between workers and their employers, attempting to curb the worst abuses. The state sets labor standards, including a minimum wage, extra pay for overtime work, the prohibition of child labor and homework, and the payment of workers' compensation and unemployment insurance. All these laws were violated in the Los Angeles garment industry.

The problem worsened in the 1980s. When Governor George Deukmejian took office in 1983, he weakened labor-standard enforcement efforts. The enforcement staff was small and penalties were light, making law violation worth the minimal risk of getting caught. Moreover, evasion of the law was all too easy. When a contractor got into trouble, he could close his shop and open again under a new name. A worker at Las Familias summed up the situation: "The law is so weak it's a joke."

Contractors felt trapped by the laws the state imposed on them. One of them complained: "We have to pay time-and-a-half for overtime, but we don't get paid overtime by the manufacturer. The minimum wage goes up, the cost of workers' compensation goes up, and the price we get paid goes down."

Absent in the state's system of regulation was control of employer-employer relations. Contractors were considered independent business owners, not the employees of the manufacturers. Consequently, relations between manufacturers and contractors, in terms of labor standards, lay outside state jurisdiction. The blind eye turned by the state on this relationship was a key factor in the proliferation of contracting in the industry. The presence of an "independent contractor" between the manufacturer and the workers served as a mechanism for bypassing state regulation of labor standards.

Another form of state involvement concerns immigration law. In 1986, the federal government passed the Immigration Reform and Control Act (IRCA). The law held employers accountable for hiring undocumented workers by imposing sanctions on employers who knowingly hired them. It also granted amnesty to undocumented immigrants who had been stable residents in the United States since 1981.

Since most Asian immigrants were in the United States legally, IRCA had little impact on them as workers. But it was very important for Latino immigrants in the garment industry, many of whom were both undocumented and eligible for amnesty. This shift had a potential effect on contractors, including Asian contractors, as employers of the affected work force.

In 1987, hearings were held in Los Angeles to assess whether garment contractors should be allowed to bring in temporary foreign workers to offset IRCA-induced labor shortages. Some Korean contractors testified at these hearings, requesting the right to bring in workers from the Philippines.[8] Evidence for a labor shortage was unsubstantiated, and it was concluded that a temporary worker program was unnecessary (California Legislature, Assembly Subcommittee on Immigration in the Workplace, 1987).

In practice, IRCA appears to have had little impact on the Los Angeles garment industry's labor force (Loucky, Hamilton, and Chinchilla, 1989). The flow of undocumented immigrants into Los Angeles continued unabated. It was easy and cheap to obtain forged papers, and employers quickly learned that the law did not hold them accountable for the authenticity of an immigrant's documents. If the INS raided his shop, the contractor could blame the immigrants for providing false papers. Such raids were rare or nonexistent, however. Law enforcement was underfunded in this area, too, so business proceeded as usual.

The Role of the Union

The main union in the Los Angeles garment industry was the International Ladies' Garment Workers Union (ILGWU). The ILG was very weak in southern California, having dropped from 12,000 members out of 23,000 garment workers in 1946, to about 3,000 members out of 120,000 in 1990 (Laslett and Tyler, 1989).

Even in this small membership, Asian workers were underrepresented. Apart from a K-Mart warehouse that had five hundred members, one-third of whom were Filipino, Asians made up about 3 to 4 percent of ILG members. Although the ILG in New York and San Francisco has striven to organize Chinese workers, in Los Angeles the primary focus has been on Latinos, to the neglect of Asians.

Traditional unionism was difficult to establish in the Los Angeles garment industry. Manufacturers had moved to Los Angeles in part to avoid the union and were very resistant to unionization. They threatened to drive contractors out of business if their shops became unionized. And many manufacturers had the option of getting their contracting done in Mexico or elsewhere if labor conditions improved substantially in Los Angeles.

Under the National Labor Relations Act (NLRA), the federal government was supposed to protect the rights of workers to decide if they wanted representation and, if so, to select a union of their choice. Under the best of circumstances, the law was limited in terms of the ability of workers to develop real social power and bring about the kind of social change that would significantly improve their lives. But even the modest reformist achievements of the NLRA were decimated by the Reagan and Bush administrations (U.S. Congress, House, Committee on Education and Labor, 1984).

For example, although it was illegal to fire workers for union activity, filing a complaint against such a firing was useless in the Los Angeles garment industry. Delays in processing due to staff shortages meant that the charged company was likely to have disappeared. Thus contractors fired union activists with little fear of legal consequences.

The following stories illustrate the problem. The ILG made an attempt to organize a Korean-owned firm, Heng's/Dayoung International (DYI). Heng was a manufacturer and DYI a contractor with three production plants, employing three hundred, mostly Latino, workers. They produced cheap campus wear, such as sweatshirts and T-shirts, to be sold at swap meets. The union was able to sign up two hundred forty employees in support of a union representation election and established a committee of thirty committed unionists. In response, DYI shut down one of its plants, fired all the workers, reopened, and hired all new employees. It fired all thirty members of the union committee. Although the ILG filed an Unfair Labor Practice statement, the firm effectively broke the union.

In another case, the ILG organized a campaign against a Jewish-owned shoe-importing warehouse in Carson in 1988. The firm, connected to L.A. Gear, imported shoes from Korea and employed about sixty Korean workers in a work force of seventy to eighty. The union hired a young Korean to help and signed up about fifty people. The company immediately fired the union leaders. Then it gave everyone a one-dollar raise, fired some of the Korean workers, hired blacks and Latinos, and established a three-tier racial division of labor. It then moved to Ontario, California. By the time the union election was held, the union had been broken.

Asian Labor Organizing

In 1979, the Korean Labor Association (KLA) was founded by a group of young men who had been student activists in Korea. Although professionals themselves, they were concerned with helping Korean immigrant workers organize. They set up an office in Koreatown, put an advertisement in the local Korean newspapers, and responded to phone calls. Even though they did not actively search for opportunities to organize labor, many Korean workers sought their help. In three cases, the KLA became involved in organizing union election drives. Two of them were with nongarment shops, and the third was in a knitting company called French Rags.

French Rags was a sweater manufacturer in Culver City that did all its knitting in-house. It produced quality sweaters that sold for two hundred dollars and employed about ninety workers, two-thirds of whom were Koreans. Some Korean women came to the KLA office, complaining that the company was doing good business but paying them poorly. With assistance from the Amalgamated Clothing and Textile Workers'

Union (ACTWU), the KLA was able to sign up more than half the workers and filed for an election with the NLRB.

The company hired two union-busting lawyers, one Anglo and one Korean. Their tactic was to divide the workers, pitting Mexicans against Central Americans, and Latinos against Koreans. The campaign was very emotional, and in the election the KLA fell short by only twelve votes. According to a KLA official, because of the union drive, the owner decided to scale down the business from $9–10 million to $1.5–2 million and cut her work force to twenty. That is how far some owners will go to avoid a union.

Who Benefits?

It is clear from Figure 5.1 that at the bottom of this industry, at the level of the workers, the suffering was considerable and the conditions were dehumanizing. Garment workers were obviously exploited, but by whom? Who benefited from their hard lives?

Asian (and other) contractors appeared to be the immediate beneficiaries of the difficult conditions confronted by garment workers. Asian contractors suffered hardship, too, however. True, their lives were not nearly as pressed as the workers. They could usually afford decent housing and could send their children to college. But they often worked very hard, to the point where their health could be impaired, and felt caught between implacable forces. Still, despite the fact that contractors were themselves victimized by the system, they bore some responsibility for the exploitation and gained some, albeit a relatively small, portion of the surplus taken from the workers.

At each level of the hierarchy of the industry, markups accrue. *Business Week* (1988) estimated that, for a dress that retailed for $100, $15 went to labor, including both workers and contractors. Material costs were $22.50, and the manufacturer's profit and overhead came to $12.50. The retailer doubled the manufacturer's price, taking out $50 in expenses and profit. Banks and factors, as well as allied industries such as advertising, took their share.

The beneficiaries were not only the stockholders and owners of these firms, and the benefit was not only accrued in the form of profits. It also was incorporated into salary scales. Manufacturers, retailers, and bankers paid some of their employees handsome salaries, whose high levels could be attributed in part to the low levels paid garment workers. For example, in fiscal year 1989–1990, the president of The Gap, a major apparel retailer, received a salary of $1.7 million.

In manufacturing, retailing, and banking/factoring, there was a stratum of very well paid employees and one of low-paid, exploited workers. A direct relationship exists between the minimum-wage and no-benefits earnings of garment workers, and the six-to-seven-digit salaries plus handsome benefits of retailing, manufacturing, and banking professionals and managers.[9] The widening divide, observed by Ong (1989), was produced and reproduced through the processes described for this industry.

The garment industry reveals starkly some of the problems of capitalism and how it helps construct racial and ethnic antagonisms. The illegality found at all levels of the industry was a product of the system of private ownership and competition, which drives people to engage in a ruthless struggle for survival and advantage. Checks on the worst excesses, whether by the state or by opposing forces, were weak or nonexistent, in part because capitalists were able to exert considerable influence over the government and through it subvert the efforts of opposing forces. The result was social decay: a dog-eat-dog world in which the unprotected were left to be ravaged by the strong and powerful.

Latino (and some Asian) immigrants were severely oppressed in this industry. Asian contractors were their immediate oppressors. That created a volatile situation of interethnic hostility, leading to the potential for serious social cleavages.

Notes

1. For studies of Chinese in the New York industry, see International Ladies' Garment Workers Union, Local 23-25, and New York Skirt and Sportswear Association, 1983; Kwong, 1987; Lin, 1989; and Wal-

dinger, 1986. Studies of Chinese in the San Francisco garment industry include Lan, 1971; Loo and Ong, 1982; Nee and Nee, 1974, chap. 12; and Wong and Hayashi, 1989.

2. Research for this chapter included interviewing about forty people knowledgeable about the garment industry, mainly during the summer of 1989. Several garment factories were visited, and state registration data on garment factory ownership were obtained and analyzed. I am grateful to Patricia Domingues and Jane Bonacich for laboriously punching 4,589 business names, addresses, and ethnicities into the computer, and to Phillip Bonacich for assistance in analyzing them. Special thanks go to Patricia Hanneman, who conducted the main analysis.

3. Figure 5.1 is a simplification that could be elaborated by the addition of other actors related to the industry. They include the owners of the properties rented by garment contractors, advertising agencies, newspapers and magazines that publish articles and advertising, customs brokers, insurance companies, sewing machine factories, textile producers, business consultants, accountants, lawyers, and academics who study the industry. In other words, the industry is surrounded by allied businesses and professions. All of them can be seen as beneficiaries of the low-wage system at the bottom, but because they are more peripheral players, I am choosing to ignore them here.

4. In a few cases, partners were listed. I chose not to do a special analysis of them, however, because database fields were cropped in the state printout to thirty-five characters for names, and the names of partners were sometimes incomplete. Partners were simply coded with one ethnic designation. In the rare case in which the partners seemed to be of different ethnicities, I arbitrarily chose the clearer one. Some error no doubt occurred in this coding, although I was able to check some of the names with a Korean, a Vietnamese, and a Chinese colleague. (Thanks go to Chris Lee, Yen Espiritu, and Paul Ong for their help.) In addition, I obtained the membership lists of the Los Angeles Chinese and Korean contractors' associations, which helped verify more than 150 cases. Using established ethnic names from these two sources, I was able to employ the computer to clear up some discrepancies.

5. Examining state unemployment insurance claims in the garment industry, Paul Ong (personal communication, 1989) found that, for Los Angeles County in 1988, 75 percent were made by Latino workers, 13 percent by non-Hispanic whites, 7 percent by Asians, and 4 percent by blacks. Over 50 percent of the non-Hispanic whites

were clerical and management employees, unlike the case in the other groups.

6. These interviews were conducted in 1988 by Hye Kyung Chang under the auspices of Lucie Cheng.

7. The contractors occupy a position that fits comfortably into the concept of "middleman minorities" (Bonacich, 1987; Bonacich and Modell, 1980). They are ethnically distinctive. They serve as go-betweens between an elite and a subordinated population. They become the shock absorbers of the system, dealing with antagonisms both from above and from below. I am avoiding introducing the concept into the body of the chapter, however, because it carries too much baggage and controversy. Moreover, the situation of Asians in the Los Angeles garment industry speaks for itself, and the concept of middleman minorities adds little to it.

8. This request is the only indication I have of the presence of Filipino workers in the industry. That they were specifically asked for suggests either that they have a significant presence in the industry already or that people are aware of the industry in the Philippines and see it as a source of recruits.

9. Some may argue that the higher-paid employees "deserve" their high pay. They are being rewarded for their productivity and their investment in education, which make them valuable to their employers. In answer, I argue choosing how to allocate rewards is a social decision. Even if one can demonstrate that salary levels are driven entirely by market forces (a dubious proposition), the decision to allow the market to drive salaries so far in opposite directions remains a decision, and not just a force of nature.

References

Arax, Mark. 1987a. "Many Refugees Work while Getting Welfare." *Los Angeles Times,* 9 February, pp. 1, 8, 16.

———. 1987b. "Refugees Called Victims and Perpetrators of Fraud." *Los Angeles Times,* 10 February, pp. 2, 3, 26.

Bonacich, Edna. 1987. "'Making It' in America: A Social Evaluation of the Ethics of Immigrant Entrepreneurship." *Sociological Perspectives* 30 (October): 446–466.

Bonacich, Edna, and John Modell. 1980. *The Economic Basis of Ethnic Solidarity: Small Business in the Japanese American Community.* Berkeley: University of California Press.

Business Week. 1988. "Why Made-in-America Is Back in Style." 7 November, pp. 116–120.

California Legislature, Assembly Subcommittee on Immigration in the Workplace. 1987. *A Status Report on California's Garment Industry.* Sacramento.

Dinh, Le Kim. 1989. "18 Little Saigon Firms Cited on Wage Policies." *Los Angeles Times,* Orange County edition, 5 October, Part 2.

Efron, Sonni. 1989. "Sweatshops Expanding into Orange County"; "Mother's Plight Turns a Home into a Sweatshop"; "'Hot Goods' Law Revived as Anti-Sweatshop Tool." *Los Angeles Times,* 26–28 November, Part A.

Emshwiller, John R. 1989. "'Mr. Fix-it' Helps Immigrants to Go from Rags to Riches: Mr. Cho's Korean-American Garment Group Provides a Pattern for Others." *Wall Street Journal,* 15 March, p. B2.

Fernandez-Kelly, M. Patricia. 1983. *For We Are Sold, I and My People: Women and Industry in Mexico's Frontier.* Albany: State University of New York Press.

Fernandez-Kelly, M. Patricia, and Anna M. Garcia. 1989. "Hispanic Women and Homework: Women in the Informal Economy of Miami and Los Angeles." In *Homework: Historical and Contemporary Perspectives on Paid Labor at Home,* ed. Eileen Boris and Cynthia R. Daniels, pp. 165–179. Urbana: University of Illinois Press.

Forman, Martin, and John Gilbert. 1976. *Factoring and Finance.* London: Heinemann.

Fröbel, Folker, Jürgen Heinrichs, and Otto Kreye. 1980. *The New International Division of Labour: Structural Unemployment in Industrialised Countries and Industrialisation in Developing Countries.* Cambridge: Cambridge University Press.

Fuentes, Annette, and Barbara Ehrenreich. 1984. *Women in the Global Factory.* Boston: South End Press.

Hess, Darrel Eugene. 1990. "Korean Immigrant Entrepreneurs in the Los Angeles Garment Industry." Master's thesis, University of California, Los Angeles.

Hoffman, Kurt, and Howard Rush. 1988. *Micro-Electronics and Clothing: The Impact of Technical Change on a Global Industry.* New York: Praeger.

International Ladies' Garment Workers Union, Local 23-25, and New York Skirt and Sportswear Association. 1983. *The Chinatown Garment Industry Study.* New York: International Ladies' Garment Workers Union.

Jacobs, Brenda. 1988. "The 807 Option: New Trade South of the Border." *Bobbin* (May): 26–33.

Jin, Hyung-ki. 1981. *A Survey on the Economic and Managerial Status of Sewing Factories Owned and Operated by Korean Contractors in the Los Angeles Area*. Pomona: California State Polytechnic University, Industrial Research Institute for Pacific Nations.

Kwong, Peter. 1987. *The New Chinatown*. New York: Hill and Wang.

Lan, Dean. 1971. "The Chinatown Sweatshops: Oppression and an Alternative." *Amerasia Journal* 1 (November): 40–57.

Laslett, John, and Mary Tyler. 1989. *The ILGWU in Los Angeles, 1907–1988*. Inglewood, Calif.: Ten Star Press.

Li, Peggy, Buck Wong, and Fong Kwan. 1974. *Garment Industry in Los Angeles Chinatown, 1973–74*. Working Papers on Asian American Studies no. 5. Los Angeles: University of California.

Lin, Jan. 1989. *The Social Geography of Garment Production in Lower Manhattan*. REALM, Working Papers Series no. 4. New York: New School for Social Research.

Loo, Chalsa, and Paul Ong. 1982. "Slaying Demons with a Sewing Needle: Feminist Issues for Chinatown's Women." *Berkeley Journal of Sociology* 27:77–88.

Loucky, James, Nora Hamilton, and Norma Chinchilla. 1989. "The Effects of IRCA on Selected Industries in Los Angeles: A Preliminary Report." Unpublished.

Malnic, Eric, and Hector Tobar. 1989. "31 Plucked from Burning Building." *Los Angeles Times*, 6 December, Part B.

Maram, Sheldon L. 1980. *Hispanic Workers in the Garment and Restaurant Industries in Los Angeles County: A Social and Economic Profile*. Working Papers in U.S.–Mexican Studies no. 12. San Diego: University of California.

Mitter, Swasti. 1986. *Common Fate, Common Bond: Women in the Global Economy*. London: Pluto.

Moskowitz, Louis A. 1977. *Dun and Bradstreet's Handbook of Modern Factoring and Commercial Finance*. New York: Thomas Y. Crowell.

Nee, Victor G., and Brett De Bary Nee. 1974. *Longtime Californ': A Documentary Study of an American Chinatown*. Boston: Houghton Mifflin.

Noyelle, Thierry J. 1987. *Beyond Industrial Dualism: Market and Job Segmentation in the New Economy*. Boulder, Colo.: Westview Press.

Olney, Peter. 1989. "Some Strategies for Change: The Rising of the Million." *LA Weekly* (24 February–2 March): 28–29.

Ong, Paul M. 1989. *The Widening Divide: Income Inequality and Poverty in Los Angeles*. Los Angeles: Research Group on the Los Angeles Economy, Graduate School of Architecture and Urban Planning, University of California.

Rothstein, Richard. 1989. *Keeping Jobs in Fashion: Alternatives to the Euthanasia of the U.S. Apparel Industry.* Washington, D.C.: Economic Policy Institute.

Safa, Helen I. 1981. "Runaway Shops and Female Employment: The Search for Cheap Labor." *Signs* 7 (Winter): 418–433.

Sahagun, Louis. 1990. "City Cracks Down on Garment District." *Los Angeles Times,* 29 April, Part B.

U.S. Congress. House. Committee on Education and Labor. 1984. *The Failure of Labor Law: A Betrayal of American Workers.* Report of Subcommittee on Labor-Management Relations. Washington, D.C.: Government Printing Office.

U.S. Congress. Office of Technology Assessment. 1987. *The U.S. Textile and Apparel Industry: A Revolution in Progress—Special Report.* OTA-TET-332. Washington, D.C.: Government Printing Office.

U.S. General Accounting Office. 1988. *Sweatshops in the U.S.: Opinions on Their Extent and Possible Enforcement Options.* Washington, D.C.: Government Printing Office.

Waldinger, Roger D. 1986. *Through the Eye of the Needle: Immigrants and Enterprise in New York's Garment Trades.* New York: New York University Press.

Wong, Bernard. 1987. "The Role of Ethnicity in Enclave Enterprises: A Study of the Chinese Garment Factories in New York City." *Human Organization* 46 (Summer): 120–130.

Wong, Diane Yen-Mei, with Dennis Hayashi. 1989. "Behind Unmarked Doors: Developments in the Garment Industry." In *Making Waves: An Anthology of Writings by and about Asian American Women,* ed. Asian Women United of California, pp. 159–171. Boston: Beacon Press.

6. The Migration and Incorporation of Filipino Nurses

Paul Ong and Tania Azores

One striking difference between today's Asian immigration waves and those of earlier periods is class composition. As stated in earlier chapters, unskilled workers dominated the earlier waves. Most immigrants were incorporated into the U.S. economy as laborers, and a smaller number found a limited avenue of economic mobility through the use of ethnic resources to start small businesses. Today it is just as likely that an Asian immigrant comes from a professional background as from a lower-class background, and a sizable number of those with high education and specialized skills have entered the professions of their choice. The process, however, is neither simple nor automatic. Incorporation of the highly skilled is problematic, the product of the interaction of economic, institutional, and personal factors. This chapter examines this process through a case study of Filipino nurses.

The focus on this ethnic-occupational group stems from the fact that the Philippines has been the major source of foreign-trained nurses working in the United States. According to available immigration statistics, more than seventy thousand foreign nurses entered the country between 1965 and 1988, most of them from Asia. Although Korea, India, and Taiwan are Asian sending countries, the Philippines is by far the biggest supplier of nurses. Filipinos comprise over 90 percent of the nonimmigrant entries and over half the immigrants, and they are the most highly visible foreign-trained nurses in the United States. We estimate that at least twenty-five thousand Filipino nurses migrated to the United States between 1966 and 1985. The dominance of Filipino nurses among those with temporary working visas is even greater. Among all foreign-trained nurses in the United States with temporary working visas, seven out of ten from 1985 to 1988 (Puleo, 1989) and three out of four in 1989 were Filipinos (*Interpreter Releases*, 1989). In 1984, the United States had an estimated twenty-six thousand registered nurses (RNs) who had been trained in the Philippines. Thus, it could be argued that a discussion of immigrant Asian nurses, indeed of foreign-trained nurses in general, is predominantly about Filipino nurses.

The Nursing Shortage

The primary underlying economic factor for the migration of Filipino nurses to the United States is an endemic and recurring shortage of nurses in this country. The rapid growth in the demand for health care has outpaced the growth in the supply of nurses, creating a dynamic shortage. The demand also fluctuates with the economy, causing severe shortages during expansionary periods. Despite repeated governmental efforts to increase the supply through expanding and reforming nursing education, structural factors have made it nearly impossible to eliminate these shortages. These factors include the changing character of U.S. medical care, reflected in the shift from private doctors to health management organizations (HMOs) and hospitals; the tendency of hospitals to act in collusion and to use sex-based discrimination to hold down wages; and the existence of poor working conditions in the nursing labor market.

The increased demand for health care can be seen in the statistics on personal consumption. Between 1965 to 1990, medical expenditures increased by 220 percent (after adjusting for inflation), while total expenditures increased by only 117 percent. During this same period, medical expenditures as a proportion of total expenditures grew from 7.4 percent to 11.2 percent. Government programs have also added to the increased demand. Both the Medicare and Medicaid programs were established in 1965, and by 1990 their total cost stood at $159 billion. Taken together, private and public expenditures on health care now account for 12 percent of the gross national product.

The number of nurses has risen with the growth in the demand for health care. In 1965, there were 621,000 registered nurses; by 1988, there were 2,033,000, an increase of 227 percent

(Moses, 1990). Despite this dramatic increase, over half of all hospitals experienced either a mild or severe shortage of nurses in 1986. In 1987, the American Hospital Association reported a vacancy rate of 11.3 percent. Although the shortage has abated since then, it has not disappeared. It is only the most recent in a series of critical shortages over the last two or three decades (Jackson, MacFalda, and McManus, 1989; Yett, 1975, 19–29).

The recurring shortages are not just a problem of supply and demand. In a competitive market, increased demand for labor would force wages upward, which, in turn, would provide greater incentives for persons to enter the profession. When future increases in demand and the potential for higher wages are foreseen, there should be enough individuals willing to invest in the required training so that future supply will keep up with future demand. That clearly has not happened in nursing. One reason for the sluggish supply response could be that there have been too few schools, creating a bottleneck for those wishing to respond to the economic incentives. Given the substantial public and private investments in building nursing schools, however, that should not be the determining factor. In fact, data on enrollment, discussed later, indicate that at least since the mid-1970s, there has been excess capacity. Another reason could be that individuals have misjudged the growth in demand for nurses. Thus, too few choose nursing. But in light of the continued discussion in both the public and professional media on the chronic shortages and the growth in the demand for health care, it is hard to believe that not enough people are aware of the trends.

This occupation is prone to spells of severe shortages because wages have not risen to the levels needed to stimulate the necessary growth in the supply of nurses. When labor demand grows continuously over a protracted period, the labor market cannot be in equilibrium but instead experiences a dynamic shortage (Arrow and Capron, 1959). The size of the shortage, however, is determined by the prevailing wage rate. In the nursing field, one would expect that growing demand would lead to large increases in wages because the supply is relatively unresponsive in the short run.[1] Since nursing care is only a fraction of the total cost for health care, and the growth in demand for health care has been robust despite real price increases, the observed increased medical expenditures should, under competitive conditions, generate significant increases in wages that would help ensure a strong response in the supply of new nurses. This rapid increase may have indeed happened in the early 1960s, when the average monthly salary of full-time nurses grew by 26 percent in real terms, compared to only a 13 percent increase for all full-time workers (Yett, 1975, 155). The increases since the mid-1970s, however, have been less dramatic. Between 1976 and 1986, real wages for nurses rose by only 2 percent (calculated from data in American Nurses' Association, 1987, 162). These increases have not been sufficient to eliminate the shortages.

The disequilibrium in the nursing labor market is not merely the result of the dynamic mismatch between supply and demand. The shortage is tied to wages that have remained below market level because hospitals, which employ about 70 percent of the nurses, have colluded to set rates. Under monopsonistic conditions, which exist when there is one buyer of labor and many sellers of labor, a firm can maximize profits by setting wages below the market rate. Consequently, there is excess demand, or its equivalent, labor shortage, at the prevailing wages, and the value derived from the employees is greater than the wage bill. When there is more than one firm, monopsony outcomes are achieved through employers acting in unison to set wage rates. Both empirical and legal evidence show that hospitals have indeed operated in such a fashion (Cleland, 1989, 166–167; Yett, 1975). Hospitals have been able to collude because their product market is local in scope; thus the number of buyers of labor is sufficiently small that employers can act as a cartel. For example, facilities in southern California operated through their local hospital association to keep wages down (Hunter, 1986, 132). The ability to pursue such actions has been enhanced by the recent trends in mergers in the health care field, which not only increase corporate profits (Woolley, 1989) but also facilitate monopsonistic behavior in the labor market by shrinking the number of hospitals per local market.

Nursing wages are further depressed by sex-based wage discrimination at the occupational level. One of the realities of the United States's labor market is a significant degree of segregation by gender, which produces many occupations that are predominantly male or female. Through both economic and institutional mechanisms, the gender composition of an occupation influences wage levels independent of personal and other structural characteristics, with wages falling as the female proportion increases (Sorensen, 1989). Wage levels in nursing, which remains overwhelmingly female, have been kept low through this form of sex discrimination. Although alternative job-evaluation models yield widely varying and sometime conflicting estimates of the impact of occupation-based discrimination, the results for registered nurses consistently show that their wages should be increased to achieve equity, by anywhere from a low of 14 percent to a high of 68 percent (Aaron and Loughy, 1986, 33–35).

Although it is difficult to disentangle the effects of monopsonistic behavior and sex-based discrimination on the wage rate for nurses and its growth, one consequence is clear. The growth in the supply has been painfully sluggish despite increasing demand for health services, leading to the observed shortage. Nurses have responded to the glaring wage disparity through unionization and comparable-worth suits (Blum, 1991, 104–08; Hunter, 1986, chap. 7). These factors have been offset by recent changes in the health industry, generating reimbursement policies that tend to keep nursing wages from growing rapidly.

Over the last few decades, the long-run economic and political swings in the United States described in Chapter 1 have driven structural changes in this sector. Economic growth in the 1950s and 1960s enabled more firms to offer health insurance as a part of the benefits package that bought industrial peace, and one of the concessions to the social movements of the 1960s and early 1970s was the creation of two public health programs, Medicare for the elderly and Medicaid for the poor. The resulting rapid increase in the demand for health care has been accompanied by a sharp rise in costs. While the rate of inflation from 1965 to 1990 for all items was 315 percent, the rate for medical care was 546 percent. Not only has health care taken a larger share of all income over the last quarter-century, but each dollar is now purchasing less, even after accounting for overall inflation.

Since the economic crisis of the late 1970s, both the private and public sectors have called for constraints on medical costs. As companies face increased competition in the global market or seize the initiative while labor is weak, trimming benefits has been one way to cut labor costs. This move has translated to more workers without employer-paid health insurance and to less coverage for those who are still insured (Renner and Navarro, 1989). The economic crisis in health has not been limited to the private sector. With an increasingly strained budget and the dominance of a conservative administration, the government also sought to constrain the costs associated with Medicare and Medicaid. In response to cost-containment strategies that limit total per capita expenditure and standardize payments for treatments of diagnosis-related illnesses, the health industry has been restructured through an expansion of health maintenance organizations and preferred physician organizations, as well as hospital mergers and buyouts.

The drive to contain cost has intensified pressures on hospitals to operate with lower cost outlays, including efforts to keep nurses' wages low. The financial problems are particularly severe for inner-city public hospitals, which depend on state and local funding at a time when these governments are facing budgetary crises. Moreover, these hospitals must pay higher wages to attract nurses to compensate for inner-city-related problems such as a high crime rate (Hendricks, 1989).

The nursing profession is not only having difficulty finding a new supply of nurses, but also suffers from a high exit rate. Of the more than two million registered nurses in 1988, one in five was not working in her or his profession (Moses, 1990, 5), and this figure does not include the many who decided to forgo renewing their licenses. Burnout is not unusual, given the hard physical work and long hours. Additional stress is associated with treating patients with severe illnesses and having to deal with death. Along with these problems, nurses suffer from a lack of job control (Vogt, 1983). Despite their critical role in providing health care, nurses are subordinate to physicians, who are reluctant to relinquish key decisions. Moreover, some doctors exhibit a range of abrasive behavior that alienates nurses, leading to lower retention rates (Moore and Fraser, 1989, 156).

Recent developments at the societal level are likely to aggravate the current shortage. In the past, women entered nursing because it was one of the few professions open to them. The problems of gender subordination and low prestige are part and parcel of this occupation. The women's movement has generated fundamental changes that have made nursing a less desirable choice. A survey sponsored by the magazine *Working Woman* places nursing among the ten least-desirable professions (Jackson et al., 1989, 6). At the same time, new opportunities have opened up in much more lucrative fields, such as medicine, law, and engineering, which are attracting an increasing share of those pursuing higher education (Buerhaus, 1987). By 1987, more women college freshmen indicated that they wanted to pursue a career in medicine than in nursing (Jackson et al., 1989, 9–10). As a consequence of the changes in attitudes and values, admissions to nursing schools fell from a high of 112,523 in 1975–1976 to 90,693 in 1986–1987 (Cleland, 1989, 81).

The chronic labor shortage and the dismal prospects for the future have contributed to a continued preferential treatment of nurses in the immigration laws. Nursing remains one of the few occupations still on the Department of Labor's Schedule A, which provides blanket certification to certain professions for the purpose of qualifying for permanent immigration.[2] As we show later, various legislative acts have enabled many on temporary visas to become permanent residents and have simplified the recruitment of foreign nurses as temporary workers.

Although foreign-trained nurses make up only a fraction of the nursing work force, (4% in 1984), they are nonetheless seen as a valuable source of labor by many hospitals, particularly inner-city facilities in older metropolitan areas facing fiscal difficulties. Consequently, these hospitals actively recruit nurses throughout the world, some through their own recruiters, others through recruiting firms based in the United States or abroad. Although many hospitals want to target Western countries such as Great Britain and Canada, Asia, particularly the Philippines, has been the largest source of foreign nurses.

The Supply of Filipino Nurses

In many ways, the migration of Filipino nurses is merely an extension of the broader movement of people from the Philippines. Historical and economic forces have prompted more than three-quarters of a million Filipinos to migrate to the United States since 1970 and have created a reservoir of countless others waiting for an opportunity to do so. Certainly, the huge disparity in the standards of living between the two nations and the dream of finding the good life in the United States are fundamental reasons for out-migration that are not unique to the Philippines but applicable to many other less-developed Asian nations. Nevertheless, the widespread desire among Filipinos to go to the United States is distinctive, because the historical colonial relationship between the two countries Americanized many Filipino values and aspirations. This colonial history stimulated migration not only by shaping individual attitudes but also by creating institutional practices that perpetuate the process of Americanization.

Two legacies of U.S. colonialism in the Philippines are the use of English as the lingua franca throughout the archipelago[3] and the establishment of an educational system patterned after that of the United States. The Philippines also maintains extensive links with the United States through trade, foreign assistance, and military bases.[4] In 1988, there were more than a quarter-million U.S. nationals in the Philippines, making it the largest concentration in Asia. Long after decolonization, U.S. influence is still very much present despite attempts by the Philippine government to establish an independent and unique national identity. These historical and contemporary linkages have made the Philippines the largest source of Asian immigration to the United States, second only to Mexico among all nations.

The migration of Filipino nurses, although part of the larger migration, is distinctive not only because nurses are extremely overrepresented among those leaving, but also because their migration involves a specific set of institutions and processes. This labor force must first be created through extensive training. In the Philippines, the establishment of a pool of nurses is a product of institutional response and individual motivation. The degree to which this pool becomes an effective supply, however, is determined by occupation-specific immigration regulations and licensing requirements in the United States. Both elements influence the flow, status, and employment of Filipino nurses.

The Labor Pool. The Philippines has led the developing nations in establishing an extensive nursing education system in recent history. The participation of thousands of Filipino nurses in the U.S. State Department's Exchange Visitors Program after World War II attests to the early role of the United States as a mentor in the area of nursing education and practice.[5] Indigenous nursing schools, however, played a much larger role in creating an expanding pool of nurses. Richard Joyce and Chester Hunt (1982) report that from 1950 to 1970 the number of nursing schools in the Philippines rose from 17 to 140 and that the cost of training increased as well. Nursing schools proliferated, not just in the greater Manila area but also in the provinces. One potential benefit of this expansion was a relatively high number of health providers. By 1965, there were 8.8 nurses for every 10,000 persons, a ratio that easily surpassed those for South Korea (3.3), Taiwan (1.3), or Indonesia (0.8), as reported by the World Bank (1988) and Taiwan's Council for Economic Planning and Development (Republic of China, 1987). The rapid expansion of nursing education slowed in the mid-1970s, when the enrollment of nursing students began to decline. Nonetheless, the educational system still graduates thousands each year. The *1989 Philippine Statistical Yearbook* reported that there were more than sixty-five thousand newly registered nurses in the period from 1979 to 1988.

The expansion of nursing schools could not have taken place without an underlying demand for training, a demand due in part to the high prestige of health practitioners in the Philippines (Carino, 1977). This is not the only reason, however, especially in light of the financial realities that make the choice of a nursing career in the Philippines economically unwise. Increased impoverishment during and after the Marcos dictatorship created a dire need for health care, but the decline in per capita income cut the ability of the people to pay for it. One study found that over a third of the nurses in the Philippines were either underemployed or unemployed, and many, particularly those educated in private colleges, could not recover the cost of their training from local wages (Ongkiko and Suanes, 1984). Given the lack of effective domestic demand for nurses and the deteriorating economic conditions, the Philippines has had a surplus of nurses despite large-scale out-migration to the United States, Europe, and the Middle East (Rimando, 1984).

Global rather than domestic employment opportunities have been the driving force behind the early expansion of nursing education and the continued high level of enrollment. For many Filipinos, becoming a nurse is seen as a way to secure meaningful employment abroad rather than pursuing professional practice at home. The average salary for a registered nurse in the United States is about twenty times that in the Philippines, which is only one hundred dollars per month (Berkman, 1988). According to Charles Stahl (1987, 39), even those who go to the oil-rich Middle East countries as temporary workers can earn two to three times as much by working abroad.

Not every Filipino nurse wants to migrate, and not everyone who wants to migrate is able to do so. Nonetheless, there are enough examples of employment abroad to affect individual choice. The chance to earn high wages overseas prompts thousands to pay for the training. Some schools play on the desire of applicants by promising job placements abroad after graduation, particularly in the United States, although, as we discuss later, the chance of achieving this goal can be marginal. Nonetheless, Philippine nursing schools have produced thousands of graduates to meet the high demand for nurses in the United States, Europe, and the Middle East. The perception that nursing is a means of escaping a depressed economic situation will persist so long as there is a foreign demand for the profession.

The desire to migrate by becoming a nurse is not based merely on a narrow calculation of individual gains. The family's welfare plays a major role. Nursing is seen as a way to move the entire family from the Philippines to the United States. Once they become permanent residents or naturalized citizens, nurses can petition for admission of their immediate relatives. The first to be sponsored are often the parents, and once the parents themselves are naturalized, they in turn can sponsor their other children for entry to the United States. When nursing is perceived as the profession that will best serve the interests of the family, this course of study is often prescribed for the appropriate member of the family, irrespective of that individual's personal career choice.

Immigration Regulation. Although employment opportunities abroad create a pool of Filipino nurses, the number who have the opportunity to practice their profession in the United States is controlled by immigration laws and regulations, as well as by licensing requirements (discussed later). The international movement of people can be controlled by both the sending and receiving countries. In the case of the Philippines and the United States, however, only the latter has attempted to regulate the movement of Filipino nurses. The Philippines has had few restrictions on emigration in general, a by-product of a belief in the right of personal choice that is deeply embedded in the political ideology inherited from the United States (Carino, 1987). Moreover, the Philippines promotes this trend and relies heavily on labor "exports" as a means of generating badly needed foreign currency (Stahl, 1987).

On the other hand, the United States regulates the inflow of Filipino nurses. Laws, regulations, and rulings by the Immigration and Naturalization Service (INS) and the Department of Labor have alternately limited and expanded the supply of foreign-trained nurses. Before the full implementation of the 1965 Immigration Act, the major avenue of entry was the Visitors Exchange Program, whose expressed objective was to assist other nations by giving foreign nurses the opportunity to receive advanced training in the United States. In practice, some hospitals exploited this program by using the "trainees" as cheap labor to supplement their work force, and these abuses contributed to the ultimate demise of this program in the late 1970s. As with other aspects of contemporary immigration, the 1965 Immigration Act was a watershed in the movement of Filipino nurses. The overall effect was to open new opportunities to work in the United States. But there have been important modifications that are, not surprisingly, tied to labor market conditions.

The 1965 national nursing shortage, particularly in the inner cities of major urban areas, prompted the U.S. secretary of labor to rule that nurses could receive automatic labor certification without the prior sponsorship of an employer (Schedule A), allowing foreign-trained nurses to enter the United States as immigrants under the occupational preference quotas. Foreign-trained nurses could also enter the country on temporary work

(H-1) visas to fill temporary positions. Five years later, the 1970 immigration amendment allowed H-1 visa holders to fill permanent positions, which dramatically expanded the number of positions that could be filled by temporary foreign workers (*Congressional Quarterly Almanac*, 1970, 236). The 1970 act also amended the two-year foreign residency requirement for exchange visitors, permitting them, under certain conditions, to apply for H-1 visas without leaving the country. Since then, the H-1 visa category has been a major venue through which foreign nurses have entered the United States.

The use of temporary visas became more important after the ending of highly favorable treatment of nurses under the immigration quotas in response to the economic crisis of the mid-1970s. In 1976, the secretary of labor removed the automatic waiver of labor certification for nurses. That made it more difficult, although not impossible, for Filipino nurses to migrate as occupational immigrants. Nevertheless, the continued shortage of nurses and the reliance on foreign nurses led to accommodations on the part of the federal government to allow temporary workers to prolong their stay in the United States. In 1977, H-1 nurses who had failed to pass their licensing exams within the prescribed time period were given a stay of deportation and three years to retake the exams (*Federal Register*, 1979, 53852). In September 1985, an INS interim policy statement permitted the issuance of H-1 visas for an initial period of three years with one two-year extension. In "extraordinary circumstances," another year could be added, for a total maximum allowable time of six years.[6] This stopgap measure of visa extension was continued in the 1988 amendments to the Immigration Act. With no end in sight to the critical nursing shortage, Congress passed the Immigration Nursing Relief Act of 1989 (INRA), allowing nurses who entered the United States with H-1 visas before 1 September 1989, and who had worked in nursing for three years, to adjust to permanent status without regard to per country caps on immigration.[7]

One shortcoming of INRA was its treatment of foreign nurses who moonlighted at other hospitals or accepted other unauthorized employment. In order to adjust their status, they were required to apply for immigrant visas overseas. Since

moonlighting is a common practice among nurses, strict implementation of INRA had a detrimental impact on the supply of
nurses. Congress was once again forced to act, this time by including a provision in the Immigration Act of 1990 that allowed
foreign nurses who accepted unauthorized employment to file
applications for adjustments for themselves as well as for their
accompanying spouses and children.

The shifts in immigration regulations have altered the Filipino
nurses' modes of entry. From the mid-1960s to the mid-1970s,
the nurses came as exchange students and as occupational immigrants. During this time, nurses, including exchange students
who met their two-year foreign residency requirement, could get
visas relatively quickly under the third preference. Since the
mid-1970s, these visas have become increasingly difficult to obtain, with the number of principal recipients of third-preference
visa categories averaging around five hundred to six hundred a
year. Although foreign nurses can still apply to enter the United
States under an occupational category, this route is effectively
closed to nurses from the Philippines, where the waiting period
for third-preference visas is currently longer than sixteen years.
The decline of immigrant nurse entries is more than offset by the
vast number of nurses coming in as temporary workers under
the H-1 visa classification. In 1985, 1,519 nurses from the Philippines were admitted in this category. Because of the nurse shortage that began in 1986–1987, this number rose to 6,239 in 1988.

Despite the multitude of laws and regulations, the United
States has not been able to regulate the flow of Filipino nurses
through the occupational provisions under the immigration
quotas or the temporary work programs. These regulations have
not been absolutely effective in controlling the movement and
stay of Filipino nurses, since the nurses make use of modes of
entry other than those directly related to their occupation. Specifically, many Filipino nurses use family reunification provisions. Others adjust their nonimmigrant status to that of immigrants by marriage to a U.S. citizen. At the expiration of their
temporary working visas, nurses are required to return to their
home country unless they can stay in the United States through
other means. Given the current situation, it is no surprise that
many nurses choose to adjust their status by marriage. But the

use of family reunification provisions is not limited to temporary workers who adjust their status to permanent workers. Increasingly, Filipino nurses have been able to enter the United States either by being sponsored by a relative already in the United States or by initially entering as temporary visitors (Liu, Ong, and Rosenstein, 1991).

Licensing Barriers. In addition to immigration laws and regulations, licensing requirements operate to regulate the effective supply of Filipino nurses practicing in the United States. Of the estimated ninety to one hundred thousand foreign nurses who have entered the United States as immigrants, exchange students, or temporary workers since 1965, the number actually added to the pool of registered nurses (RNs) in the country is considerably smaller, because, like practitioners of other professions, foreign nursing graduates (FNGs) must be credentialed. Regardless of mode of entry, all foreign-trained nurses are subject to the same credentialing requirements.

The process of credentialing has become more stringent. In the 1960s and early 1970s, when the Exchange Visitors Program was in full swing and many foreign nurses came from Europe and Canada, most FNGs, including a majority of Filipinos, received licenses by endorsement. So long as an FNG had received the required education and license in her home country, she could become a registered nurse in the United States. In the early 1970s, the requirement shifted as an increasing number of states began requiring that FNGs pass a state test before they could receive a license. This process often proved to be a major barrier. In 1975, for example, 84 percent of foreign nursing graduates failed to pass state boards on their first try, and many continued to fail even on their second and third attempts (*American Journal of Nursing,* 1978, 359). Without credentials, many Filipino nurses became part of a pool of skilled but unlicensed workers who were frequently exploited by unscrupulous employers. These FNGs were hired as nurse's aides while continuing to carry out the duties of a registered nurse.

The late 1970s witnessed a move to implement premigration testing. Concerns about safe delivery of health care as well as the exploitation of foreign nurses led to the creation of the Commission on Graduates of Foreign Nursing Schools (CGFNS) in 1977, cosponsored by the American Nurses' Association and the National League of Nursing. The commission established a program whereby FNGS seeking to work in the United States would be screened and tested in their home countries.[8] The expectation was that nurses who successfully completed CGFNS requirements before leaving their country would have a better chance of passing state licensing examinations in the United States. This goal has been realized. Since CGFNS exams were introduced as a screening mechanism in 1978, 89 percent of FNGS who have taken the licensing examinations have obtained their RN credentials (Maroun and Serota, 1988), a dramatic improvement over the performance in the prior decade. The greater success of FNGS in taking state licensing exams is not due solely to CGFNS screening, however. State Board Test Pool Exams (SBTPE), which were administered until 1982, when the National Council Licensure Examination (NCLEX) was put into place, proved to have a cultural bias and were found to be discriminatory against foreign nursing graduates. Removal of the problematic items and the substitution of job-related questions greatly improved the chances of passing by foreign nursing graduates taking the new NCLEX exams.

The new testing procedure did not entirely eliminate the problem of unlicensed FNGS. Even with the CGFNS, a substantial number continue to fail the state examinations. Moreover, Filipino nurses entering through family reunification provisions are not required to take the premigration exam and are thus less likely to be screened and more likely to fail the tests given in the United States. Because of the risk of failure, many Filipino nurses also take the test for a licensed vocational nurse (LVN) credential at the same time they are trying to become licensed as RNS. A few never make it beyond the LVN. Despite their facility with the English language, Filipino nurses have a poor record in passing state licensing examinations, even after successfully clearing the hurdle of the qualifying exams. In California, for example, Filipinos had a 13 percent passing rate for first-time takers of the SBTPE in 1983. This figure was well below the success rate of 55 percent overall and 31 percent for other Asian nurses who took the test at the same time. In our survey of Filipino nurses in Los Angeles,[9] about half said they passed the licensing test the first time they took it. One-third of those surveyed became LVNs within a year of their arrival, becoming RNs the following year. For 20 percent of the respondents, however, it took more than two attempts to pass the licensing examination.

Labor Recruitment. The recurring nursing shortage combined with immigration regulations to produce a system that encourages active labor recruitment, involving recruiters and immigration lawyers on both sides of the ocean. Because the severity of the nursing shortage varies considerably across facilities, hospitals with high vacancies and turnover have the greatest incentive to recruit abroad. Although foreign recruitment may require additional expenses, it still makes economic sense for U.S. health facilities. A study by Barbara Shockey (1989) shows how, within thirteen weeks, the high cost of temporary staffing and double shifts more than offset the recruitment cost of foreign nurses. The underlying economic factors that lead hospitals to recruit overseas are mitigated by current regulations, which require hospitals to submit a statement detailing what they have done to attract U.S. nurses and how hospital services would be affected without the foreign nurses. Hospitals are prohibited from sponsoring new foreign nurses if they have laid off a domestic nurse in the prior twelve-month period.

Organized recruitment takes three forms. In the first, an institution, for example, a hospital or nursing home, undertakes the recruitment effort on its own. In the second, the institution contracts with an agency in the foreign country to do the recruiting. In the third form, a combination of the first two, the institution sends someone to the foreign country to work with a local recruitment firm (Shockey, 1989). Foreign nurse recruiters are paid two thousand to five thousand dollars per nurse, depending on their particular arrangement with prospective employers. When they go on recruiting trips, they are given a weekly salary, and their air fare and hotel expenses are covered (Arbeiter, 1988). Another form of recruitment employed by hospitals is word of mouth, whereby staff nurses recruit their friends in other states or in the Philippines when on vacation. This method is perhaps less predictable, but it is more economical for hospitals.

The extent of recruitment activity can be seen in advertisements in the Philippine press. On one visit to Manila, for example, we found three prominent announcements of job openings in one issue of the *Manila Bulletin*, a major daily newspaper. One advertised for two hundred nurses to work for a Boston nursing home chain, and another called for one hundred nurses needed by several New York City hospitals. The third was from a hospital in New York advertising the benefits of working for it and openly trying to lure nurses away from other recruiters.

The recruitment process is not without flaws. Recruiters can be very aggressive in their hunt for nurses to bring to the United States, even to the point of providing misinformation to FNGS. For example, recruiters sometimes claim that CGFNS will accept experience as a substitute for educational credentials. Some recruiters also give false information regarding test dates and sites. The psychological cost of such misinformation pales, however, when compared to what happens when FNGS quit their jobs and celebrate with family and friends after being prematurely and erroneously notified by a recruiter that they passed the CGFNS exam (Maroun and Serota, 1988). Worst of all, some recruiters or their agents demand a "fee" from the nurses before they can be recruited. Although we do not know the extent to which this practice occurs in the Philippines and other Third World countries, it does happen, and there is no mechanism in place to monitor it.

Incorporation

For Filipino nurses who overcome the immigration and licensing hurdles, their incorporation into the health field is influenced by the specifics of the labor shortage and recruitment as well as by their economic motivations. Not surprisingly, a disproportionately large number of them are concentrated in those settings where the labor shortage is most acute and where there is a history of recruitment and use of FNGS. Filipino nurses' underlying financial objective to earn high wages is manifested by a willingness to work hard and long hours, with the payoff being higher-than-average incomes. Although Filipinos tend to have long careers as hospital nurses, relatively few move into administrative positions. The alternative has been to establish temporary agencies. The persistence of ethnicity in defining employment outcomes is a clear indication that the incorporation of Filipino nurses is far from complete.

Sectoral and Geographic Distribution. As a result of active recruitment and employer sponsorship, Filipino nurses tend to locate in the settings and geographic areas where U.S. employers have had trouble attracting domestically trained workers. Filipino nurses are disproportionately present in hospitals, particularly in jobs that have been difficult to fill. According to our analysis of the 1984 National Sample Survey of Registered Nurses (Moses, 1984), an overwhelming majority (82%) of the estimated twenty-seven thousand Filipino registered nurses in the United States worked in hospitals. By comparison, only 53 percent of non-Filipinos were in similar settings. This difference persists even after accounting for the number of years with a license. For example, of those who had been registered nurses for five to eight years, 92 percent of the Filipinos worked in a hospital while only 70 percent of the non-Filipinos did.

Filipinos are more likely than other nurses to be employed as staff nurses in critical care units of large metropolitan hospitals, partly because of the circumstances of their immigration: Filipino nurses are recruited to fill the shortages in these areas. In our Los Angeles survey, where 90 percent of the respondents were immigrants, we found that in many cases at least two-thirds of the nurses working in critical care and medical-surgical units, especially on the evening and night shifts, were Filipinos. The setting and working conditions of Filipino nurses, as well as the critical functions they perform, are typified in an excerpt from the statement of a New York hospital administrator at an immigration hearing:

[H-1 nurses] tend to be concentrated in certain services and units. . . . The areas where there is the most significant risk of stress and

burnout in the profession are the intensive care units and the medi-
cal/surgical services. Therefore, while every individual nurse is valuable, those working in these areas are virtually irreplaceable and of
critical importance to our health care system. (McEachen, 1989, 198)

Although this statement makes specific reference to H-1 nurses,
it applies equally to immigrant Filipino nurses, many of whom
were formerly temporary workers themselves.

Recruitment and employer sponsorship also influence the
geographic distribution of Filipino nurses. Although Filipinos
have traditionally settled in the West (52% of U.S. Filipinos were
California residents in 1990), large numbers of Filipino health
practitioners can be found in the East and Midwest (Liu et al.,
1991). In 1984, 46 percent of the Filipino nurses who had received their licenses within the last four years resided in those
two regions. One consequence of this geographic pattern of incorporation is the formation of Filipino communities dominated
by professionals. The proportion of Filipinos who are in the
health professions (including doctors and nurses) in Chicago
and New York is more than twice that in Los Angeles and more
than six times that in San Francisco (Azores-Gunter, 1987). Because of heavy recruitment from the Midwest and the eastern
seaboard, these areas have large concentrations of nurses on H-1
visas. New York City represents the extreme, employing 63 percent of the country's foreign nurses (*Hospitals*, 1990, 67). Filipinos comprise 18 percent of the RN staff of New York City hospitals and 83 percent of the foreign nurses employed there.

The initial geographic patterns are not stable, because many
Filipino nurses later relocate to the West Coast. This pattern was
evident in our 1988 survey, which showed that Filipino nurses
who lived in Los Angeles since they first arrived in the United
States came to this country with approved immigration visas,
while those who initially entered with exchange visitor or H-1
visas moved to Los Angeles from the East Coast or the Midwest
after the expiration of their contracts. The attraction of Los
Angeles stems from its favorable climate, its large Filipino community base, and the greater likelihood of finding friends and
relatives in the community. Relocating is not a trivial matter,
however, given the cost entailed. Nurses who are licensed in

New York must take another licensing exam in California to practice there. In our survey, we found two nurses who were RNS on the East Coast but were temporarily working as LVNS while awaiting licensing in California. The relocation process also has an impact on recruitment in Los Angeles. According to administration officials and a nurse recruiter in Los Angeles, recruitment of nurses from the Philippines was not necessary in the late 1980s, since Filipino nurses from other parts of the country filled many of the vacancies in the Southland. On the other hand, hospitals in the East and Midwest must continue to rely on overseas recruitment to replace the foreign workers who have relocated.

Earnings. As we have stated earlier, many Filipinos pursue nursing as a way to find better-paying employment abroad. The money they earn supports not only themselves and their families in the United States, but also relatives in the Philippines. These obligations have made Filipino nurses high-income target earners who remain active in the profession long after their non-Filipino colleagues have left the practice. In 1984, 91 percent of the Filipinos who had been licensed four years or less worked full-time as nurses, compared to 72 percent of non-Filipinos. For those with nine or more years of licensure, 73 percent of the Filipinos worked full-time as nurses, compared to only 45 percent of the non-Filipinos. One outcome of the high level of economic activity is a higher average income. Data from the 1984 National Sample Survey of Registered Nurses (Moses, 1984) show that Filipinos had the highest earnings from their nursing employment among all groups, averaging almost five thousand dollars more annually than white nurses. A regression analysis of the data shows that Filipinos had higher earnings even after accounting for age, years of licensure, educational level, employment setting, and geographic region.

Filipino nurses use various strategies to increase their earnings. One-fifth of our Los Angeles respondents observed that Asian nurses tend to work in the evenings and at night, shifts that pay a 10 percent premium. According to one respondent, "Filipino nurses are more in 3 P.M. to 11 P.M. shifts in my ward [medical/surgical], maybe because not too many nurses apply.

Other groups, they don't stay long, specially if they are young."
The respondents also mentioned that some Filipino nurses work
double shifts and in inner-city hospitals, which offer salaries
higher than the national average.

Given the willingness of Filipino nurses to work under the
least desirable conditions, there has been concern that they
would depress wages of U.S. workers. The INS commissioned a
study precisely to look into this problem (Booz, Allen & Hamilton, 1988). Noting the high proportion of H-1 nurses in New
York City, the study compared their wages with the prevailing
wage levels in the area but found no adverse impact on U.S.
nurses.

Not everyone agrees with this finding, however. The AFL-CIO,
for example, contends that the INS-sponsored study was not
based on sufficient evidence regarding salaries, working conditions, and the recruitment and training of nurses over a period
of time. It cites Bureau of Labor Statistics data to show that New
York City, with the heaviest use of H-1 nurses among several
metropolitan areas, had much lower real wage increases for
nurses than other areas between 1978 and 1985. According to the
AFL-CIO, these data suggest that the H-1 nurses did have an adverse effect on the wages of nurses in New York and on the
ability of New York to attract domestic nurses (Guthrie, 1989).
We believe that the small increases have much more to do with
the fiscal problems of the state than the presence of foreign
nurses. The lack of an adverse impact is not surprising, given
the way wages are set. As stated earlier, hospitals have acted in
a monopsonistic fashion, and the financial pressure from cost
containment places a cap on the wages that are offered. Under
these conditions, many of the positions would go vacant in the
absence of FNGS.

Mobility. Although many Filipinos are initially incorporated
into the health system through direct placement or recruitment
with a specific hospital, they frequently move in search of better
employment. We have already discussed the geographic relocation of H-1 nurses. Immigrants, both permanent residents and
naturalized citizens, tend to be mobile in another way. They
move from one hospital to another within the same locality, es-

pecially during the early years of their careers. For example, the nurses in our survey who came as immigrants and settled in Los Angeles from the very beginning changed employers as often as four times in the first six years. They tended to stabilize after the third or fourth employer or after six to eight years in Los Angeles.

Although Filipino nurses have long careers working in the hospital sector, a disproportionately small number of them rise to management level positions. Only 9 percent of employed Filipinos work as administrators, supervisors, or head nurses, compared to 18 percent of all employed nurses. Although the presence of a large population of temporary workers lowers this figure, and the question of a possible glass ceiling for Filipino nurses comes to mind, the issue of upward mobility is more complex than may be indicated by these factors. Certainly, the perception of Filipino nurses as being cliquish, reticent, "less professional," and lacking social skills (Sarsfield, 1974) works against their being seriously considered or being invited to apply for managerial positions. The other side of the issue is that there is a real hesitancy on the part of many Filipino nurses to seek higher positions. Being a head nurse is a twenty-four-hour responsibility with no overtime pay or shift differential. A staff nurse doing double shifts or working with nursing registries can make considerably more money than a head nurse and not have as much responsibility. For Filipino nurses, fulfilling family obligations generally comes before professional advancement.

Working through a registry represents a better avenue of mobility for Filipino nurses. Working through these temporary agencies is still a minor phenomenon but one that has grown dramatically. For example, 3 percent of all U.S. registered nurses in 1988 obtained their principal nursing position through a temporary employment service. This proportion was a 55 percent increase over 1984 figures for nurses working under these conditions. Another indicator of interest in registry work is the number of nursing registries that are owned, managed, or operated by (or cater to) Filipinos. From 1984 to 1991, the number of such registries advertising in the Los Angeles section of the *Filipino Directory* rose from nine to twenty-three.

Although nurses who work exclusively through a registry

must buy their own insurance and receive no benefits from the hospitals, there are offsetting advantages. Nurses choose this type of employment for two reasons: to earn supplemental income and to gain better control of their working conditions. In our Los Angeles survey, we found that registries not only pay higher hourly rates but also provide nontraditional bonuses, such as trips to Hawaii or thousand-dollar premiums, offers that few hospitals are willing to make. Another feature of registry work that draws nurses is flexibility: they have control of when, where, and how much they want to work. To increase their flexibility and choice, the nurses are often on the rolls of more than one agency. Registries are able to offer higher wages and still thrive because they charge the hospitals high fees for their services. For their part, hospitals find it more economical in the long run to pay registry fees than to pay regular staff for double shifts to cover transient and seasonal fluctuations in the demand for nurses or to fill positions when a permanent person is on vacation or ill.

Nurses on temporary working visas are not allowed to work for other than their sponsors, but permanent residents and naturalized citizens see registry work as a viable option. For one-tenth of the nurses we interviewed, primary employment was through the registry, while another one-fifth were regular hospital employees but were also working elsewhere through a registry. It was not uncommon to find a Filipino nurse holding one full-time job in a hospital in downtown Los Angeles and another full-time job at a second hospital on the other side of town.

The use of registries is not just an avenue of mobility for nurses as workers. It is also a means of advancement for those who open and operate a registry. This strategy appears to be a recent but growing phenomenon among Filipino nurses. The move from being an employee at a hospital to being an owner of a temporary agency requires new managerial and administrative skills. According to one Filipino owner of a nurse registry business, registry nurses must be credentialed, evaluated, and oriented. Besides scheduling nurses, the owners spend time developing market strategies to place their nurses. Initially, they make calls on directors of nursing to introduce their firm and to show them a portfolio of the kinds of nurses they have on call. Nurses who have not previously worked at a hospital do so free of charge to the hospital as part of their orientation. These nurses are still paid by the registry, however, and this offer is seen as an investment in developing new markets. Registry ownership not only changes the status of an individual but is transforming a segment of Filipino nurses from the professional class to the managerial class.

Ethnic Issues. Although Filipino nurses have been incorporated into the health field, particularly hospitals, the incorporation is far from complete because of the persistence of ethnicity. Ethnicity has asserted itself in the hospital setting in the form of visible clustering of Filipino nurses in certain hospitals in large metropolitan areas. The origin of many of these clusters is the process of selective recruitment discussed earlier. The establishment of social support systems in some facilities also contributes to the clustering of Filipino nurses. Filipinos with job seniority can facilitate the mentoring process. For newly arrived workers, having other Filipinos in the work environment minimizes culture shock. Despite a familiarity with the English language, there are significant cultural differences between the world in which the Filipinos were socialized and the world in which they work.

The presence of Filipino clusters enables ethnic-based behavior. For example, there is a tendency for the nurses to speak in their native language. Although those who do so are considered rude and are suspect because Americans do not know what they are talking about, it is very difficult for the nurses not to speak their native language among themselves: among bilingual Filipinos, the use of English can be a reflection of psychological distance and/or power relations between speakers. Filipino culture dictates that group members speak to one another in the native language at least some of the time if they are on a friendly basis. Even in a professional setting, speaking only English to another Filipino can mark one as a snob and an outsider and can have a negative effect on both personal and working relationships. Thus, while it is true that Filipinos can use the native language to keep other people in the dark about their conversations, that is not usually the intent.

Electing to work late hours and speaking a native language, such as Tagalog, can also be regarded as ways in which Filipino nurses minimize the stresses of the work environment. According to some of the nurses we talked to, it is easy to work the night and evening shifts, when most patients are asleep and fewer people are on the floor. The Filipinos are more relaxed working under these conditions. And while nurses sometimes resort to speaking Tagalog as a way of releasing tension, reverting to the native language can also be seen as an attempt to reaffirm their identity in the midst of what to them is a foreign environment and thus, in some way, gain control of that environment.

Although this use of a native language is understandable, it has been a source of conflict. Domestic nurses do not always react favorably to Asian nurses who are difficult to understand, unlike western Europeans, whose accents they often find "charming." Asian nurses who speak to one another in their native language because it is more "natural" for them to do so can also alienate doctors, other nurses, and even patients, who wonder if they are being talked about. In their desire to maintain control over all situations, some hospitals are driven to impose an "English only" rule at all times, in violation of individual rights. A case in Pomona, California, filed in 1991, which has drawn national attention, involves a Filipino nurse who sued her employer for demoting her for speaking Tagalog while on duty. The court ruled that the hospital retaliated unfairly and ordered that the nurse be transferred, with back pay, to a position comparable to the one she had held previously (Chang, 1991). But the policy that banned the use of Tagalog on the shift where the nurse worked was ruled to be nondiscriminatory, despite the fact that speaking Spanish was allowed on the floor. This ruling was appealed in 1991, and an out-of-court settlement was reached in 1992 (Henry, 1990; Imahara, 1993; Mydans, 1990; Ochoa, 1991).

The role of ethnicity extends beyond the hospitals. For example, the temporary agencies discussed earlier represent a form of ethnic labor market. Interviews with two Filipino owners revealed that 80 to 90 percent of their listings of available nurses are Filipinos. A common ethnic identity also plays a role in the formation of Filipino nurses' associations, whose primary function is to sponsor social events. Although these associations are based on ethnic bonds, they are nonetheless colored by their particular class interests and concerns. The associations have on occasion sponsored seminars and workshops for professional advancement. Some of these organizations have also taken on a political role in lobbying the states and the federal government regarding testing and visa requirements.

The importance of the Filipino nurses is not based on their impact and contribution to the health care system in the United States. It would be unfair to state that this country has grown dependent on Filipino nurses, although there are many hospitals that have. Even when thousands of Filipino nurses were entering the country, they comprised at most only a small percentage of the total supply. The case of the Filipino nurses, however, does reveal much about an important element of contemporary Asian migration, that of highly educated labor.

The migration and incorporation of highly educated labor are not simple processes. They involve structural problems in the United States (recurring labor shortages), institutional responses in the Philippines (the expansion of nursing education), policies and regulations (Filipino laissez-faire and dependency on labor export, as well as U.S. immigration laws and their occupational provisions), and individual actions (Filipinos using nursing in an instrumental fashion to find better employment opportunities abroad). Incorporation into the U.S. economy hinges on achieving professional standing, in this case, an RN license. Although many Filipino nurses have been able to find work in their chosen career, the incorporation is far from being complete because of the persistence of ethnicity.

Things are not likely to change in the near future. Economic conditions in the Philippines are still precarious, and any improvement will not soon close the huge wage differences between the two countries. The 1989 Nursing Immigration Relief Act might enable several thousand foreign nurses to work "permanently" in the United States, but it will have only a minor impact on the shortage of domestic nurses, estimated at 370,000. The pressure to recruit and admit more foreign nurses will continue. Although the latest immigration laws have placed new restrictions on the future importation of foreign nurses, historical evidence suggests that exceptions will once again be made as the needs arise. The role of ethnic-professional organizations is likely to become more important over time as membership increases and as testing and immigration issues become more politicized.

Notes

1. The economic term for this situation is an *inelastic supply,* in which a given percentage increase in wages generates a smaller percentage increase in supply. A recent estimate using 1984 data places the elasticity at 0.49, which is comparable to earlier estimates (Buerhaus, 1991). Thus a 10 percent increase in wages would increase supply by less than 5 percent.
2. This is a determination and certification by the secretary of labor to the secretary of state and the attorney general that there are not sufficient workers in the United States who are able, willing, qualified, and available to perform such skilled or unskilled labor.
3. English is becoming less and less a lingua franca since the public schools shifted to Pilipino as the language of instruction in the mid-1970s. Pilipino is the Tagalog of the Greater Metropolitan Area of Manila and is also the language of social protest. The use of the term "Pilipino" in mass media has contributed greatly to its gain in popularity.
4. The United States gave up Clark Air Force Base after the disaster caused by the 1991 eruption of Mt. Pinatubo. In 1992, the Philippine senate did not ratify a treaty to renew the United States–Philippine military bases agreement, which had expired in September 1991. As a result, all U.S. bases, including Clark and Subic, have been removed from the Philippines.
5. The policy of importing nurses has a history that dates back at least to the period after World War II with the implementation of the State Department's Exchange Visitor Program, created under the Information and Educational Exchange Act of 1948. The American Nurses' Association was an authorized sponsor of the program, and it directly recruited foreign nurses along with many U.S. hospitals. Designed to promote cultural understanding and technology exchange between the United States and Third World countries, the

program attracted scores of nurses from Asia, with large contingents from the Philippines.

6. In the past, H-1 visas were issued for only a two-year initial period, with one-year extensions for an indefinite period of time.

7. In 1991, H-1 visas expired for nurses who were hired after the effective date of the act and had not adjusted to permanent residency status. Employers not willing to risk sanctions terminated these nurses as their visas expired.

8. CGFNS administers qualifying exams semiannually in forty-three cities worldwide to test the language competency and nursing proficiency of applicants who are already licensed or certified in their home country as first-level nurses. (According to the International Council of Nurses, a first-level nurse must have a high school diploma and must have graduated from a government-approved nursing school with a minimum two-year program, including theory and clinical practice in the five areas of nursing: medical, surgical, obstetrics, pediatrics, and psychiatry.) FNGs who pass the exam are given a CGFNS certificate, which is required before the INS will issue an H-1 or occupational visa to enter the United States. Once in the United States, the FNG is expected to take the RN licensing examination at the next scheduled examination date (it is given every February and July in all fifty states). Depending on the state, an FNG may or may not be allowed to practice nursing before passing the examination. In California, an interim permit is issued that allows the candidate to work before taking the examination and while awaiting the results.

9. The survey was conducted in 1988. One hundred fifty questionnaires were distributed to the Filipino nursing community through the Philippine Nurses Association of Southern California and through personal contacts in area hospitals. Only forty questionnaires were returned. They represented men and women who worked in fifteen health facilities, including two county hospitals, a health maintenance organization, three private general hospitals, several small community and convalescent hospitals, and three outpatient clinics. Because of the voluntary nature of the survey, there was uneven representation from the different types of health facilities.

References

Aaron, Henry, and Cameran Loughy. 1986. *The Comparable Worth Controversy*. Washington, D.C.: Brookings Institution.

American Journal of Nursing. 1978. "Pre-immigration Tests Start in October for Foreign Graduate Nurses." March, p. 359.

American Nurses' Association. 1987. *Facts about Nursing, 1986/87*. Kansas City, Mo.

Arbeiter, Jean S. 1988. "The Facts about Foreign Nurses." *RN* 51(9):56–63.

Arrow, Kenneth, and William Capron. 1959. "Dynamic Shortages and Price Rises: The Engineer-Scientist Case." *Quarterly Journal of Economics* 73 (May):292–308.

Azores-Gunter, Tania Fortunata M. 1987. "Status Achievement Patterns of Filipinos in the United States." Ph.D. dissertation, University of California, Los Angeles.

Begun, James W., and Rogger Feldman. 1989. "Policy and Research on Health Manpower Regulation: Never Too Late to Deregulate?" *Advances in Health Economics and Health Services* 11:79–110.

Berkman, Leslie. 1988. "U.S. Hospitals Are Stepping Up Use of Foreign Nurses." *Los Angeles Times*, 19 June, pp. 1, 9.

Blum, Linda. 1991. *Between Feminism and Labor: The Significance of the Comparable Worth Movement*. Berkeley: University of California Press.

Booz, Allen & Hamilton. 1988. *Characteristics and Labor Market Impact of Persons Admitted under the H-1 Program: Final Report, June 1988*. Booz, Allen & Hamilton, Management Consultants.

Buerhaus, Peter. 1991. "Dynamic Shortage of Registered Nurses." *Nursing Economics* 9 (September–October):317–328.

Carino, Benjamin. 1987. "Brain Flow from the Philippines: Facts, Causes, and Consequences." Paper prepared for the Brain Flow Workshop sponsored by the Center for Pacific Rim Studies, University of California, Los Angeles, 22–26 June.

Carino, Ledevina. 1977. "Philippines: Patterns from the U.S.A." In *Professional Structure in Southeast Asia*, ed. T. H. Silcock, pp. 166–224. Canberra: Australian National University.

Chang, Irene. 1991. "Ruling on Foreign Language Ban Criticized." *Los Angeles Times*, 26 October, p. B3.

Cleland, Virgina. 1989. *The Economics of Nursing*. Norwalk, Conn.: Appleton and Lange.

Congressional Quarterly Almanac. 1970. 91st Cong., 2d sess., vol. 26. Washington, D.C.: Congressional Quarterly News Features.

Federal Register. 1979. 44: 53852.

Filipino Directory of California: A Guide to American Life. Southern California Edition. 1984. Los Angeles: Fil-Am Enterprises.

Filipino Directory of the United States and Canada. 1991–92. Los Angeles: Filipino Directory in American.

Guthrie, Robert. 1989. "Statement of Robert Guthrie, Assistant Director, Department for Professional Employees, AFL-CIO." Testimony before the House Subcommittee on Immigration, Refugees, and International Law during hearings on H.R. 1507 and H.R. 2111, Immigration Nursing Relief Act of 1989. 101st Cong., 1st sess., Serial no. 13, pp. 221–241. Washington, D.C.: Government Printing Office.

Hendricks, Ann M. 1989. "Hospital Wage Gradients within U.S. Urban Areas." *Journal of Health Economics* 8(2):233–246.

Henry, Sarah. 1990. "Fighting Words." *Los Angeles Times Magazine*, 10 June, pp. 37–38.

Hospitals. 1990. 5 February, p. 67.

Hunter, Frances. 1986. *Equal Pay for Comparable Worth*. New York: Praeger.

Imahara, Kathryn K. 1993. Phone interview of Kathryn K. Imahara, attorney for Aida Dimaranan, Asian Pacific American Legal Center, by Tania Azores, 7 March.

Interpreter Releases: Report and Analysis of Immigration and Nationality Law. 1989. 66 (4 December):1316.

Jackson, Janet, Pamela MacFalda, and Kathleen McManus. 1989. "Status of the Nursing Shortage and Projections." In *Managing the Nursing Shortage*, ed. Terence Moore and Earl Simendinger, pp. 1–11. Rockville, Md.: Aspen Publishers.

Joyce, Richard E., and Chester L. Hunt. 1982. "Philippine Nurses and the Brain Drain." *Social Science Medicine* 16:1223–1233.

Liu, John M., Paul M. Ong, and Carolyn Rosenstein. 1991. "Dual Chain Migration: Post-1965 Filipino Immigration to the United States." *International Migration Review* 25(3):487–513.

McEachen, Irene. 1989. "Testimony of Irene McEachen, Vice-President, Nursing, Beth Medical Center." Testimony before the House Subcommittee on Immigration, Refugees, and International Law during the hearings on H.R. 1507 and H.R. 2111, Immigration Nursing Relief Act of 1989. 101st Cong., 1st sess., Serial no. 13, pp. 193–199. Washington, D.C.: Government Printing Office.

Manila Bulletin. 1986. July 27.

Maroun, Virginia M., and Carol Serota. 1988. "Special Report: The Nursing Shortage. Demanding Quality When Foreign Nurses Are in Demand. *Nursing and Health Care* 9(7):360–363.

Moore, Terence, and Carolyn Fraser. 1989. "The Medical Staff's Influence in Nurse Recruitment and Retention." In *Managing the Nursing Shortage*, ed. Terence Moore and Earl Simendinger, pp. 150–159. Rockville, Md.: Aspen Publishers.

Moore, Terence, and Earl Simendinger, eds. 1989. *Managing the Nursing Shortage*. Rockville, Md.: Aspen Publishers.

Moses, Evelyn B. 1984. *National Sample Survey of Registered Nurses, November 1984* [Computer file]. Rockville, Md.: Bureau of Health Professionals [producer].

———. 1990. *Findings from the Sample Survey of Registered Nurses, March 1988*. Washington, D.C.: U.S. Department of Human and Health Services, Division of Nursing.

Mydans, Seth. 1990. "Pressure for English-Only Job Rules Stirring a Sharp Debate across U.S." *New York Times*, 8 August, p. A12.

National Economic and Development Authority, National Census and Statistics Office. 1982. *Philippine Yearbook, 1983*. Manila.

———. 1989. *Philippine Statistical Yearbook*. Manila.

Ochoa, Cecile C. 1991. "Rights Lawyers Fight 'No Tagalog' Ruling." *Los Angeles Filipino Bulletin*, 21 November–15 December, p. 1.

Ongkiko, Ricardo, and Gerard Suanes. 1984. "A Rate of Return Analysis of the Nursing Profession in the Philippines." A.B./B.S. thesis, University of the Philippines, Manila.

Puleo, James. 1989. Hearings before the House Subcommittee on Immigration, Refugees, and International Law on H.R. 1507 and H.R. 2111, Immigration Nursing Relief Act of 1989. 101st Cong., 1st sess., Serial no. 13, pp. 61–67. Washington, D.C.: Government Printing Office.

Renner, C., and Victor Navarro. 1989. "Why Is Our Population of Uninsured and Underinsured Persons Growing? The Consequences of the Deindustrialization of America." *Annual Review of Public Health* 10:85–94.

Republic of China. 1987. *Taiwan Statistical Data Book*. Taipei: Council for Economic Planning and Development.

Rimando, Carlos. 1984. "The Migration of Filipino Nurses: Its Implication for the Domestic Market." Unpublished paper, University of the Philippines, Manila.

Sarsfield, Nancy Ann Chiavacci. 1974. "An Acculturative Study of the Filipino Nurse in New Jersey Hospitals." Ph.D. dissertation, New York University, New York.

Shockey, Barbara L. 1989. "Foreign Nurse Recruitment and Authorization for Employment in the United States." In *Managing the Nursing Shortage*, ed. Terence Moore and Earl Simendinger, pp. 252–263. Rockville, Md.: Aspen Publishers.

Sorensen, Elaine. 1989. "The Wage Effects of Occupational Sex Composition: A Review and New Findings." In M. Anne Hill and Mark Killingsworth, eds., *Colloquium on Comparable Worth*. Ithaca, N.Y.: Cornell University-I.L.R. Press.

Stahl, Charles W. 1987. "Manpower Export and Economic Development: Evidence from the Philippines." In *International Labour Migration in the Philippines and Southeast Asia*, pp. 27–47. A Roundtable Report. Berlin: German Foundation for International Development.

U.S. Congress. House. Committee on the Judiciary. Subcommittee on Immigration, Refugees, and International Law. 1989. Hearings on H.R. 1507 and H.R. 2111, Immigration Nursing Relief Act of 1989. 101st Cong., 1st sess., May 31, Serial no. 13. Washington, D.C.: Government Printing Office.

U.S. President. 1991. *Economic Report of the President.* Washington, D.C.: Government Printing Office.

Vogt, Judith. 1983. *Retaining Professional Nurses: A Planning Process.* St. Louis: C.V. Mosby Company.

Woolley, J. Michael. 1989. "The Competitive Effects of Horizontal Mergers in the Hospital Industries." *Journal of Health Economics* 8(2):271–291.

World Bank. 1988. *World Development Report.* New York: Oxford University Press and World Bank.

Yett, Donald E. 1975. *An Economic Analysis of the Nurse Shortage.* Lexington, Mass.: Lexington Books.

7. Chinese-Vietnamese Entrepreneurs in California

Steve Gold

A growing body of research has considered the ability of various immigrant and ethnic groups to adapt economically to host societies through ethnic self-employment (Cohen, 1969; Cummings, 1980; Kim, 1981; Light, 1972; Min, 1988; Portes and Bach, 1985). Ethnic economies have also been studied in terms of their effects on the restructuring of advanced industrial societies.

Although the restructuring process can occur independently of the presence of immigrant workers and entrepreneurs, observers have associated these two social phenomena and attempted to clarify the connection between them (Castells, 1989; Sassen, 1988; Waldinger, 1986). Studies of immigrants and restructuring generally concern one of two populations: unskilled, sometimes undocumented, manual workers such as Latinos and Caribbeans; and professional or entrepreneurial groups such as Chinese and Koreans. Usually left out of this analysis is the role played by refugees, a group numbering well over a million in the United States since the mid-1970s (Office of Refugee Resettlement, 1990).

While the difference between refugees and immigrants is a matter of continuum rather than simple categorization, the social, motivational, and demographic characteristics of refugees clearly contrast with those of economically motivated immigrant groups (Bernard, 1977). Further, because they receive refugee status from the U.S. government, they occupy an exclusive relationship with the state. Accordingly, refugees engage in certain unique patterns of economic adaptation (Gold, 1988).

A major distinction between refugees and immigrants involves their ability to prepare for and accept the difficulties of living in a new culture (Portes, 1984; Rumbaut, 1986). Immigrants often make extensive preparations before their foray into a new nation, carrying substantial amounts of capital and freely returning home to arrange business deals, recruit countrymen, or borrow money (Kim, 1981; Mangiafico, 1988). In contrast, refugees flee their homeland in order to survive (Bonacich, 1973; Ngan, 1982; Reimers, 1985; Teitelbaum, 1985). They have little opportunity to plan for their new life, learn English, or collect capital, and they generally arrive without assets and cannot return at will.[1]

Immigrants often make migration decisions on the basis of economic considerations and hence possess labor market characteristics that are desired in the host society (Burawoy, 1976; Castles and Kosack, 1973; Simon, 1986). In contrast, refugee populations include many persons who would be unlikely to leave home on a voluntary basis. They are far from being a self-selected labor force. Instead, their numbers include many unemployables: young children, elderly individuals, religious and political leaders, and people in poor mental and physical condition (Portes and Rumbaut, 1990). Accordingly, refugees have much lower rates of labor force participation than other immigrant groups (Office of Refugee Resettlement, 1990).

Finally, refugees occupy a legal status distinct from that of most other recent migrants. They receive legal resident status, refugee cash assistance (RCA) for a period ranging from eight to thirty-six months depending on their year of arrival in the United States, and are entitled to the same welfare benefits and services as U.S. citizens. Thus, in comparison to most other recent immigrant groups, refugees are characterized by a combination of personal and economic disadvantages and legal privileges. In the southern California economy, they occupy a rather singular situation as a sizable low-income group with legal resident status. This chapter considers the role of one of the most economically active refugee groups to enter the United States in recent years: the Chinese-Vietnamese.[2]

Southeast Asian Chinese refugees draw on their business experience in Southeast Asia and their links with co-ethnics both overseas and in the United States. Their business capacity is illustrated by the fact that many of the largest refugee enterprises in West Coast cities, including Seattle, San Francisco, Oakland, San Jose, Los Angeles, Monterey Park, and Westminster, are owned by the "Viet Hoa" (ethnic Chinese). Further, among larger businesses that are owned by refugees—wholesale, import/export, real estate development, and manufacturing concerns—the ethnic Chinese exercise almost complete dominance. Such businesses are capable of generating numerous jobs. They are also vital to the development of integrated ethnic economies like those associated with the most successful populations of immigrant entrepreneurs and may play a significant role in reorganizing economic relationships in the larger society (Light, 1972 and 1980; Portes and Manning, 1986; Waldinger, 1987; Wilson and Martin, 1982).

The Chinese-Vietnamese Refugees

In the two thousand years of relations between China and its southern neighbor, thousands of Chinese have migrated to Vietnam. Most came from Guangdong Province, including Canton and Fukien. Their degree of assimilation to Vietnamese culture varied. Some Chinese were nearly totally assimilated; others lived in Chinese enclaves, sent their children to Chinese schools, and spoke Chinese dialects rather than Vietnamese (Chen, 1987). Like overseas Chinese in other Asian nations, many Chinese in Vietnam occupied a classic middleman role (Bonacich, 1973). They became an economically powerful minority group and were often subject to the hostility of the ethnic Vietnamese (Purcell, 1965; Whitmore, 1985). Under the Diem regime (1958–1963), laws were enacted to require Chinese to serve in the military, take on Vietnamese citizenship, and in other ways encourage assimilation.

Despite their many cultural similarities, China and Vietnam have a tradition of conflict. Although North Vietnam and China cooperated during the Vietnam War, soon after (in 1978), hostilities heated up again. As a result of the Vietnam-China conflict, the Hanoi government decided to rid Vietnam of its Chinese minority. Three reasons were cited for Vietnam's ejection of the Chinese. First, the loyalty of the Chinese was doubted. Second, the Communist government was in the process of rebuilding Vietnamese society and wished to remove this staunchly capitalistic minority group. Finally, by charging the ethnic Chinese hundreds or thousands of dollars in gold as an exit fee, the new government was able to obtain badly needed cash (Chen, 1987; Long and Kendall, 1981; Purcell, 1965; Reimers, 1985; Teitelbaum, 1985).

As a result of these historical developments, since 1978 a sizable number of ethnic Chinese have fled Vietnam as "boat people" and resettled in the United States (and other nations). Similar factors have brought smaller flows of ethnic Chinese refugees from Cambodia and Laos.

Patterns of Adaptation. Ethnic Chinese refugees from Vietnam occupy a paradoxical economic position within the Southeast Asian refugee community in the United States. Many of the most successful refugee entrepreneurs are of Chinese ethnicity; community activists estimate that up to 40 percent of entrepreneurs in Orange County's Little Saigon (the largest Vietnamese community outside Southeast Asia) are Chinese-Vietnamese. As a group, however, "even after personal and contextual variables are controlled for, the Sino-Vietnamese resettled in the United States are still at a disadvantage with respect to both acculturation and economic adaptation" when compared to other Vietnamese refugees (Desbarats, 1986, 425; Rumbaut, 1986).

Levels of economic disadvantage are striking. The elite Vietnamese refugees who entered the United States between 1975 and 1977 have made remarkable strides, but the more recently arrived—including most Chinese-Vietnamese—have encountered difficulty in adjusting to America (Office of Refugee Resettlement, 1987).[3] One study of Vietnamese in San Diego found 61 percent to be at or below the poverty level (Rumbaut, 1986, table 3). These Southeast Asian refugees also display high rates—64 percent—of welfare dependency (Office of Refugee Resettlement, 1987, 35). Only 31 percent of Southeast Asian refugee households in the United States are fully self-supporting (Office of Refugee Resettlement, 1988, 140).[4] "Ten years after Southeast Asian refugees first entered the United States, 50 percent of California's 400,000 refugees, making up 43,000 families, are fully reliant on welfare" (Arax, 1987, 1). Because of the low level of support provided by welfare and refugee cash assistance, of those Southeast Asians who rely on it, 64 percent live below the poverty level (Caplan, Whitmore, and Bui, 1985, 189).

Statistics concerning the economic status of refugees by ethnicity are relatively rare, but those that do exist indicate that the ethnic Chinese confront considerable difficulties. A federally funded study of 1,384 Vietnamese, Chinese-Vietnamese, and Lao refugee families who entered the United States after 1978 found that of the three groups, the Chinese-Vietnamese had the lowest rate of employment and were the least likely to be self-supporting. Moreover, Chinese-Vietnamese who were working earned less per hour than employed Vietnamese (Caplan et al., 1985, tables III.A.4 and IV.E.2). Thus, the Chinese-Vietnamese are relatively unique among Asian immigrants, as they constitute an ethnic population that includes both affluent business owners and poverty-stricken, welfare-dependent refugees.

The settlement of Chinese-Vietnamese refugees in southern California and their involvement in self-employment can be best understood when placed in its particular context, one that involves the simultaneous occurrence of several local, national, and international factors. Since 1975, greater southern California has become home to the largest population of Vietnamese and other Southeast Asians outside their home nations. Current estimates place this population at around 200,000. Ethnic Chinese make up about a third of all Vietnamese in this area (Tran, 1986). Starting about a decade earlier and increasing rapidly during the same time period, vast numbers of other Asians have also arrived in southern California, yielding an Asian population of over 1.2 million in Los Angeles and Orange counties by 1990 (Turner and Allen, 1991). Estimates of Orange County's Vietnamese population alone range upward of 85,000 (Brody, 1987).

As a result of the arrival of these Asian immigrants, many middle-class areas of southern California have been transformed into Asian suburbs. While the Chinese-Vietnamese often live in the same areas as nonrefugee Asian immigrants, because of their origins and their status as refugees they are generally less educated and have fewer assets than other Asian groups (Mangiafico, 1988; Office of Refugee Resettlement, 1990; Portes and Rumbaut, 1990).

It is in these Asian neighborhoods—both traditional Chinatowns and new Asian suburbs—that most refugee businesses are located. The three areas of greatest Chinese-Vietnamese business concentration in southern California are Chinatown in downtown Los Angeles; Monterey Park and Alhambra in the San Gabriel Valley of eastern Los Angeles County; and Westminster and Garden Grove in Orange County, a development so large that it is identified by a "Little Saigon" exit sign on the Garden Grove Freeway. The presence of the considerable and relatively concentrated population of Asian immigrants in southern California has much to do with the development of a Chinese-Vietnamese economy in this area (Portes and Bach, 1985).

Multiple Connections. Most literature on ethnic economies is concerned with the forms of connection, integration, and solidarity that occur within a single ethnic group. For example, Alejandro Portes and Robert Bach (1985) show how established Cuban entrepreneurs work together and hire recently arrived co-ethnics in order to develop a powerful ethnic economy in Miami. Illsoo Kim (1981) makes a similar argument about New York's Koreans. Less attention has been devoted to the ways that ethnic entrepreneurial groups take advantage of their connections with other populations, institutions, and social developments to play important economic roles.

Nevertheless, some promising research on this issue has been carried out. Ivan Light and Edna Bonacich (1988), Pyong-Gap Min (1988), and Roger Waldinger and colleagues (1990) have shown how certain skilled immigrant groups have positioned themselves in the social and ethnic stratification systems of industrial societies to take special advantage of preexisting captive labor, consumer markets, and other favorable social and economic conditions. These groups take the place of a shrinking native middle class; hire recently arrived, distressed immigrant workers at low wages; and sell products and services to underserved minority populations in such a way as to yield profits for themselves and the larger economic system while furthering the restructuring process. The findings of these studies allude to the role that many Chinese-Vietnamese entrepreneurs play in U.S. society.

The economic role of the Chinese-Vietnamese involves multiple connections. They bring together various groups and, in so doing, make a living for themselves and foster social and economic connections on local, regional, and international levels. Orange County's Little Saigon illustrates this process.

Little Saigon is a large ethnic shopping district. Most of the strip and enclosed malls that house retail stores, restaurants, and offices in the area were built by Chinese-Vietnamese real estate developers using overseas Chinese capital. The majority of customers and many shop owners are Vietnamese. Other entrepreneurs are Chinese-Vietnamese and nonrefugee Chinese immigrants. Goods in many shops (food, clothing, herbs, and toys) are imported from Asia, some by Chinese-Vietnamese who cooperate with overseas Chinese to obtain and transport merchandise.

In addition to retail operations, many medical offices are located in Little Saigon. They are run by Vietnamese doctors whose patients' health care is often paid for by refugee benefits made available by the state and federal governments. Most of the janitors and other laborers in the area (such as the men collecting shopping carts outside the Taiwanese American "99 Market") are Latinos. Beyond the retail sector of Little Saigon, small factories (for food production, electronics, garments) and import/export operations are run in warehouses. Owned by Chinese-Vietnamese and Vietnamese, these businesses rely on Latinos and refugees as a work force.

In sum, the Chinese-Vietnamese economy involves the intersection of several ethnic and nationality groups and institutions. The Chinese possess and mobilize ties with overseas Chinese, Chinese Americans, Southeast Asian refugees, Latino laborers, and the U.S. welfare system to obtain capital, imported goods, labor, jobs, customers, community connections, and social services. Without each participant, the present system could not exist. The Chinese-Vietnamese bring these groups together in such a way as to catalyze the economic transformation of southern California. The enclave is multiethnic, and the Chinese-Vietnamese provide the glue that links the various actors. In so doing, they reestablish a middleman economic role similar to the one that they occupied in Southeast Asia.

Extent of Vietnamese Economic Activity

It is difficult to estimate the precise size of Vietnamese economic activity in southern California. Limited data suggest the degree of business development within this community. From the late 1970s to 1989, commercial rents in Orange County's Little Saigon increased from 35 cents to $2.50 per square foot, exceeding rents in adjacent, nonethnic shopping areas. Asian entrepreneurs have developed $75 million worth of property, including a 150,000-square-foot, $10 million enclosed mall (Brody, 1987; Jordan, 1986). Land prices for prime commercial acreage have increased tenfold, from $7 to $70 per square foot, since the early 1980s.

In interviews, informants estimated that Vietnamese run more than two thousand businesses in Los Angeles and Orange counties, employing five thousand to six thousand or more workers. Many operations that I visited were very small and hired few workers—for example, family-run restaurants, an herbalist, and a photography studio. Other "cottage industries," such as sewing, auto repair, food preparation, accounting, translation, entertainment, swap meet sales, and tutoring, are operated on a part-time basis out of refugees' homes. Certain businesses are sizable, however. I interviewed a food distributor and importer who employs fourteen, a restaurateur whose business is part of a chain that has thirty employees, an appliance dealer who has thirty-two workers, and the owner of two grocery stores who has fifty employees. Two other Little Saigon operations that are jointly owned by Taiwanese and Chinese-Vietnamese employ a total of 185 workers.

Economic Viability

The Chinese-Vietnamese have used various resources to build ethnic economic activities in southern California. These resources include capital, imported goods, ethnic-based cooperation in business, the availability of low-cost immigrant workers, the concentration of refugee enterprise, and the antigrowth environment of certain southern California municipalities.

Capital. As refugees, few Chinese-Vietnamese were able to transfer assets from Vietnam to the United States. Nevertheless, by relying on ethnic connections, including their access to overseas funds, their participation in U.S.-based ethnic associations, and their ability to amass resources within extended families, many have been able to capitalize businesses (Gold, 1988).

Capital made available by overseas Chinese is an important resource for Chinese-Vietnamese entrepreneurs in the United States. Affluent Chinese from Hong Kong and Taiwan seek to invest in the United States, often as a means of transferring funds for their eventual relocation. This capital is put to work in banking and real estate transactions. Without this source of overseas capital, it is unlikely that the real estate that houses many Vietnamese and Chinese-Vietnamese businesses—worth more than $75 million—could have been developed.

The importance of links between Vietnamese-Chinese and other Chinese is reflected in the fact that many leading Chinese-Vietnamese have changed their names from Vietnamese to Chinese. A Chinese-Vietnamese journalist described the international financial networks used to capitalize businesses in the United States.

> And the Chinese, we help together. Say I am Chinese, I come from Vietnam. Example, you are Chinese and you come from Taiwan or maybe Singapore, or maybe Hong Kong. I need money—I need you to help support my business. How come you help me? I would like to tell you. Because I have good experience and I have good credit. You have the money, but you don't know how to run a business. So you check on my credit and ask the other people. I want to buy this restaurant. You help me, maybe you become partner, because you believe in my ability. Maybe you are partner, or maybe I give you interest after six months. It works because we are all Chinese.

Several Chinese-Vietnamese dialect associations have been created by southern California's refugees. Their members share capital and business advice and enter into joint investments. They provide social welfare services and direct the recently arrived to suitable employment. They also offer a base for rotating credit associations. Although some refugee entrepreneurs claimed the Hui (Vietnamese rotating credit association) is rare and of little importance in the United States, others said such activities are widespread and sizable, able to provide ten thousand dollars or more to solve a business's cash-flow problems on short notice. According to the president of the Los Angeles Chinatown Chamber of Commerce and a Chinese-Vietnamese journalist, dialect groups engage in occupational specialization: Hainan-origin entrepreneurs own grocery stores, Chao Zhou refugees are restaurateurs, Ha'kanese are herbalists, and so on.

In interviews, several respondents described how family-based networks are used to raise money and secure trustworthy employees. Members of extended families and other networks sometimes horizontally integrate their small businesses to attenuate the intense competition common to ethnic business districts. For example, certain restaurants, grocery stores, tailor shops, and other companies have several branches located in close proximity in areas of refugee concentration. Toward the same end, business owners try to obtain exclusive leases from landlords—ones that exclude potential competitors from a given commercial development.

Sources of Imported Goods. Chinese-Vietnamese use their linguistic and cultural skills and overseas connections to import consumer items of the type desired by Asian consumers in the United States. Since labor costs are much lower in Asian countries, imported agricultural and manufactured goods are often inexpensive when compared to those available in the United States.

Because certain Asian products preferred by Vietnamese consumers are not generally exported to the West, personal contacts are vital for organizing their acquisition and shipment. Importers claim that organizing international trade in such perishable commodities is extremely difficult and would be virtually impossible without their competence in Chinese, co-ethnic connections, and travel to Asia. Dealers in this merchandise have little competition, however, and thus find the endeavor profitable. Consequently, the Chinese-Vietnamese and their trading partners are bringing various products and firms into the world economy for the first time.[5]

Ethnic Cooperation. According to many respondents, a general spirit of negotiation and trust pervades the Chinese-Vietnamese business community. Wholesale prices, credit, due dates for payment, various business services, and bank loans are worked out in a manner that refugees feel is more cooperative and flexible than would be the case with established U.S. banks, contractors, landlords, or wholesalers.

To participate in this blizzard of economic activity, even U.S.-owned banks and companies hire Chinese employees able to breach ethnic barriers. Vietnamese business owners extend credit to their co-ethnic customers in a manner more lenient than is available from U.S. retailers, thereby stimulating business. (Such businesses often charge high prices for goods and levy exorbitant interest rates, however.)

The ability of the Chinese-Vietnamese to develop good relations with other Chinese businesspeople in the United States is essential to the establishment and growth of their economic activity. Several respondents described how common language skills allowed refugees to be hired by established Taiwanese with whom they later became partners. Others explained that Chinese landlords frequently leased commercial real estate to Chinese-Vietnamese entrepreneurs under preferable terms.

Similarly, a Chinese-Thai who functioned as a major importer of Vietnamese-style foods to Los Angeles preferred dealing with co-ethnic Chinese-Vietnamese retailers, claiming that the ethnic Vietnamese are poor credit risks: "Most of my customers are Chinese-Vietnamese. Real Vietnamese not too good. They are not honest. They just take, don't want to give. Most of the Chinese are more trustworthy. And when you have trust, like we Chinese have, we work out okay."

Ethnic Labor. Family members and co-ethnics provide Chinese-Vietnamese entrepreneurs with a source of reliable, low-cost, and knowledgeable labor. Unlike many other Asian immigrant groups, the Southeast Asian refugee population includes a fairly large number of unskilled workers who are willing to accept low-paying jobs in the ethnic economy (Kibria, 1989; Rumbaut, 1989). At the same time, however, hardworking, low-wage Latino laborers are frequently hired to do cleaning, factory work and other physical tasks.

Ethnic Concentration. The existence of the large number and tight concentration of Vietnamese businesses in southern California provides many advantages for entrepreneurs. Partly because of the presence of numerous refugee doctors (paid by government benefits to care for refugees) who buy advertisements, the area has active ethnic media, including more than thirty-three newspapers and magazines, a Vietnamese Business Directory (Yellow Pages), and several hours of cable television and radio programs weekly. These outlets help businesses find customers and allow business owners to buy and sell enterprises, get advice, and locate employees. Many tertiary businesses—construction, cleaning, advertising, consulting, banks, accountants, restaurant furnishers, and sign makers—have grown up to support existing ethnic operations.

As the ethnic economy grows in size and visibility, it attracts Vietnamese refugee tourists from around California and the United States. Moreover, high rates of secondary migration to southern California from other parts of the United States provide a steady influx of consumers, workers, and entrepreneurs (Office of Refugee Resettlement, 1990).

Antigrowth Environment. Ironically, the antigrowth (anti-Asian) environment in communities that house suburban Asian enclaves may have positive effects on Chinese-Vietnamese entrepreneurs. Many of the suburban southern California cities with major populations of Asians have reacted with hostile, antigrowth programs to discourage further development by Asian businesses. Such was the case in both Monterey Park and Westminster (see Chapter 8).

Because a large and relatively affluent Asian population now lives in these areas, however, there exists a sizable consumer demand for Asian goods. Yet established corporations are generally unprepared to serve Asian customers and may be unwilling to enter an uncertain environment.

Consequently, Chinese-Vietnamese entrepreneurs who were willing to take such a risk (or, perhaps because of their lack of knowledge about the United States, were unaware of the degree of risk involved) stepped in to fill the void. As a result, many of the major Asian grocery stores in Los Angeles and Orange counties are now owned by Chinese-Vietnamese. A Chinese American city official from a predominantly Asian suburb described the conditions that led Chinese-Vietnamese into a near monopoly in the grocery business.

> The Chinese-Vietnamese are from the merchant class, so they look from that level. And that compounds with the urban policy. We have a very strong antigrowth policy in our city and therefore, as a result, the major conglomerates, businesses like Lucky (a major grocery chain) were extremely uncertain if this marketplace was safe for major developments.
>
> Normally, these big companies are a leader with demographic changes such as an increased Asian population. They will step in to serve them. But because of the antigrowth policy, the conglomerates were unwilling to do so.
>
> Therefore, conditions created a vacuum for the Vietnamese-Chinese business people. They had the flexibility, they had the audaciousness, the nerve, and they will take a risk that no one else is willing to take. It was a combination of factors, and they were very lucky. Now they're very successful.

The Limitations. Despite the evidence of a growing enclave of Chinese-Vietnamese entrepreneurs, this population continues to suffer economic problems. Not all enterprises are successful, and not all those involved in the enclave are doing well. One major difficulty encountered by refugee businesspeople is access to the skilled employees who are needed to manage the growth from "mom and pop" stores to corporate businesses. The owner of four electronics stores commented:

> Certainly it is difficult to find a good manager. Sometimes the owner does not have enough trust in other people. The owner doesn't have enough business skill to run a big corporation. It's my case also. It's a growing stage, and it's very difficult.
>
> And to hire MBA or graduate from school here, we cannot compete with the salary. MBAS can get $30,000 a year [from other com-

panies]; we cannot afford it. The most is about $20,000, and we cannot compete, salarywise.

Other problems include limited capital, a lack of knowledge about business practices, and poor planning before startup. Excessive reliance on co-ethnic consumers and on the Little Saigon setting also yields difficulties. As suggested by Portes' enclave model, the ethnic Chinese need to sell products and locate themselves where non-Vietnamese will buy from them (Portes and Manning, 1986). Though developers and community activists hope that Little Saigon will become a major attraction for non-refugee customers and tourists, Vietnamese still account for the vast majority of shoppers.

While some ethnic practices, including the spirit of flexible negotiation, rotating credit associations, and paternalistic labor relations, are advantageous to Chinese-Vietnamese entrepreneurs, other ethnic traditions hinder business growth. Some refugees are unable to obtain investment funds from major lenders because they refuse to submit to the bank's review of their financial status. Although reliance on undocumented workers and other sources of employees that do not comply with labor laws may yield short-term profits, in the long run these practices often become counterproductive because they result in an unstable staff, shoddy workmanship, and may even government penalties.

Chinese-Vietnamese entrepreneurs have to deal with competition from other groups who also seek to serve refugee customers. For example, the largest import company, grocery, and restaurant in Little Saigon are owned by immigrants from Thailand, Taiwan, and Hong Kong, respectively. Though competitors take business away from Chinese-Vietnamese entrepreneurs, they also attract customers to shopping areas, hire co-ethnic workers, and make business for Vietnamese service enterprises (i.e., Vietnamese auto mechanics and insurance agents benefit when refugees buy cars from non-Vietnamese auto dealers). Also, such companies train Vietnamese workers and support the ethnic media. Of course, Chinese-Vietnamese businesspeople serving a nonrefugee clientele must deal with a host of competitors.

Ethnic partnerships and associations sometimes fall apart, taking businesses with them. Finally, a growing number of gangs prey on the Vietnamese refugee community and often demand payments from entrepreneurs (Emmons and Reyes, 1989; Vigil and Yun, 1990).[6]

Chinese-Vietnamese and Economic Restructuring. The Chinese-Vietnamese entrepreneurial presence has had an impact on the social, spatial, and economic restructuring process that is ongoing in the region. The effects of this presence include transforming urban neighborhoods, providing and employing low-cost ethnic labor, encouraging further internationalization of the Southland economy, and selling inexpensive goods and services to low-income consumers.

Transforming Urban Neighborhoods. The restructuring process is, in part, a spatial one. Here the Chinese-Vietnamese have played an important role, transforming cities in both inner-city and suburban neighborhoods. One major result has been the revitalization of urban Chinatowns. In the mid-1960s, pundits described the disappearance of North American Chinatowns. This process began to be reversed by the Chinese migration following the Immigration Act of 1965 and was accelerated by the arrival of Chinese-Vietnamese refugees.

In Los Angeles's Chinatown, this transformation becomes especially apparent as one compares the sparsely populated areas and aging structures directed toward non-Chinese tourists (representing the "old Chinatown") with the newly built, teeming, ethnic-oriented retail stores, malls (one is labeled Saigon Plaza), offices, banks, and restaurants, many of which bear Vietnamese as well as Chinese signs. The president of the Los Angeles Chinatown Chamber of Commerce estimated that one-third of the neighborhood's restaurants are now Chinese-Vietnamese–owned, as well as a growing number of grocery markets and clothing stores.

Similar developments are evident in other North American Chinatowns, in Seattle, San Francisco, and Oakland, and in Toronto and Vancouver, Canada. With less access to capital than their co-ethnics from Taiwan, Singapore, and Hong Kong, the

Chinese-Vietnamese are nevertheless energetic and ambitious. They are the "foot soldiers"—the small businesspeople, workers, managers, and consumers—of much of the real estate development and restructuring initiated by offshore and migrant investment.

In this way, the Chinese-Vietnamese are involved in an ethnic succession process. They play an important role in maintaining the economic, spatial, and social institution of the American Chinatown. Chinatowns are locations for inexpensive leisure, import/export businesses, and sweatshops. Often acting as buffer zones between rich and poor districts, they have become undesirable settings for second-generation Chinese Americans and affluent immigrant Chinese, who prefer to enter the professions and reside in suburbs rather than carry on in the inner-city location of previous generations (Lyman, 1974; Mangiafico, 1988). The less affluent Chinese-Vietnamese are willing to sustain and even expand these settings, thus maintaining this social institution and the social and economic benefits it provides. The president of the Chinatown Chamber of Commerce noted:

> Gradually, more and more of them [Chinese-Vietnamese] are moving into most of Chinatown, Broadway Street. There are a lot of small dress shops; then there are some number of restaurants and supermarkets. The Chinese-Vietnamese people almost take over because they sell cheaper.
>
> You see the old Chinese people, their children go to UCLA and the old people are retiring from small business. So I say, there is a good chance [for the Chinese-Vietnamese]. They bring more business to Chinatown. This is a two-way street because there's more competition but there's more growth.

A similar Chinese-Vietnamese vitalization of urban areas has occurred in suburbs such as Monterey Park and Little Saigon in southern California and in the Tully Road area of San Jose. Here sleepy suburban areas were extensively developed as a result of Chinese-Vietnamese entrepreneurship. Though the Chinese-Vietnamese did not construct these areas alone (rather, development occurred in conjunction with others, as described above), they played a central role in the process of urban transformation.

These suburban enclaves provide a setting for ethnic communities, whose labor and consumer needs are economically exploited. Low-cost goods and services are made available to immigrant workers. Once urban backwaters, they are now municipal assets, culturally rich and ripe for further gentrification.

Providing Low-Cost Labor. Chinese-Vietnamese refugees play an important part in restructuring by making available a low-cost labor force. As entrepreneurs, they work on slim profit margins, massing family resources and exploiting themselves to maintain marginal or undercapitalized enterprises. In addition, making use of their connections to other Southeast Asian refugees, they sometimes hire these distressed workers for low wages in factories, restaurants, and food-processing industries and for homework. Mr. Tran, a Vietnamese entrepreneur and adviser to a refugee business development program, described the use of co-ethnic workers by Chinese-Vietnamese entrepreneurs:

> It is a rumor that refugees get hired for long hours and low wages. We have to understand the employer's position—they need to make a profit. It doesn't look nice if the employee is not treated properly. But if we are on employer's side—they are doing the right thing. If there is an agreement between the employer and the employee, they cannot expect to get the same wage as a unionized worker. But they accept the offered wage and work hard and make money. It is good for employer and for the employee. At least it looks fair.
>
> The wage is not as good—but they couldn't apply for a job in another company due to their lack of English. They might have a skill, but cannot understand the instruction of their supervisor, so it is a minus point for them. It is good business to pay as little in wages as possible.

While business owners seek to hire co-ethnic workers, refugees are well aware of the undesirable features of employment in the ethnic economy and take such positions only as a last resort. In contrast to the ethnic enclave model that stresses the rewards of employment in an ethnic context (Portes and Bach, 1985), job-seeking Vietnamese almost universally prefer jobs in large U.S. companies to those in ethnic businesses (Johnson, 1988). They hold that U.S. jobs offer better wages, shorter shifts, more security, health benefits, and opportunities to learn English.

Finally, there is a growing reliance on out-group labor in large operations run by Chinese-Vietnamese in southern California. Rather than employ fellow refugees, they increasingly rely on Mexican, Chicano, and Central American workers. Entrepreneurs cited several advantages associated with hiring Latinos. They were physically strong and worked very hard; lacking legal residency, they were easy to control; and as cultural outsiders who did not speak the owner's language, they were unlikely to open a competing enterprise or use a job as an opportunity to engage in "inside job" crimes such as embezzlement or protection rackets. Finally, Latino workers could not demand favors based on common ethnicity.

In contrast to their positive characterization of Latino labor, Vietnamese employers described co-ethnic workers as disrespectful, overly ambitious, unwilling to do hard physical labor, potentially criminal, and generally more difficult to manage and fire. By 1989, reliance on Latino workers had become so common in Orange County's Little Saigon (an area where almost all signs were in Vietnamese or Chinese) that many stores posted "Help Wanted" placards in English. The manager of several properties that house ethnic businesses in Little Saigon commented: "As far as the labor pool, I sure don't see a lot of the Southeast Asian people doing real labor. All the big companies here hire Mexican labor. In the workplace here, it's not uncommon to see Hispanic laborers going from door to door asking for work in the Vietnamese stores."

A Chinese-Vietnamese journalist offered a similar explanation: "Mexican, no green card, so you pay cheap. I pay you $5 an hour, but I pay Mexican $3 an hour. And Mexican are strong, and if I need to fire him, he just goes."

Since the middle 1980s, a growing number of Vietnamese entrepreneurs have become involved in the garment assembly business in southern California. As a highly competitive, labor-intensive industry, it relies heavily on a low-cost labor force of refugees and Latinos. Recent reports document various abuses in this industry, including child labor, homework, subminimum wages, and nonreported earnings (Gold and Kibria, 1993;

Thompson, 1990). A *Los Angeles Times* article noted some four hundred garment businesses in Orange County, employing more than five thousand workers (Efron, 1989). Industrial sewing equipment was sold by Chinese entrepreneurs in several refugee neighborhoods, and I saw these machines in refugees' homes. According to the manager of one sewing machine shop, Chinese-Vietnamese entrepreneurs frequently purchased machines on a time-payment plan. The availability of a low-cost and marginal labor force of Vietnamese refugees and Latino immigrants was central to the existence of this growing sector of refugee enterprise.

Vietnamese refugees' involvement in the garment industry is important in terms of sociological theory because it marks their first large-scale participation in providing goods for a nonethnic market—a major criterion of ethnic business success, according to several theories of the ethnic economy (Light, 1972; Portes and Manning, 1986). As the Chinese-Vietnamese become increasingly involved in entrepreneurship, the benefits of low-cost labor are passed on to larger companies and perhaps to consumers. At the same time, by institutionalizing such low-paying, low-power working conditions, the ethnic economy serves to impoverish further the region's already hard-pressed working class (for an extensive discussion of these issues, see Chapter 5).

Internationalization. The small importing enterprises of the Chinese-Vietnamese generally do not function on the scale of the import/export operations of the better-capitalized, and longer-established Japanese, Koreans, or Taiwanese. Nevertheless, the Chinese-Vietnamese are increasingly active in import/export businesses. Those I contacted in southern California generally deal in food and related items such as herbs, tea, and cookware.

Vietnamese consumers, who are the target market of many Chinese-Vietnamese import/export activities, have unique tastes. They seek Vietnamese-style products—rice, cookware, sauces, vegetables, teas, spices, and types of fish—that are not generally imported into the United States. The business of importing these goods is described by those involved as an extremely difficult endeavor, requiring language skills, overseas travel, and ethnic ties. A Chinese-Vietnamese herbalist explained:

Sometimes you just cannot afford to bring goods in. Taxes, transportation costs, and everything. If you are not moving it in a large quantity, your costs would be tremendous.

One thing is dealing with foreign contacts and agents, and another is going to the location. You don't know the territory, and there's no way you have control over the foreign agents, foreign brokers. You have to know their weaknesses. Don't play with their strengths.

So I'm familiar with that. We also work with people in Taiwan, Hong Kong, and China. We do go over once or twice a year. They're not going to do the best, especially since, you know, a lot of things are not going right over there now. You might order something that they showed you as a sample, but then they give you a different quality. A lot of people ended up losing their business because they didn't know what was going on over there. If someone ties up your letter of credit, your money, over here you have your prospects waiting for your merchandise.

And a lot of things are prohibited by U.S. customs. They can tie it up for another two or three weeks, and you are lucky if the products are not contaminated. If the label is not right, the ingredients are not specified, they burn the entire container.

In their role as importers, Chinese-Vietnamese entrepreneurs have established or expanded trade links with parts of the world that formerly had very limited trade with the United States. These new trade patterns are developed through links with overseas Chinese in Asian nations. In so doing, Chinese-Vietnamese entrepreneurs bring new nations, regions, and commodities into the world system.

In addition, Chinese-Vietnamese maintain social and economic ties with relatives, regional/dialect groups, and other organizations throughout the world. In interviews, several described participating in international overseas Chinese meetings. Such connections are important sources for international trade contacts. Chinese-Vietnamese claimed that their involvement in international trade provided affluent Chinese migrants from other nations, especially Taiwan, Hong Kong, and Singapore, with a means to elude government regulations on currency transfer and to bring their assets into the United States. A Little Saigon entrepreneur and community activist commented:

I think there is a desire for a lot of Hong Kong people and also Taiwanese to move over here. Sometimes the laws in Hong Kong and Taiwan do not allow them to get their money out of the country. But if they do business, it's easier for their Taiwan products to become U.S. dollars, and the U.S. dollars to stay here.

That's why I think that maybe the ethnic Chinese succeed because of the desire of the Taiwanese and Hong Kong people to transfer their capital to the United States. And also investment in homes, property, businesses, whatever.

Finally, Vietnamese refugees send millions of dollars in remittances and goods to relatives in Vietnam and in refugee camps, generally through companies that provide both goods and shipping. Since before 1994 the United States and Vietnam were politically hostile, shipments to Vietnam had to be accomplished through a third party, usually Air France. Companies that provided these services were ubiquitous in refugee neighborhoods.

Provision of Low-Cost Goods and Services. Saskia Sassen asserts that an important part played by immigrants in restructuring economies involves their provision of goods and services to other low-income populations:

> The growing low-income population also contributes to the proliferation of small operations and the move away from large standardized factories and large chain stores for low-priced goods. Small establishments relying on family labor . . . typically meet the consumption needs of the low-income population. (1991, 86)

In their involvement in retail sales, food, and import/export businesses, the Chinese-Vietnamese certainly play this role, filling the needs of Southeast Asian refugees, Asian Americans, and other low-income groups. In addition, their dealings in commercial real estate create settings where other entrepreneurs, most notably Vietnamese, also serve this function.

The proliferation of nail and hair salons (163 such operations, ranging in location from African American Inglewood to affluent Huntington Beach, are listed in the 1991 *Vietnamese Consumers' Guidebook of Southern California*) provide women with access to the grooming they require to hold jobs in the expanding service economy. In a similar manner, doughnut shops, which are frequently owned by Southeast Asian refugees, provide a low-cost food source.

The Mixed Blessings of Entrepreneurship. In many ways, Chinese-Vietnamese entrepreneurship benefits the southern California economy. Chinese-Vietnamese businesspeople invest their capital, labor, and energy in the region. They provide jobs that employ marginal workers such as refugees and Latino migrants, revitalize declining neighborhoods, and invent innovative and often low-cost ways of delivering goods and services that invigorate the social and cultural life of the area. Their endeavors create an ethnically oriented social and economic environment that allows a newly arrived population to feel a degree of territorial control and cultural familiarity in an exotic and unfamiliar society.

Chinese-Vietnamese entrepreneurship also has its negative effects. Usually, they are consequences of the larger economic conditions within which refugee proprietors must function and hence are not the sole creation of Chinese-Vietnamese businesspeople. Such effects are chiefly attributable to the more socially and economically powerful institutions and processes of the world system. Nevertheless, these outcomes do have serious implications for the larger society.

One of the most apparent negative consequences of immigrant entrepreneurship involves its effects on wages and working conditions (Castles and Kosack, 1973; Min, 1988). As already noted, wages and working conditions for both owners and employees of many Chinese-Vietnamese businesses are far from ideal. As recently arrived refugees who are struggling to survive, some businesspeople exploit themselves and their labor force. A spirit of cannibalistic competition marks many of their economic activities, resulting in frequent business failures (Leba, 1985; Trankiem, 1986). While some entrepreneurs are successful, others clearly lose out. In addition, Chinese-Vietnamese proprietors often employ the most distressed workers available—recent refugees and undocumented Latinos (many of whom are women)—and offer them starvation wages (Efron, 1989; also see Chapter 5).

According to several reports, Vietnamese and Chinese-Vietnamese economic activities are associated with the informal economy (Baker and North, 1984; North, 1988; Sassen, 1991). The *Los Angeles Times* claimed that "an estimated 25 percent of California's refugee families are supplementing welfare payments with in some instances as much as $25,000 a year in unreported income" (Arax, 1987, 1). Jobs in the informal economy are generally poorly paid and without traditional fringe benefits. Moreover, since they are unregulated, such positions deprive the refugees of safe working conditions and the public coffers of tax contributions.

Little Saigon and the "Enclave Debate." The findings of this chapter are relevant to the "ethnic enclave" debate, which concerns the returns (in relation to human capital) ethnic group members receive by working for co-ethnics or in the larger economy. Portes and Bach (1985) assert that immigrants benefit from co-ethnic employment, while Jimy Sanders and Victor Nee (1987) find little to substantiate such assumptions. The highly detailed data required to resolve this question accurately in terms of the Vietnamese are lacking. Even with these limitations, however, we can contribute some insight by considering available, though incomplete, information.

Studies by Jacqueline Desbarats (1986), Phyllis Johnson (1988), and Ruben Rumbaut (1986 and 1989), which compare employment and ethnicity within Southeast Asian refugee populations, conclude that Chinese-Vietnamese are disproportionately involved in an ethnic economy. That is, they work for co-ethnics and rely on ethnic connections for job referrals much more frequently than the ethnic Vietnamese. In addition, Chinese-Vietnamese have lower incomes, do more part-time work, have fewer opportunities for advancement, and receive fewer benefits than ethnic Vietnamese (Caplan et al., 1985).

Although such findings suggest that co-ethnic employment is an unrewarding enterprise for the Chinese-Vietnamese, we cannot determine its real impact, since, as a group, they possess less desirable labor-market characteristics than the ethnic Vietnamese. For example, the Chinese-Vietnamese have fewer years of education, less skill in English, less job training, and a shorter period in the United States than the Vietnamese (Rumbaut,

1989). Notwithstanding the difficulty of comparing Chinese-Vietnamese to Vietnamese, both Desbarats (1986) and Johnson (1988) clearly state that the ethnic economy contains few opportunities for upward mobility. Johnson concludes: "A long-term consequence of ethnic employment seems to be lower wages relative to those in non-ethnic employment. Our findings suggest that future occupational attainment may be . . . permanently limited for the group who had initial Asian employment" (1988, 17).

At the community level, then, there is little to suggest that the Chinese-Vietnamese ethnic economy offers greater returns to workers than that of the larger society. When the development of the Chinese-Vietnamese economy is considered in light of a fine-grained perspective, however, more evidence of its ability to generate benefits for group members can be found.

First, as described throughout the chapter, the growing Chinese-Vietnamese ethnic economy appears to be providing relatively highly paying jobs for a significant number of refugees. Co-ethnics who have close ethnic or familial ties to successful entrepreneurs are often able to use this social capital to obtain employment or become self-employed in ways that promote upward mobility (Bailey and Waldinger, 1991; Coleman, 1990; Gonzales, 1991).

Further, the available studies that suggest poor returns from the ethnic economy should be considered in terms of the timing of their data collection. Much of the research into Chinese-Vietnamese economic status was conducted five years or less after most of these refugees' date of entry to the United States. These data clearly capture a very early point in the history of ethnic business development, when this population experienced a traumatic exit and arrived without financial assets. Hence, available information regarding the rewards associated with Chinese-Vietnamese entrepreneurship is probably overly pessimistic in view of the more contemporary context described in this chapter.

In a similar vein, the research here has shown that Vietnamese employees active in the ethnic economy often receive low initial wages but increased incomes later on. "Paternalistic exploitation" and training systems eventually provide higher incomes via the skills or self-employment "invested in" during the initial low-wage period (Bailey and Waldinger, 1991).[7]

Finally, as Ivan Light and colleagues (1992) observe, when considering relative earnings associated with an ethnic economy, one should realize that some self-employed persons might be unwilling or unable to find employment in the larger economy and hence have a greater income than would be the case if they remained unemployed. Since Vietnamese refugees have less than ideal labor market characteristics, their ability to find existing jobs is often quite limited. Accordingly, self-employment can be an especially valuable means of support (Gold, 1992; Gold and Kibria, 1993; Office of Refugee Resettlement, 1988).

In sum, then, despite limited data, we can conclude that at the aggregate level the experience of the Vietnamese ethnic economy offers little evidence to support the enclave thesis. At the same time, however, it is apparent that refugees who possess meaningful links to successful ethnic entrepreneurs probably do have access to a viable path of mobility that offers more options than that of the larger society. Finally, for refugees who are unwilling or unable to find jobs in the larger economy, the ethnic economy offers the sole venue for employment.

The Chinese-Vietnamese of southern California have created an ethnic economy. Their entrepreneurship corresponds to many of the conditions associated with other groups of successful immigrant entrepreneurs. International links and forms of co-ethnic cooperation and integration appear to be especially valuable entrepreneurial resources. In addition, these immigrants have positioned themselves in such a way as to gain economic advantages from relations with a variety of groups and institutions in U.S. society. They include Chinese Americans, overseas Chinese, other Southeast Asian refugees, Latino labor, and the U.S. welfare system.

Through these social and economic relations, Chinese-Vietnamese entrepreneurs not only have established an economic niche for themselves but have contributed to the ongoing social, economic, and spatial restructuring of southern California. They have played a part in the ethnic and economic transformation of neighborhoods, the provision of low-cost labor (often under exploitative conditions), the further internationalization of the regional economy, and the delivery of low-cost goods and services to immigrant and minority populations.

Notes

Acknowledgment: This research was supported by a grant from the John Randolph Haynes and Dora Haynes Foundation.

1. For example, 61 percent of the members of the first wave of Vietnamese refugees to arrive in the United States in 1975 had less than twenty-four hours to prepare for their exit, and 83 percent had less than one week (Liu, Lamanna, and Murata, 1979, 15). Although later-arriving Vietnamese had more time to prepare for leaving, such plans were limited in scope because they were made under conditions of extreme duress (Long and Kendall, 1981; Teitelbaum, 1985).
2. I collected data from 1982 to 1990 through fieldwork and in-depth interviews with forty-five entrepreneurs in northern and southern California as well as others who were knowledgeable about Southeast Asian entrepreneurship. Research subjects included Chinese-Vietnamese business owners and their employees, Vietnamese entrepreneurs, officials employed in cities where many Chinese-Vietnamese enterprises are located, and nonrefugee Chinese who have extensive dealings with Chinese-Vietnamese entrepreneurs. Relying on snowball sample techniques in a single geographical region, I collected information about the role of the ethnic community, shown to be a key factor among the most successful populations of ethnic entrepreneurs (Cohen, 1969; Cummings, 1980; Light, 1972; Portes and Manning, 1986). Finally, I did extensive participant observation fieldwork while working as a grant writer in the small business development program of a Vietnamese resettlement agency in San Francisco in 1983 and 1984.
3. The Office of Refugee Resettlement (1988) reports that the Vietnamese who arrived in 1975 have achieved income parity with the larger U.S. population. The 1975 arrivals are, however, only a small proportion of the total Vietnamese American population (130,000 out of 500,000). Their numbers include few ethnic Chinese. The quick adaptation of the 1975 arrivals can be attributed to their higher levels of skill and education.
4. Because the Office of Refugee Resettlement reports economic data

in aggregate categories, we must sometimes rely on aggregate statistics for all Southeast Asian refugees rather than Vietnamese alone. This population is about 70 percent Vietnamese, with the remainder consisting of Laotians and Cambodians. Vietnamese have higher levels of education and urban experience than the other two nationalities (Office of Refugee Resettlement, 1990).

5. For example, Asian nations such as Taiwan, Hong Kong, Japan, and Korea have heavily export-oriented economies with financial and legal regulations and institutions set up to facilitate international trade (Light and Bonacich, 1988). These arrangements can be an asset to ethnic entrepreneurs in the United States. Other nations, such as Thailand and the Philippines, where Southeast Asian entrepreneurs buy their stock, have less organized trade economies. Consequently, more groundwork and supervision are required for importers to obtain these products.

6. Gangs and crime were identified as the number-one fear in a 1989 survey of Orange County Vietnamese (Emmons and Reyes, 1989).

7. On the other hand, as Herbert Gans (1992) notes, given the nation's poor economic performance since the 1970s, pundits may be overgeneralizing from the early economic successes of Vietnamese refugees.

References

Arax, Mark. 1987. "Refugees Called Victims and Perpetrators of Fraud." *Los Angeles Times*, 10 February, Part I, pp. 2, 3, 26.

Bailey, Thomas, and Roger Waldinger. 1991. "Primary, Secondary, and Enclave Labor Markets: A Training Systems Approach." *American Sociological Review* 56(4):432–445.

Baker, Reginald P., and David S. North. 1984. *The 1975 Refugees: Their First Five Years in America.* Washington, D.C.: New Transcentury Foundation.

Bernard, William S. 1977. "Immigrants and Refugees: Their Similarities, Differences, and Needs." *International Migration* 14(4):267–281.

Bonacich, Edna. 1973. "A Theory of Middleman Minorities." *American Sociological Review* 38 (October): 583–594.

Brody, Jeffrey. 1986. "Vietnamese: Statistics Belie the Image of the Superachiever." *Orange County Register*, 12 May, pp. A5–6.

———. 1987. "Frank Jao: Real Estate and Power Broker." *Orange County Register*, 11 January, pp. C1, 4–5.

Burawoy, Michael. 1976. "The Function and Reproduction of Migrant Labor: Comparative Materials from Southern Africa and the United States." *American Journal of Sociology* 81:1050–1087.

Caplan, Nathan, John K. Whitmore, and Quang L. Bui. 1985. *Southeast Asian Refugee Self-sufficiency Study*. Office of Refugee Resettlement Report. Ann Arbor, Mich.: Institute for Social Research.

Castells, Manuel. 1989. *The Informational City*. Oxford: Basil Blackwell.

Castles, Stephen, and Godula Kosack. 1973. *Immigrant Workers and Class Structure in Western Europe*. New York: Oxford University Press.

Chen, King C. 1987. *China's War with Vietnam, 1979: Issues, Decisions, and Implications*. Stanford: Hoover Institution Press.

Cohen, Abner. 1969. *Custom and Process in Urban Africa: A Study of Hausa Migrants in Yoruba Towns*. Berkeley: University of California Press.

Coleman, James. 1990. *Foundations of Social Theory*. Cambridge: Belknap/Harvard University Press.

Cummings, Scott, ed. 1980. *Self-Help in Urban America: Patterns of Minority Business Enterprise*. Port Washington, N.Y.: Kennikat Press.

Desbarats, Jacqueline. 1986. "Ethnic Differences in Adaptation: Sino-Vietnamese Refugees in the United States." *International Migration Review* 20:405–427.

Efron, Sonni. 1989. "Sweatshops Expanding into Orange County." *Los Angeles Times*, 26 November, pp. 1, 38.

———. 1990. "Few Viet Exiles Find U.S. Riches." *Los Angeles Times*, 29 April, pp. 1, 34–35.

Emmons, Steve, and David Reyes. 1989. "Gangs, Crime Top Fear of Vietnamese in Orange County." *Los Angeles Times*, 5 February, pp. 3, 35.

Finnan, Christine Robinson, and Rhonda Cooperstein. 1983. *Southeast Asian Refugee Resettlement at the Local Level*. Office of Refugee Resettlement Report. Menlo Park, Calif.: SRI International.

Gans, Herbert. 1992. "Second-Generation Decline: Scenarios for the Economic and Ethnic Futures of the Post-1965 American Immigrants." *Ethnic and Racial Studies* 15(2):173–192.

Gold, Steven J. 1988. "Refugees and Small Business: The Case of Soviet Jews and Vietnamese." *Ethnic and Racial Studies* 11-4:411–438.

———. 1992. *Refugee Communities: A Comparative Field Study*. Newbury Park, Calif.: Sage.

Gold, Steven J., and Nazli Kibria. 1993. "Vietnamese Refugees and Blocked Mobility." *Asian and Pacific Migration Review* 2(1):27–56.

Gonzales, Juan L. 1991. *The Lives of Ethnic Americans*. Dubuque, Iowa.: Kendall Hunt.

Johnson, Phyllis. 1988. "The Impact of Ethnic Communities on the Employment of Southeast Asian Refugees." *Amerasia Journal* 14(1):1–22.

Jordan, Hallye. 1986. "A Shopping Mall with Room for Culture." *Orange County Register*, 12 August, p. 8.

Kelley, Gail P. 1986. "Coping with America: Refugees from Vietnam, Cambodia, and Laos in the 1970s and 1980s." *The Annals* 487 (September): 138–149.

Kibria, Nazli. 1989. "Patterns of Vietnamese Refugee Women's Wagework in the U.S." *Ethnic Groups* 7:297–323.

Kim, Illsoo. 1981. *New Urban Immigrants: The Korean Community in New York*. Princeton: Princeton University Press.

Leba, John Kong. 1985. *The Vietnamese Entrepreneurs in the U.S.A.* Houston: Zieleks.

Light, Ivan H. 1972. *Ethnic Enterprise in America: Business and Welfare among Chinese, Japanese, and Blacks*. Berkeley: University of California Press.

———. 1980. "Asian Entrepreneurs in America." In *Self-Help in Urban America: Patterns of Minority Business Enterprise*, ed. Scott Cummings, pp. 33–57. Port Washington, N.Y.: Kennikat Press.

Light, Ivan, and Edna Bonacich. 1988. *Immigrant Entrepreneurs: Koreans in Los Angeles, 1965–1982*. Berkeley: University of California Press.

Light, Ivan, Georges Sabagh, Mehdi Bozorgmehr, and Claudia Der-Martirosian. 1992. "Ethnic Economy or Ethnic Enclave Economy?" Paper presented at the annual meeting of the American Sociological Association, Pittsburgh, 20–24 August.

Liu, William T., Maryanne Lamanna, and Alice Murata. 1979. *Transition to Nowhere: Vietnamese Refugees in America*. Nashville, Tenn.: Charter House.

Long, Nguyen, with Harry Kendall. 1981. *After Saigon Fell*. Research Papers and Policy Studies no. 4. Berkeley: Institute of East Asian Studies, University of California.

Lyman, Stanford. 1974. *Chinese Americans*. New York: Random House.

Mangiafico, Luciano. 1988. *Contemporary American Immigrants: Patterns of Filipino, Korean, and Chinese Settlement in the United States*. New York: Praeger.

Min, Pyong-Gap. 1988. *Ethnic Business Enterprise: Korean Small Business in Atlanta*. Staten Island, N.Y.: Center for Migration Studies.

Ngan, Nguyen Ngoc. 1982. *The Will of Heaven: The Story of One Vietnamese and the End of His World*. Toronto: Van Lang.

North, David. 1988. "Aliens and the Regular and Irregular Labor Markets." Paper presented at the U.S. Department of Labor Conference on Immigration, Washington, D.C., 15–16 September.

Office of Refugee Resettlement (ORR). 1984, 1986, 1987, 1988, 1989, 1990. *Report to Congress: Refugee Resettlement Program.* Washington, D.C.: U.S. Department of Health and Human Services.

Portes, Alejandro. 1984. "The Rise of Ethnicity: Determinants of Ethnic Perceptions among Cuban Exiles in Miami." *American Sociological Review* 49:383–397.

Portes, Alejandro, and Robert Bach. 1985. *Latin Journey: Cuban and Mexican Immigrants in the United States.* Berkeley: University of California Press.

Portes, Alejandro, and Robert Manning. 1986. "The Immigrant Enclave: Theory and Empirical Examples." In *Competitive Ethnic Relations,* ed. Susan Olzak and Joanne Nagel, pp. 47–68. Orlando, Fla.: Academic Press.

Portes, Alejandro, and Ruben G. Rumbaut. 1990. *Immigrant America: A Portrait.* Berkeley: University of California Press.

Purcell, Victor. 1965. *The Chinese in Southeast Asia.* London: Oxford University Press.

Reimers, David M. 1985. *Still the Golden Door: The Third World Comes to America.* New York: Columbia University Press.

Rose, Peter I. 1985. "Asian Americans: From Pariahs to Paragons." In *Clamor at the Gates: The New American Immigration,* ed. Nathan Glazer, pp. 181–212. San Francisco: Institute for Contemporary Studies.

Rumbaut, Ruben G. 1986. "The Structure of Refuge and Southeast Asian Refugees in the U.S.: A Portrait of a Decade of Migration and Resettlement, 1975–1985." Paper presented at the annual meeting of the American Sociological Association, New York City, 30 August–3 September.

———. 1989. "The Structure of Refuge: Southeast Asian Refugees in the United States, 1975–1985." *International Review of Comparative Public Policy* 1:97–129.

Sanders, Jimy, and Victor Nee. 1987. "Limits of Ethnic Solidarity in the Ethnic Enclave Economy." *American Sociological Review* 52:745–767.

Sassen, Saskia. 1988. "New York's Informal Economy." In *The Informal Economy,* ed. Alejandro Portes, Manuel Castells, and Lauren A. Benton, chap. 3. Baltimore: Johns Hopkins University Press.

———. 1991. "The Informal Economy." In *Dual City: Restructuring New York,* ed. John Hull Mollenkopf and Manuel Castells, pp. 79–101. New York: Russell Sage Foundation.

Simon, Julian L. 1986. "Basic Data Concerning Immigration into the United States." *The Annals* 487 (September): 12–56.

Teitelbaum, Michael S. 1985. "Forced Migration: The Tragedy of Mass Expulsions." In *Clamor at the Gates: The New American Immigration,* ed. Nathan Glazer, pp. 261–283. San Francisco: Institute for Contemporary Studies.

Thompson, Mark. 1990. "Threadbare Justice." *California Lawyer* (May): 28–32, 84–85.

Tran, Anh K. 1986. *Economic Base of the Vietnamese Community in the Los Angeles and Orange County Area.* Los Angeles: Asian American Studies Center, University of California.

Trankiem, Luu. 1986. *Economic Development Opportunities for Indochinese Refugees in Orange County.* California Community Foundation.

Turner, Eugene, and James P. Allen. 1991. *An Atlas of Population Patterns in Metropolitan Los Angeles and Orange County, 1990.* Northridge: Department of Geography, California State University Northridge.

Vigil, James Diego, and Steve Chong Yun. 1990. "Vietnamese Youth Gangs in Southern California." In *Gangs in America*, ed. C. Ronald Huff, pp. 145–162. Newbury Park, Calif: Sage.

Waldinger, Roger. 1985. "Immigrant Enterprise and the Structure of the Labor Market." In *New Approaches to Economic Life*, ed. Bryan Roberts, Ruth Finnegan, and Duncan Gallie, pp. 66–88. Manchester: Manchester University Press.

———. 1986. *Through the Eye of the Needle: Immigrants and Enterprise in New York's Garment Trades.* New York: New York University Press.

———. 1987. "Changing Ladders and Musical Chairs: Ethnicity and Opportunity in Post-Industrial New York." *Politics and Society* 15(4): 369–401.

Waldinger, Roger, Howard Aldrich, Robin Ward, and associates. 1990. *Ethnic Entrepreneurs: Immigrant Business in Industrial Societies.* Newbury Park, Calif.: Sage.

Whitmore, John K. 1985. "Chinese from Southeast Asia." In *Refugees in the United States: A Reference Handbook*, ed. David Haynes, pp. 59–75. Westport, Conn.: Greenwood Press.

Willette, JoAnne L., Marion F. Shaycroft, and Carl V. Haub. 1985. *The Sociology of Minority Business Enterprise: An Overview.* Report submitted to Minority Business Development Agency. Arlington, Va.: Development Associates.

Wilson, Kenneth L., and W. Allen Martin. 1982. "Ethnic Enclaves: A Comparison of the Cuban and Black Economies in Miami." *American Journal of Sociology* 88(1):135–160.

Part IV
Political Struggles

Introduction

Yen Espiritu

Focusing on macroeconomic changes, much of the literature on restructuring and immigration neglects to analyze the effects of these changes on everyday urban life. Addressing this oversight, this section examines the impact of the post-1965 Asian immigration on politics, that is, on the distribution and exercise of, and the struggle for, power and resources. Instead of adapting to the dominant power structure, new Asian immigrants have restructured the political face of Los Angeles, challenging and transforming existing ethnic and class hierarchies. This challenge has generated contentious as well as coalitional relations among Asian subgroups and between Asians and non-Asians.

In Chapter 8, Leland Saito and John Horton discuss changing power relations between old and new residents in Monterey Park, a nearby suburb of Los Angeles. Dubbed "America's first suburban Chinatown," Monterey Park has undergone rapid and complete ethnic transformation, from more than 80 percent white in 1960 to more than 50 percent Asian in 1990. Many of the residents are wealthy professionals and businesspersons from Taiwan and Hong Kong. The minoritization of whites and the visibility of Asians have ethnicized political concerns, transforming slow-growth and linguistic issues into nativistic and anti-Asian movements. These reactionary movements have, in turn, politicized immigrant and established Asian residents, encouraging them to coalesce with each other and with non-Asians in order to promote issues of quality of life and political representation. Although their numerical dominance, professional status, and wealth are important political resources, the political prospect of Asians in Monterey Park largely depends on their ability to build coalitions that cut across generational, ethnic, and class boundaries.

New Asian immigrants have also collided with African Americans. As Paul Ong, Kye Young Park, and Yasmin Tong discuss in Chapter 9, the growing presence of Korean immigrant businesses in African American neighborhoods in Los Angeles (and in other cities) has antagonized impoverished customers and competing shop owners, resulting in African American–organized boycotts of Korean stores and even racial violence. Like the established residents in Monterey Park, African Americans regard Korean immigrants not as fellow Americans but as "foreigners" who take advantage of the African American communities. This nativistic sentiment makes scapegoating more readily acceptable. It also leads to a clash of ideologies between the two groups. As immigrants, Koreans perceive the United States as the land of opportunity; in contrast, African Americans (especially the underclass) view the United States as the land of opportunity denied. In addition to racial, economic, and cultural factors, this ideological opposition worsens Korean–African American relations.

Whereas most studies of intergroup relations have focused on hostility between blacks and whites, the Korean–African American conflicts direct attention to antagonisms among nonwhite minorities. Conflict among nonwhites is distinct from traditional black-white hostility. In black-white conflicts, the two groups involved are distinguishable in terms of the power resources they possess, with whites having more of every resource; in contrast, conflicts among nonwhites occur principally between disadvantaged groups. In the context of declining opportunities and increasing competition for economic subsistence in urban America, the potential for confrontation between nonwhite groups is ever increasing. Because of their ethnic and cultural differences, the new immigrants are perfect targets for the displaced hostility of the traditional inhabitants of urban areas.

The new Asian immigration has also affected the development of racial solidarity among Asian American subgroups. Since the late 1960s, Asian Americans have organized along racial lines (i.e., as Asians) in order to enlarge their capacities to protect and promote their interests in modern racial politics. With the arrival of the post-1965 immigrants, the Asian American population has become much more fragmented in both class and ethnic terms. The preference for highly educated labor in immigration legislation—and the post–World War II removal of racial barriers in the economic sector—has expanded the rank of the professional-managerial class, splintering the Asian American population along class lines more clearly than in the past. The post-1965 immigration has also brought new ethnic constituencies into the pan-Asian fold; many are unfamiliar with or indifferent to the pan-Asian concept.

Despite the importance of ethnicity, in Chapter 10 Yen Espiritu and Paul Ong suggest that class divisions represent the greatest obstacle to racial solidarity among Asian Americans. Ironically, class polarization is most evident within the very pan-Asian organizations that purport to promote racial unity. Because these organizations are dominated by middle-class professionals, they preclude a broad-based membership, thereby undercutting the use of race as their organizing principle. Class differences often correlate with ethnicity, so that internal conflicts over power and control appear to be along ethnic lines. In Los Angeles, the competition for jobs, money, and power among Asian Americans has occasionally been bitter, with some subgroups opting to pursue their interests outside the pan-Asian framework. Faced with charges of ethnic chauvinism and inadequate representation, some pan-Asian organizations have instituted outreach programs to attract new Asian immigrants into their fold.

In sum, shaped by a rapidly changing world economy, the post-1965 Asian immigration has, in turn, reshaped intergroup relations in the urban United States. It has fostered divisive conflicts that pit one ethnic minority against another in competition for political power and material resources. On the other hand, as the new immigrants become more politicized, they have also organized (hitherto unlikely) interethnic and class coalitions that allow them to combat systems of inequality and ethnic chauvinism both inside and outside the Asian American community.

8. The New Chinese Immigration and the Rise of Asian American Politics in Monterey Park, California

Leland T. Saito and John Horton

In response to discrimination and opportunities for empower-ment brought about by the post-1965 influx of Asian immigrants, immigrant and established Asian American residents are nego-tiating a new pattern of Asian American politics. This new pat-tern is most apparent in Monterey Park, a nearby suburb of Los Angeles, where Asian American "minorities" have become the numerical majority. In this suburb and the surrounding San Gabriel Valley region, immigrant and established Asian Ameri-cans ally with each other (and with non-Asians) to shift the lo-cal power structure from Anglo domination to growing Asian American and Latino influence. Thus, instead of assimilating into the mainstream, Asian immigrants are important actors in shaping local politics.

Monterey Park is an especially significant site for studying the impact of the post-1965 Asian immigration on local politics. First, it is the only city in the United States, outside Hawaii, that has a majority Asian population (57% in 1990). It is also located in greater Los Angeles, the metropolitan statistical area with the largest number of Asian Americans in the United States. Second, Monterey Park is a regional locus of political activism. A training ground for local politicians aspiring for higher offices, the San Gabriel Valley has been called the "incubator" of minority poli-tics (Estrada, 1991). Anti-Asian activities, demographic changes, and the need for Asian American political representation have combined to make Monterey Park a focal point for Asian Ameri-cans in the Los Angeles area who wish to support Asian Ameri-can politics. This unity is built on broad goals that most Asian Americans can support: Asian American representation within a diverse, pluralistic society with a multicultural rather than Euro-centric orientation.

Our research is based primarily on ethnographic fieldwork in Monterey Park since 1987 and on exit poll data from the 1988 and 1990 city council elections, which identify Asian American and immigrant voting patterns. Focusing on relations between immigrants and Asian Americans, the ethnographic data offer insight into the day-to-day process of constructing Asian power.

The Demographic and Economic Conditions for Political Change

Minutes east of downtown Los Angeles, Monterey Park has historically been a step on the ladder of mobility out of the poorer urban centers to the middle-class suburbs of the San Gabriel Valley. The ethnic composition of the city changed dramatically between 1960 and 1990 (Table 8.1). In 1960, Monterey Park was an Anglo city reluctantly giving way to the suburban aspirations of Latinos and Japanese Americans. By 1980, the accelerated immigration of second- and third-generation Latinos (predominantly Americans of Mexican descent) and of the Nisei (second-generation Japanese Americans) had changed the ethnic map of the city. There was also a small but growing population of African Americans.

Table 8.1. Ethnic Composition of Monterey Park, 1960–1990

	Percentage of City Population			
Ethnicity	1960	1970	1980	1990
African American	0.003	0.2	1.2	0.6
Anglo	85.4	50.5	25.0	11.7
Asian/Pacific Islander	2.9	15.0	35.0	57.5
Latino	11.6	34.0	38.8	29.6

Sources: Monterey Park Planning Department, 1974; Ong, 1991.

In the 1980s, because of the influx of Chinese immigration from Taiwan, Hong Kong, and elsewhere in Asia, the ethnic proportions in Monterey Park once again shifted. As indicated in Chapter 1, the new Chinese immigration to California was sparked by more lenient U.S. immigration laws, political and economic restructuring in Asia, and the dream of a prosperous and peaceful life in the expanding Pacific Rim economy. Encouraged by developers and realtors selling Monterey Park in Taiwan, Hong Kong, and the United States as the "Chinese Beverly Hills" and attracted by the city's relatively affordable housing, proximity to downtown Los Angeles, and regional access provided by freeways bordering the city on three sides, Asians moved to Monterey Park in large numbers. By 1990, the city had a majority Asian population.

The high percentages of Asian Americans in Monterey Park (57.5) and in Los Angeles (9.8), as compared to the United States as a whole (2.9), suggest that the Los Angeles area is one of the major destination points for Asian immigrants (Table 8.2). The Asian American population grew tremendously from 1980 to 1990, more than doubling in the United States and in California. In absolute numbers and as a percentage of the population, the Asian American population greatly expanded in Monterey Park between 1960 and 1990 (Table 8.3).

Table 8.2. Asian American Population and Growth, 1980–1990

Area	No. of Asian Americans, 1990	% Asian American 1980	1990	% growth of Asian Americans, 1980–1990
Monterey Park	34,898	33.7	57.5	90.6
Los Angeles	341,807	6.6	9.8	74.4
California	2,845,659	5.3	9.6	127.0
United States	7,272,662	1.5	2.9	107.8

Sources: Anderson, 1991; UCLA Asian American Studies Center, 1991.

Table 8.3. Asian American Population Growth in Monterey Park, 1960–1990

Year	No. of Asian Americans	City Total Population	Asian American Population as % of City Total
1960	1,113	37,821	2.9[a]
1970	7,540	49,166	15.3
1980	18,890	54,338	34.8
1990	34,898	60,738	57.5

Sources: Monterey Park Planning Department, 1974; U.S. Bureau of the Census, 1983, 1991.

[a]Includes "others."

The census also details the demographic transition among the Anglo, Asian American, and Latino populations in Monterey Park. In 1970, the Japanese Americans were the largest Asian American group, comprising 61.4 percent of the Asian American population (Table 8.4). By 1990, their numbers had declined by 19.2 percent, and they constituted only 17.4 percent of the Asian American population. In contrast, the Chinese population more than quadrupled in the 1980s and made up 63 percent of the Asian American population in 1990. Vietnamese, Koreans, and Filipinos also entered the city from 1970 to 1990, although in much smaller numbers than the Chinese.

As a result, Monterey Park today is a town in transition from a middle-American, racially mixed, suburban bedroom community to a financial and service center for the local and regional Chinese and Asian populations. Chinese signs and Asian businesses line the major commercial streets, and condominiums are invading what had been the domain of single-family dwellings. Faced with these changes, old-timers are leaving, resisting change, or facilitating the incorporation of immigrants.

Table 8.4. Monterey Park's Changing Asian American Population, 1970–1990

Year	Chinese	Japanese	Korean	Vietnamese	Filipino	Pacific Islander/ Other
1970	2,202	4,627	118	n/a	481	112
1980	7,735	7,528	1,180	862	807	778
1990	21,971	6,081	1,220	2,736	1,067	1,823
Percentage change						
1970–80	251.3	62.7	900.0	—	67.8	594.6
1980–90	184.1	−19.2	3.4	217.4	32.2	134.3
Percentage of Asian American population						
1970	29.2	61.4	1.6	—	6.4	1.5
1980	40.9	39.9	6.2	4.6	4.3	4.1
1990	63.0	17.4	3.5	7.8	3.1	5.2

Sources: Monterey Park Planning Department, 1974; U.S. Bureau of the Census 1983, 1991.

Factors Dividing and Uniting Asian Americans. As the two largest Asian population groups in Monterey Park, the Japanese and Chinese differ generationally and politically, making it difficult for them to unite as Asian Americans (Saito, 1989 and 1993b). The first Asian group to enter the city in large numbers, Japanese Americans are primarily second-generation Americans, long-established residents, and Democrats. In contrast, most of the Chinese in Monterey Park are immigrants, newcomers to the city, and, when they become citizens, tend to register Republican or have no party affiliation. According to our interviews, despite these differences, Chinese and Japanese in the city have at times united as Asians to promote Asian American politics.

Like established Latino and Anglo residents, many Japanese Americans resent the Chinese newcomers and the ways they have changed the city. One Nisei, a long-term Monterey Park resident, pointed out some of the differences he sees between Japanese and Chinese:

> First of all, I think that the Nisei and Sansei [third-generation Japanese Americans] can speak English a lot better than the Chinese can. And I think we probably behave better in public than they do: we're not as boisterous in public, we're not pushy in public as the Chinese are. I mean you don't see a Japanese person crowding in line or talking at the top of his voice.

To emphasize the negative impact of the Chinese on Monterey Park, he quoted his son's remarks on returning home after a few years of military service overseas: "God damn, dad, where the hell did all these Chinese come from? Shit, this isn't even our town anymore." As this Nisei went on to explain, however, non-Asians seldom recognize the differences between established Japanese American residents and Chinese newcomers:

> I think it's kind of a bad thing for us, that the Caucasian categorizes us as Chinese. I would like the Caucasian people to think that there is a difference between the Japanese and the Chinese, but they don't do it here in Monterey Park because they see me, they think, hey, here's another Chinese.

He jokingly told us, "They should wear buttons saying, 'I'm Japanese, not Chinese,' just like some Chinese who wore buttons during World War II, 'I'm Chinese, not Japanese.'"

Although this Nisei felt strongly about the differences between Japanese Americans and Chinese newcomers, he also recognized the need for "Asian American" representation when he
voted in 1982 for Lily Chen, a Chinese immigrant, for city council. He said, "I backed her . . . and I said, all right, if that's what
you say you're going to do, and you're going to stick up not
only for the Chinese, but for all the Asians, that's including the
Filipinos, Samoans, Japanese, whatever."

It is also difficult to build political unity *within* an Asian ethnic
group (Agbayani-Siewert and Revilla, forthcoming). For example, as newcomers, Chinese immigrants may organize along
family, regional, and linguistic lines, instead of or in addition to
the "Chinese" line. Moreover, since the Chinese immigrants in
Monterey Park have come from various places, such as Taiwan,
the People's Republic of China, Hong Kong, and Vietnam, another level of difference exists. Even Chinese immigrants acknowledge how hard it is to get the hundreds of different Chinese organizations in Los Angeles to agree on anything. They
also talk about the generational differences between Chinese immigrants and the "ABCs" (American-born Chinese), suggesting
that the latter have lost their Chinese culture.

Given these political, ideological, and generational differences
among Asians, what events and circumstances in the history of
the United States and Monterey Park can unite them politically
as Asian Americans? An important part of the answer is their
shared history of discrimination.

First, the history of Asian groups in the United States has
been marked by anti-Asian laws and movements, including the
only laws to limit immigration and naturalization based on region of origin. Examples are the Chinese Exclusion Act of 1882,
Gentlemen's Agreement of 1907–1908, California Alien Land
Laws of 1913 and 1920, and the World War II internment of Japanese Americans. Laws passed in 1790 and 1870 limited the right
of naturalization to whites (including Latinos) and African
Americans, leaving Asians as the only group without that right.
The possibility of naturalization did not come for Chinese immigrants until 1943, Filipinos (laws fluctuated) and Asian Indians
until 1946, and Japanese until 1952 (Hocking, 1980). Anti-Asian
actions have existed among groups that vary in ideology and

class position: the glass ceilings faced by Asian Americans in the managerial and executive levels of Fortune 500 companies (Suzuki, 1977), anti-Asian practices by labor groups (Saxton, 1971), and the United States Communist Party's expulsion of its members of Japanese ancestry during World War II (Yoneda, 1983).

Second, Monterey Park has been the scene of a number of anti-Asian activities. For example, the city council passed Resolution 9004 in 1986 (since rescinded only to be reinstituted as a state constitutional amendment) declaring English the city's official language (Horton and Calderon, 1992). Between 1988 and 1990, councilman and mayor Barry Hatch used city hall as a platform for his nativist views, giving speeches on how "immigration built America, and immigration will destroy America unless controlled." Anti-Asian sentiment also emerged in the slow-growth movement, as some established residents sought to impose their definition of what is appropriately "American" on the design and regulation of commercial property. Nativist forces point to business signs covered with Chinese characters as evidence that the immigrants do not want to become a part of the United States, that they want to create a "Hong Kong of the West." Revealing the Eurocentric character of their beliefs, the very same people who claim that foreigners should adapt to "our ways" consider it appropriate to remodel Atlantic Square, the largest shopping mall in the city, in "Mediterranean" style. The unstated message is that European American is preferable to Asian American.

Third, Asian American unity can be forged in reaction to the many personal incidents of discrimination, ranging from fights in local high schools to a cross burned into the lawn of a Chinese resident in the nearby city of Arcadia. Our interviews provided numerous examples of personal discrimination. One elderly Japanese American woman described how she was attacked by an Anglo woman:

> I got attacked in March of 1986 by a Caucasian lady, that's blond and blue eyes, you know. She disabled my arm and my wrist and my hand. I had to have it in a cast for a whole month. [Her voice rises with emotion, getting louder and higher pitched.] I mean, I was just sitting in the store, and just looking at stuff. In a fabric store. *Kcccch.* [She imitates the sound of her wrist being twisted.]

She grabbed me, turned the thing where it's not supposed to turn, you know. Right after she did it, she says, "Go back to China where you belong!" Then she left; zoomed out of the store.

Every Asian American has a story to tell. In extreme cases, anti-Asianism involves violence. The Los Angeles County Commission on Human Relations (1989) reports that such anti-Asian incidents are on the rise. But anti-Asianism also includes the seemingly harmless question, asked by a non-Asian of an Asian American, "Where are you from?" meaning, you must be an immigrant and, therefore, an outsider.

In summary, what unites Asian Americans in Monterey Park are "ethnic" issues stemming from a historical legacy of discrimination that has been reactivated by the high visibility of Asian newcomers. First, non-Asians tend to treat Asians as a single group, ignoring internal ethnic, class, political, and generational differences. Second, treatment of all Asians as immigrants, as newcomers, not as "Americans," gives Asian Americans a common barrier to fight against. Finally, the externally imposed label becomes a basis for political mobilization and empowerment. This is reinforced by two other factors. One is political necessity: Japanese Americans, Taiwanese, Chinese from the People's Republic of China, and other Asian groups are too small in themselves to be effective politically. Table 8.5 shows the number of registered voters in Monterey Park in 1984 and 1989 and the growth during that period. Also shown are the figures for Chinese Americans and Japanese Americans, including their percentage of the Asian group as a whole. What is clear is that although the Chinese constituted 63 percent of the Asian American population in Monterey Park in 1990 (see Table 8.4), they made up only 59.6 percent of the Asian American registered voters in 1989. Because of their higher rate of citizenship, the Japanese represented a significant portion, 32.5 percent, of the registered Asian American voters. The other factor encouraging Asian American unity is found in the policies of the U.S. government that treat Asians as a single group, thereby encouraging organizing on a pan-Asian basis (see Espiritu, 1990; Lopez and Espiritu, 1990).

Table 8.5. Voter Registration of Monterey Park, 1984 and 1989

No. of Registered Voters	1984	1989	% Increase
City total	22,021	23,184	5.3
Asian and Pacific Islanders (API)	6,441	8,988	39.5
Chinese Americans	3,152	5,356	69.9
Japanese Americans	2,586	2,919	13.3
API of city total	29.2	38.8	
Chinese American of API total	48.9	59.6	
Japanese American of API total	40.0	32.5	

Source: Nakanishi, 1991.

The Rise of Asian American Politics. Before the mid-1980s, there were no specifically Asian American political organizations in Monterey Park. Like the Latino residents, the middle-class Japanese and Chinese Americans kept a low political profile and conformed to a political structure dominated by Anglos. Although Asian Americans and Latinos have worked behind the scenes, and three Asian Americans were elected to the city council before 1980 (Alfred Song in 1960, George Ige in 1970, and G. Monty Manibog in 1976), their electoral campaigns tended to be managed by the predominantly white power structure, which included the conservative Lions' and Kiwanis clubs and the liberal Monterey Park Democratic Club. Song recounted: "In all of the years that I have campaigned for elective office, I have never had the help, financial or otherwise, of any organized Oriental group; whatever their origin may be—Korean, Japanese, Chinese, Filipino or any others. . . . In twenty years, I think I could count the individual Asians who have come to my assistance on one hand and still have a couple of fingers left over" (Song, 1980, 16).

The election of Lily Chen, an immigrant and established resident, to the city council in 1982 was a turning point in Asian American politics. Instead of relying on the white power structure, Chen organized her own campaign with considerable funding from Asian Americans inside and outside Monterey Park. A similar pattern was followed in the 1988 election of Judy Chu, a native-born Chinese American, and the 1990 election of Samuel Kiang, a Chinese immigrant. This change signals a period of political transition, mainly the demise of the Anglo old-boy network (eroded by age and the emerging numerical and economic dominance of Asian Americans) and the rise of ethnic politics among Asian Americans as well as among Latinos (the second largest population in Monterey Park and the largest in the San Gabriel Valley).

A major goal of Asian Americans in this period of transition has been to construct the political networks and organizations needed to elect their own candidates and to bring their issues to the attention of city officials. To capture the depth of Asian American political involvement and to understand how fundamental change is occurring in the region (Nakanishi, 1991), we examined a broad range of political activities: the grass-roots participation in public hearings, the formation of new Asian political organizations, and the development of electoral politics at the local and regional levels.

This process of building Asian American politics is closely linked to the dramatic increase in the Asian American population and the high levels of affluence and education of many recent Asian immigrants. The growing involvement of immigrants in Asian American politics is due largely to the participation of Asian American professionals, who have the necessary knowledge and skills, and of businesspersons, who have learned that their interests and profits are greatly affected by local control over development. Joining forces with these two groups are established Asian Americans, who contribute their experience and knowledge of local politics, and regional groups, which supply legal, technical, and research assistance. Examples are the Asian Pacific American Legal Center of Southern California and the Asian American Studies Center at the University of California, Los Angeles.

Asian American politics is also boosted by non-Asian grass-roots groups and elected officials who recognize and want to take advantage of the potential political force of the Asian immigrant population. Because they are unfamiliar with the language and customs of the first-generation Asian immigrants, however, these non-Asians affiliate themselves primarily with native-born and long-term Asian immigrants. Whether or not these groups have actual ties to the immigrant Asians, their political know-how and fluency in English contribute to their becoming the de facto representatives of all "Asian Americans" (Espiritu, 1990; Kwong, 1987, 166–168).

Public Hearings: Defending Immigrant and Asian American Interests

Public hearings are an example of how Asian Americans in Monterey Park have mobilized to ensure that Asian American viewpoints are incorporated in the formation of city policies. This political arena is especially important for noncitizens who are ineligible to vote. As taxpaying residents, new immigrants have a stake in what happens in the community, and public hearings have become an important forum for expressing their views and applying political pressure. Participation in public hearings has led to the establishment of grass-roots networks that take advantage of the political experience and knowledge of established Asian American individuals and organizations and the numerical dominance of the new immigrants.

Whenever important or controversial issues are on the agenda, city council meetings in Monterey Park draw a full house as residents fill the roughly two hundred seats of the council chambers. Until the late 1980s, these meetings were dominated by older Anglo and Latino residents, with few Chinese immigrants participating. Responding to the increasing number of anti-Asian/immigrant movements and policies emanating from city hall, which affect *all* Asians in the area, immigrant and native-born Asian Americans have come together in protest.

An example is the issue of signage regulations. On 23 January 1989, the city council voted on the use of English and foreign

languages on commercial signs. Fighting for a strictly Euro-
centric definition of "America," council member Barry Hatch
spearheaded an effort to eliminate all use of foreign languages
on business signs—a direct attack against Chinese businesses.
For Asian Americans and their supporters, Hatch threatened the
constitutional right of freedom of speech and multiculturalism,
which supporters define as removing barriers to political and
economic equality and recognizing and respecting different languages and cultures.

Hatch lost his attempt to establish "Official English," and the
old signage regulations allowing Chinese and English remained
virtually unchanged. The victory came about through the pressure of two forces: the coalition of established immigrant
leaders, Asian Americans, Latinos, and Anglos strongly in favor
of civil rights; and the mobilization and sheer pressure of pro-
testing immigrant Asians and Asian Americans at public hearings. Councilwoman Judy Chu, a Chinese American, led a
strong multiethnic coalition during the public hearing. Asian
Americans, whether or not they could in fact read Chinese
signs, joined the coalition because they understood the anti-
Asian message implicit in the "English Only" campaigns. Politically liberal non-Asians also responded to the civil rights issue.
These political sentiments helped forge a common interest
among native-born and immigrant Asians and between Asians
and non-Asians.

Immigrant leaders also favored political coalitions. For example, the Chinese American Civil Rights and Education Foundation, a new group organized primarily by Chinese immigrants,
held a forum against sign restrictions. The speakers included
Jose Calderon, a first-generation Mexican American and the president of the San Gabriel Valley League of United Latin American
Citizens, and Kathy Imahara, a native-born Japanese American
attorney from the Asian Pacific American Legal Center of Southern California. Calderon provided a political analysis of the attack on language rights, and Imahara added a legal argument of
the constitutional right of free speech. Thus, in coalition with
each other and with non-Asians, immigrant and Asian American
organizations were able to defeat sign restrictions.

By bringing the issue to the attention of the community and

explaining the legal basis for contesting "English Only" ordinances, Asian Americans were prepared to monitor the ordinance modification process. Because signage issues first pass through the Design Review Board and Planning Commission, Asian Americans packed the public hearings to apply pressure on the city commissions. The Review Board meetings are held in the small City Hall Community Room, which resembles, and is about the size of, a high school classroom. The sparsely furnished room is usually empty except for people who have items before the board. When the sign ordinance came before the board on 19 October 1988, about eight Asians, native-born and immigrants, doubling the size of the usual number of people there, sat quietly in the room, monitoring the proceedings. The board discussion went on for several hours on the technical aspects of the sign ordinance. When the language issue came up, board members decided with little discussion to keep things the way they were.

The rather routine discussion of the signage issue belied the behind-the-scenes lobbying that took place and the significance of the sign ordinance to competing definitions of what is appropriately "American." A native-born Chinese American lawyer and resident of the community had telephoned the other Asian Americans to tell them that this issue would be on the agenda and that they should come and monitor the meeting. He had talked to several of the board members beforehand, and he believed that the general feeling of the board was that with an issue as sensitive as this one, "If it ain't broke, don't fix it." He believed that the Asian Americans in the audience acted as a moderating influence on the proceedings, letting the board know that its discussion and decisions were being closely watched.

A city hall staffperson who was present at the Review Board meeting concurred on the importance of the presence of Asian American residents at the meeting:

> *Staffperson*: I was quite surprised when all the people showed up during the Design Review Board meetings. They didn't say anything, but the pressure was there. They were watching everything that happened. You got the feeling that if something wrong happened, that they would be right on it.

Interviewer: Is it possible that the regulations might have been different if they weren't there?
Staffperson: Yes. Maybe stronger changes. Perhaps they might have added direct translation of the signs. But they had to be careful; you can't legislate against one language.
Interviewer: Sometimes I wonder how effective citizen participation is on things like that.
Staffperson: It was important.
Interviewer: It makes a difference?
Staffperson: Yes, it sure does.

The issue reached the Planning Commission on 12 January 1989, and the results were similar to those at the Review Board meeting, with a number of Asian Americans monitoring the proceedings and several Chinese Americans speaking during the public hearing in favor of keeping things the way they were.

On 23 January 1989, the issue reached the city council. The council chamber was crowded, mainly with Anglos in their fifties and sixties, Latinos, and a sprinkling of Asian Americans. The usual reporters from the *Los Angeles Times* and the Chinese daily newspapers were there. A strong coalition of Asian Americans, Anglos, and Latinos, speaking in favor of moderation and constitutional rights, helped pushed through a compromise ordinance that retained the use of foreign languages.

The presence of Asian Americans in city council public hearings is a growing trend. The experience can be intimidating, as cable television monitors focus on the speaker, the crowd voices its opinion through applause or jeers, and hostile questions arise from council members. One Chinese immigrant, who has lived in the city for more than twenty years and regularly attends and participates in public hearings, described her feelings on this matter:

A lot of Chinese people do not like to get involved, especially in our City Hall because someone can embarrass you. . . . Like me, I don't feel it. I just go there and fight back. . . . It really takes some courage. . . . I think more people would come forward even if they have a handicap with the language. . . . If they felt comfortable there. But if they go there and maybe get abused by somebody, they say forget it. (Pardo, 1990)

Asian immigrants are learning that participating in public forums is an effective way of ensuring that Asian American issues are put on the agenda and that their point of view is heard. Today fewer are saying, "Forget it." In the summer of 1991, for example, Chinese immigrant leaders organized demonstrations to support the use of bilingual dispatchers for the emergency 911 service in Monterey Park. Hundreds of demonstrators attended a city council meeting when a program of implementation was discussed. They outnumbered old-timers in the chamber, which only two years before was a bastion of reaction against immigration. They no doubt helped push the measure through by pressing for unity between the two Chinese American council members, Judy Chu and Samuel Kiang, in spite of their initial differences over how the 911 issue should be implemented.

New Local Groups: The West San Gabriel Valley Asian Pacific Democratic Club

A major force in the transition from Anglo domination to growing ethnic political power is the establishment of Asian American political organizations. In the 1980s, the western San Gabriel Valley emerged as a center for Asian American politics. A 1986 study showed that Monterey Park had the highest number and percentage of Asian and Pacific Islander registered voters of any city in Los Angeles County (Nakanishi, 1986). To institute the networks, resources, and organization needed to back issues and candidates and to work toward political empowerment, the Asian Pacific Democratic Club was formed in 1985.

Working in their respective ethnic communities during the 1960s and 1970s, the club's founding members learned two lessons. First, during this era, the idea of "Asian American" was born. Although these activists labored in separate ethnic communities, such as Chinatown or Little Tokyo, they recognized the shared political goals of all Asian ethnic groups as they worked to get funding for social services and low-cost housing and battled against the encroachment of development on their communities. Second, they realized that each group was too small to lobby effectively for government funding alone and that a pan-Asian coalition was needed (Espiritu, 1990; Kuramoto, 1980; Little Tokyo Anti-Eviction Task Force, 1976).

The club's founding members, generally in their thirties and forties, had established professional careers, mainly as attorneys and teachers. They brought knowledge, skills, networks, and resources to build an active club. One member is part of the Pacific Leadership Council, a Los Angeles–based Asian fundraising and lobbying organization, which raised about $1.2 million in 1988 (Espiritu, 1990, 134) and actively lobbied in Washington, D.C., in support of the 1990 Immigration Act. Other members have organized fundraisers for local politicians (Latinos as well as Asian Americans) and for the former California state attorney general John Van De Kamp in his run for the governorship in 1990. With political and organizing experience, the group has also provided skilled labor for the organization and day-to-day running of campaigns for local candidates. Since full membership is restricted to registered Democrats, however, few Republicans and noncitizens are active in the club.

Aware of the political potential of the Asian immigrants, the Asian Pacific Democratic Club early on organized Asian American voter registration drives. Working toward political empowerment, the club backed a Chinese American woman in a successful school board race. Club members also urged the area's state senator, assemblyperson, and congressperson (all Latinos) to hire Asian and Pacific Islander community liaisons and fought against the "English Only" initiative in Monterey Park. Other activities include forums for Democratic candidates for the Monterey Park City Council, Alhambra School Board, and Los Angeles County Supervisorial District. Getting results and fighting anti-Asian sentiments were stressed by one founding member of the group: "If Asians can't focus their political power and . . . get Barry Hatch out of office, then we might as well forget it. . . . We have to show results; otherwise, what are we doing as a club? As Asians in the political process?"

The involvement of the club in local elections was an important step in the process of replacing the white Anglo power structure. Until recently, Asian American candidates had to rely on mainstream political support because of the local political structure and type of local clubs in existence. The establishment of Asian American organizations, networks, and fundraising capacity is a significant move for the support of Asian American candidates.

Non-Asian grass-roots groups and elected officials who want to take advantage of the growing political force of the immigrant population also look to the Asian Pacific Democratic Club. During its early years, the club was continually approached by local political organizations that wanted to sponsor joint events. The Monterey Park Democratic Club, a liberal group of mainly Anglo members, helped the Asian Pacific Democratic Club write its charter. Joint events are also common with the San Gabriel Valley chapter of the League of United Latin American Citizens (LULAC), which was reorganized in 1986. The establishment of these organizations created the possibility for coalitions between Asian Americans and other groups. Recognizing the importance of coalitions in a multiethnic community, during a joint meeting between LULAC and the Asian Pacific Democratic Club a member of the Asian American group stated: "During the 1970s, we went back to our communities to work on political empowerment. To some degree, we've been successful. Now we understand the need to go beyond that, to build coalitions, to build our power base. Otherwise, we'll be fighting each other and we won't be effective."

Voting Patterns: Ethnic Politics

Asian American voting preferences in California elections have been poorly documented. Usually, they are extracted from polls that include so few Asian Americans that the results are virtually meaningless (Din, 1984; Nakanishi, 1985–1986).

Two exit polls taken for the 1988 and 1990 Monterey Park City Council elections are significant because they contain large samples of Asian American voters. John Horton's (1989) analysis of the 1988 poll found that a voter's ethnic status was a better predictor of candidate choice than age, sex, education, or income. In the 1988 election, 89 percent of the Chinese Americans and 75 percent of the Japanese Americans voted for Judy Chu, a native-born Chinese American. Using ethnographic evidence, Horton explained that the Chinese and Japanese mainly supported Chu because of the need for Asian American representation. Less support was shown by other groups: 35 percent of the Latinos and 30 percent of the Anglos voted for Chu.

In the 1990 elections, six candidates ran for three spots. The two Anglo incumbents, Patricia Reichenberger and Barry Hatch, were viewed by some Asian Americans as anti-Chinese because of their support of Resolution 9004. Another Anglo, Marie Purvis, the owner of a small business in the city, was running on a platform of controlled growth and less regulation of business. The two Latino candidates were Fred Balderrama, president of the Monterey Park Chamber of Commerce, and David Barron, city clerk. Sam Kiang, a Chinese immigrant from Hong Kong, stressed his skills and experience as an attorney and engineer to bring better management to the city's budget and development issues.

Table 8.6 shows the results of the 1990 exit poll (Horton and Tseng, 1990). As in 1988, ethnicity was the best predictor of candidate choice. Kiang, Balderrama, and Purvis won seats on the council, finishing in that order, with each candidate's highest vote percentage coming from his or her own ethnic group.

Poll data indicated that in terms of foreign-born status, party affiliation, age, and education, Japanese American voters were more like Anglo voters than like Chinese American voters. The percentage with household incomes over $50,000 was the only area in which Japanese Americans more closely resembled Chinese Americans than Anglos. Moreover, in terms of voting patterns, the percentage of Japanese Americans who favored the slow-growth Measure S and who supported bilingual education was closer to the Anglo vote than to the Chinese American vote. And yet, when it came to voting for a candidate, Japanese Americans diverged from the Anglo pattern and demonstrated the importance of Asian American ethnicity by overwhelmingly supporting Kiang. In sum, exit poll and fieldwork data indicate that despite their differences, Chinese Americans and Japanese Americans unite in their desire for ethnic representation, a desire based on the historical and contemporary factors that give them common interests as Asian Americans.

Another important finding is that ethnic candidates must ap-

Table 8.6. Voters' Profiles by Ethnicity: City Council Election, Monterey Park, 10 April 1990, in Percent

	Anglo	Chinese	Japanese	Latino
Candidates				
Balderrama	45	36	44	67
Barron	42	19	37	47
Hatch	37	10	25	19
Kiang	40	90	69	30
Purvis	53	26	34	48
Reichenberger	44	15	36	21
Foreign born	6	74	1	20
College or more	36	66	43	23
Income $50,000 or more	35	54	50	31
Party affiliation				
Republican	35	47	37	15
Democrat	59	22	59	80
None	3	22	1	3
Measure S (slow growth)				
Yes	67	51	70	65
No	19	22	15	19
Did not vote/no response	14	27	15	16
Support for bilingual education				
Yes	41	68	40	57
No	46	20	45	29
Undecided	12	7	11	11
Respondents (N)	349	239	131	255

Source: Horton and Tseng, 1990.

Note: Voters could cast up to three votes; percentages do not add up to 100.

peal to all groups in order to get the necessary votes to win an election in a multiethnic community. That is the case in Monterey Park, where Asian Americans, although the numerical majority, constitute less than 40 percent of the registered voters. Barry Hatch alienated voters with his divisive and racist attacks on immigrants and received the lowest vote total among all groups, including Anglos.

The Case of Redistricting: The Growing Scale of Asian American Politics

After each decennial census, the state political districts are reconfigured to reflect changes in population. Redistricting is critical for ethnic politics because it creates the state and federal districts from which officials are elected. Historically, politicians have divided geographic concentrations of ethnic groups into many districts, diluting their political influence. The Voting Rights Act of 1965 and the 1982 amendments prohibit minority vote dilution (Davidson, 1984). Court cases have established the legal basis for creating electoral districts that preserve the political integrity of ethnic groups by keeping communities intact within districts. The most important case for the Los Angeles region is the 1990 *Garza v. Los Angeles County*, which ruled that Latinos have been consistently divided into separate districts. As a result, the districts were redrawn, and a Latina, Gloria Molina, was elected to office in the newly created district, where Latinos became the majority population group.

Redistricting is a key issue for Asian Americans, because no Asian Americans were elected to the state legislature during the 1980s. The basis for any claim starts with raw numbers of population, and the 127 percent increase of the California Asian American population in the 1980s was due primarily to immigration. The increase of the Asian American population in the cities of the San Gabriel Valley was dramatic. Monterey Park's Asian American population grew by 90.6 percent, bringing the Asian American population to 57.5 percent of the city's population. Similarly, in nearby Alhambra, Rosemead, and San Gabriel, the

Asian American population grew by 289 to 372 percent, forming 32 to 38 percent of the population in those cities.

The Coalition of Asian Pacific Americans for Fair Reapportionment was formed in 1990 to promote the interests of Asians and Pacific Islanders to the state legislature, which was in charge of the redistricting and reapportionment process. According to a statement of goals and objectives, the statewide group was formed from more than 150 organizations representing "community members from social service agencies, academia, leaders, political organizations, private and public institutions."

The southern California branch of the coalition targeted three areas in Los Angeles County with large and rapidly growing Asian and Pacific Islander populations: central Los Angeles, the South Bay, and the San Gabriel Valley. Regional coalitions were organized and the San Gabriel Valley Asian Pacific Americans for Fair Reapportionment was formed. The coalition attended state senate and state assembly hearings around the state to advocate fair representation for the Asian and Pacific Islander community. Its major goals were reversing the fragmentation of Asian and Pacific Islander communities into separate political districts, educating the community about the politics of redistricting and reapportionment, and establishing communication links between ethnic groups in the Asian and Pacific Islander community as well as with Latinos and African Americans.

Stewart Kwoh, executive director of the Asian Pacific Legal Center and steering committee member of the southern California coalition, emphasized that this was a historic occasion because it was the first time Asians and Pacific Islanders entered the redistricting and reapportionment process as participants from the start of the proceedings. Speaking on behalf of the San Gabriel Valley coalition, Judy Chu, Monterey Park City Council member and former mayor, called attention to the fragmentation of the community in her testimony to the Assembly Committee on Reapportionment:

> Our votes are fractionalized. The cities [in the western San Gabriel Valley] . . . are divided into two supervisorial districts, three assembly districts, three senatorial districts, and three congressional districts. It is no wonder that Asians in California are virtually unrepresented anywhere beyond the local level.

Reflecting the demographic mix of the area, most of the members of the San Gabriel Valley group were Chinese Americans with some Japanese Americans. As nonpartisan and representative of the Asian American population (Nakanishi, 1991), the organization was run by both Republicans and Democrats.

One of the major fundraising events of the southern California coalition was organized by the San Gabriel Valley group and took place in Monterey Park at a large Chinese restaurant on 6 April 1991. It was very successful. About four hundred people attended, including local Latino and Asian American politicians and March Fong Eu, the secretary of state of California. Although fundraising was the primary goal of the event, it had other functions as well: drawing together diverse groups within the coalition, educating the community about redistricting and reapportionment, and demonstrating the support and interest of the community to the state legislature.

The fundraiser illustrated several characteristics about the San Gabriel Valley coalition. First, new immigrants are a vital part of the coalition. Although many of the organizers were native-born or long-term immigrants, significant numbers of the organizers and attendants were new immigrants, and the sound of Chinese languages filled the air during the reception preceding the dinner. Second, money is critical for political activities, and Asian Americans acknowledge that the new immigrants are extremely effective fundraisers. In recognition of the material and symbolic importance of Monterey Park to the Asian American community, March Fong Eu established her 1990 fundraising office there and held her election night victory party in the city. Third, ethnicity has multiple levels that are generated by the issues and goals. Many of the people present at the fundraiser attended as members of ethnic-specific Asian political or social organizations, such as the Japanese American Citizens League, Taiwanese American Citizens League, and the Chinese American Association of Southern California. Yet for important issues such as redistricting, which require the pooling of economic and political resources, the groups came together as "Asian Americans." They also reflected diversity in nativity, with some organizations consisting primarily of the native born and others including a mixture of immigrants and native born.

In summary, the case of redistricting raises several points about emerging Asian American politics. First, redistricting moves beyond the local to the regional and state arenas. Redistricting is a political process that requires technical expertise, political knowledge, and resources. Because of its large Asian American population, Monterey Park and the San Gabriel area have become a focal point for Asian Americans in Los Angeles who wish to donate money, volunteer time, and use their political and technical experience to support Asian American issues in that region.

Second, redistricting is based on population, and the added numbers provided by massive immigration gives Asian Americans a foundation for a case that they should be recognized under the Voting Rights Act. The importance of numbers emphasizes the need to unite as "Asian Americans," since no Asian American group is large enough by itself to be considered under the act.

Third, Asian Americans involved in politics are well aware of the need to work with Latinos in the redistricting process (Saito, 1993b). As newcomers to the process, Asian Americans have much to learn from Latino organizations that have gained political and legal knowledge through their successful court cases, such as *Garza v. Los Angeles County*. Asian Americans and Latinos worked together, understanding that combining their political clout by supporting one set of redistricting plans for the region would increase the likelihood that such plans would be adopted by the legislature. Latinos and Asian Americans met regularly to share information and develop plans for the San Gabriel Valley on three levels. The legal groups of both coalitions, the Mexican American Legal Defense and Education Fund and the Asian Pacific American Legal Center of Southern California, discussed the Voting Rights Act as it applied to both groups. Local grass-roots Latino and Asian American groups in the San Gabriel Valley met to construct plans for the region. Finally, the San Gabriel Valley groups met with local elected officials and flew to Sacramento to lobby legislators as one coalition, emphasizing that Latinos and Asian Americans in the region backed the same plan.

One of the common goals of Latinos and Asian Americans

was to work against fragmentation of the region in the redistricting process. Through a series of meetings on all three levels, the two groups managed to agree on plans that accomplished the complex task of protecting the political integrity of both Latinos and Asian Americans. By putting together the four cities (Alhambra, Monterey Park, San Gabriel, and Rosemead) with the largest number, highest percentages, and greatest projected growth of Asian Americans, the plans united the main Asian American population and created districts that would give Asian Americans a strong political voice. At the same time, the plans maintained the political viability of the Latino incumbents by incorporating cities with large Latino populations, creating new districts with majority Democratic registration and majority Latino populations.

On 27 January 1992, the state supreme court adopted the new redistricting plans, which incorporated the recommendations of the coalition, uniting the four cities of Asian American concentration.

Latinos control the politics of the San Gabriel Valley and as of 1993 occupy all the regional, state, and federal elected offices representing Monterey Park (assembly, state senate, Los Angeles County supervisor, and Congress). To get elected and pursue their political agendas, Asian Americans will have to make coalitions with Latinos to empower both ethnic communities.

"Asian American politics" is emerging in the western San Gabriel Valley, and Monterey Park is its symbolic and geographic focal point. Demographic and economic restructuring have created new political possibilities for established Asian Americans and Chinese immigrants in the city. In response to local nativism and a desire for increased political representation, Asian Americans have worked toward establishing networks and organizations that can support issues important to Asian Americans but often ignored by "mainstream" politics.

Organizing as "Asian Americans" is a result of the historical and contemporary conditions that generate specific issues and goals and create alliances along ethnic lines (Nagel, 1986; Olzak, 1983). The goals of the early 1990s (e.g., expanding Asian American political representation and fighting anti-Asian racism) are important and broadly defined so that most Asian Americans can support them. The future of Asian politics is uncertain, however. Issues will become more sharply defined and a number of viable Asian American candidates will emerge, representing different interests. Because the Asian American population is divided along economic, political, national, generational, and ethnic lines, the changes brought by growing numbers and economic strength may also serve to heighten differences between individuals and groups as they pursue their own interests.

Strong tendencies already exist for identifying with interests based on economic and ideological positions. Divisions between conservative business interests and progressive professionals over commercial and residential development could mirror what occurs in mainstream politics (Logan and Molotch, 1987). In July 1991, conflict over the interpretation of the firing of the Monterey Park city manager filled the ethnic and mainstream press. Native-born Asian Americans and established Chinese immigrants believed that the firing was based on the manager's overall job performance. New Chinese immigrants, displaying narrow Chinese interests and nationalism, charged that the dismissal was prompted by non-Chinese who believed that the Anglo city manager pushed too strongly for Chinese interests. Others argued that the enormous amount of publicity over the incident was the result of political maneuvering between potential Chinese American candidates. The question is, Will external factors, such as a lack of political representation or racially motivated violence, continue to generate issues that can transcend ideological and economic differences?

One of the major themes to emerge from San Gabriel Valley politics is the need for coalitions with Latinos and Anglos in this multiethnic region. Just as issues arise from specific historical conditions to unite Asian Americans, there are problems faced by Asian Americans and Latinos that multiracial coalitions can address. For example, some local city councils are dominated by Anglos even though the cities are predominantly Latino and Asian American (Rosemead is 15.9% Anglo; Alhambra, 24.3% Anglo). Coalitions would be a way to empower both ethnic communities. Some groups may favor nationalistic politics and resist coalitions, however, a development already seen in local Latino politics (Calderon, 1991).

Finally, the rise of Asian American politics in Monterey Park raises some fundamental questions about traditional notions concerning the incorporation and assimilation of immigrants into U.S. political life. Assimilation theory predicts that when immigrant groups reach the third generation, ethnic politics will disappear as economic interests take over (Dahl, 1961) and advances in educational and occupational attainment lead to integration into "mainstream" politics (Gordon, 1964). Our research in Monterey Park questions these assumptions, since it is precisely members of this group, that is, second-, third-, and fourth-generation Chinese American and Japanese American professionals and businesspersons, who have actively worked with Chinese immigrants to develop a new Asian American politics. At the same time, the new immigrants were not merely absorbed into a preexisting political order; they have changed that order. More accurately, a new order is being negotiated through the interaction between immigrants and established Asian Americans, sometimes with the help of Anglos and Latinos who see the need for coalitions in a multiethnic society.

Ethnic politics is not necessarily divisive, creating barriers between groups in the United States and leading to the fragmentation of the political order. Instead, ethnic politics, emerging from the persistence and reconstruction of ethnicity, integrates ethnic groups into the mainstream of U.S. politics. Ethnically based politics serves this function because it educates the community about U.S. politics, and contrary to the melting pot myth, ethnic politics has always been a feature of the political mainstream (Portes and Rumbaut, 1990). In view of the low participation of native-born Asian Americans in terms of voter registration (Nakanishi, 1986) and the high percentage of immigrants in the Asian American population, "ethnic" politics is an important way to integrate Asian Americans into U.S. politics. The coalitions that developed between Asian American and Latino groups to deal with redistricting demonstrate the importance of forming organizations that can serve as the bases for such alliances.

It is essential to examine the historical and contemporary conditions that give ethnicity a political meaning and importance that, at a given moment, transcend other factors such as class and gender (see Bonacich, 1972, 1976, 1980; Omi and Winant, 1986). We may indeed be living in an era when ethnic politics is evolving in response to immigration and the ongoing restructuring of the regional and world economy.

Note

Acknowledgments: We wish to acknowledge the invaluable influence of other researchers involved in the Monterey Park Project, particularly Jose Calderon, Mary Pardo, Linda Shaw, and Yen-Fen Tseng. Our research received funding from the Changing Relations Project of the Ford Foundation, which initiated a national study of relations between immigrants and established residents in six cities: Miami, Philadelphia, Chicago, Houston, Garden City (Kansas), and Monterey Park. We also received assistance from the Asian American Studies Research Center, the Institute for American Cultures, and the Academic Senate of the University of California, Los Angeles.

The Changing Relations Project produced a film for national educational television on newcomers and established residents in the six national sites, entitled "America Becoming," produced by Dai Sil Kim-Gibson and directed by Charles Burnett. Publications related to the research project include Calderon 1991; Horton 1989 and 1992; Horton and Calderon 1992; Lamphere 1992; Pardo 1990; and Saito 1989 and 1993a.

References

Agbayani-Siewert, Pauline, and Linda Revilla. Forthcoming. "Filipino Americans." In *Asian Americans: A Survey of Ethnic Groups,* ed. Pyong Gap Min. Newbury Park, Calif.: Sage.

Andersen, Patrick. 1988. "Monterey Park's Hatch Lashes Back at Critics." *Asian Week,* 16 September, p. 15.

———. 1991. "7.3 Million Asians and Pacific Islanders in U.S." *Asian Week,* 15 March, pp. 1, 17.

Bonacich, Edna. 1972. "A Theory of Ethnic Antagonism: The Split Labor Market." *American Sociological Review* 37:547–559.

———. 1976. "Advanced Capitalism and Black/White Relations in the United States: A Split Labor Market Orientation." *American Sociological Review* 41:34–51.

————. 1980. "Class Approaches to Ethnicity and Race." *Insurgent Sociologist* 10:9–23.

Calderon, Jose Z. 1991. "Mexican American Politics in a Multi-Ethnic Community: The Case of Monterey Park, 1985–1990." Ph.D. dissertation, University of California, Los Angeles.

Chu, Judy. 1991. Testimony before the Assembly Committee on Elections, Reapportionment, and Constitutional Amendments. Los Angeles. 28 June.

Dahl, Robert A. 1961. *Who Governs? Democracy and Power in an American City*. Reprint. New Haven: Yale University Press, 1973.

Davidson, Chandler, ed. 1984. *Minority Vote Dilution*. Washington, D.C.: Howard University Press.

Davis, Mike. 1987. "Chinatown, Part Two: The 'Internationalization' of Downtown Los Angeles." *New Left Review* 164:65–86.

Din, Grant. 1984. "An Analysis of Asian/Pacific American Registration and Voting Patterns in San Francisco." Master's thesis, Claremont Graduate School, Claremont, Calif.

Espiritu, Yen Le. 1990. "Cooperation and Conflict: Panethnicity among Asian Americans." Ph.D. dissertation, University of California, Los Angeles.

Estrada, Leo F. 1991. Speech presented at the San Gabriel Valley League of United Latin American Citizens Council, Annual Scholarship and Community Service Awards banquet, 21 April.

Gordon, Milton M. 1964. *Assimilation in American Life*. New York: Oxford University Press.

Hocking, Douglas. 1980. "Asian-Americans and the Law." In *Political Participation of Asian Americans: Problems and Strategies*, ed. Yung-Hwan Jo, pp. 166–185. Chicago: Pacific/Asian American Mental Health Research Center.

Horton, John. 1989. "The Politics of Ethnic Change: Grass-Roots Responses to Economic and Demographic Restructuring in Monterey Park, California." *Urban Geography* 10:578–592.

————. 1990. *Changing Relations: Newcomers and Established Residents in U.S. Communities. The Case of Monterey Park, California*. Report submitted to the Changing Relations Project Board, State University of New York, Binghamton.

————. 1992. "The Politics of Diversity in Monterey Park, California." In *Structuring Diversity: Ethnographic Perspectives on Immigrants in Five United States Cities*, ed. Louise Lamphere, pp. 215–245. Chicago: University of Chicago Press.

Horton, John, and Jose Z. Calderon. 1992. "Language Struggles in a Changing California Community." In *Language Loyalties: A Source-*

book on the *Official English Controversy*, ed. James Crawford, pp. 186–194. Chicago: University of Chicago Press.

Horton, John, and Yen-Fen Tseng. 1990. "Monterey Park City Council Exit Poll." Unpublished.

Kuramoto, Ford H. 1980. "Lessons Learned in the Federal Funding Game." In *Asian-Americans: Social and Psychological Perspectives*, vol. 2, ed. Russell Endo, Stanley Sue, and Nathaniel N. Wagner, pp. 248–259. Science and Behavior Books.

Kwong, Peter. 1987. *The New Chinatown*. New York: Hill and Wang.

Lamphere, Louise, ed. 1992. *Structuring Diversity: Ethnographic Perspectives on Immigrants in Five United States Cities*. Chicago: University of Chicago Press.

Little Tokyo Anti-Eviction Task Force. 1976. "Redevelopment in Los Angeles' Little Tokyo." In *Counterpoint*, ed. Emma Gee, pp. 327–333. Los Angeles: Asian American Studies Center, University of California.

Logan, John R., and Harvey L. Molotch. 1987. *Urban Fortunes: The Political Economy of Place*. Berkeley: University of California Press.

Lopez, David, and Yen Espiritu. 1990. "Panethnicity in the United States: A Theoretical Framework." *Ethnic and Racial Studies* 13:198–224.

Los Angeles County Commission on Human Relations. 1989. *Hate Crime in Los Angeles County*. Report to the Los Angeles County Board of Supervisors. Los Angeles.

Monterey Park Planning Department. 1974. *Population and Housing Profile*. Monterey Park, Calif.

Nagel, Joane. 1986. "The Political Construction of Ethnicity." In *Competitive Ethnic Relations*, ed. Susan Olzak and Joane Nagel, pp. 93–112. New York: Academic Press.

Nakanishi, Don. 1985–1986. "Asian American Politics: An Agenda for Research." *Amerasia* 12:1–27.

———. 1986. *The UCLA Asian Pacific American Voter Registration Study*. Los Angeles: Asian Pacific American Legal Center of Southern California.

———. 1991. "The Next Swing Vote? Asian Pacific Americans and California Politics." In *Racial and Ethnic Politics in California*, ed. Byran O. Jackson and Michael B. Preston, pp. 25–54. Berkeley: IGS Press.

Olzak, Susan. 1983. "Contemporary Ethnic Mobilization." *Annual Review of Sociology* 9:355–374.

Omi, Michael, and Howard Winant. 1986. *Racial Formation in the United States from the 1960s to the 1980s*. New York and London: Routledge and Kegan Paul.

Ong, Paul M. 1991. *Asian Pacific Islanders in California, 1990*. Los Angeles: Asian American Studies Center, University of California.
Pardo, Mary. 1990. "Identity and Resistance: Latina Activists in Two Los Angeles Communities." Ph.D. dissertation, University of California, Los Angeles.
Portes, Alejandro, and Ruben G. Rumbaut. 1990. *Immigrant America: A Portrait*. Berkeley: University of California Press.
Saito, Leland T. 1989. "Japanese Americans and the New Chinese Immigrants: The Politics of Adaptation." *California Sociologist* 12:195–212.
———. 1993a. "Contrasting Patterns of Adaptation: Japanese Americans and Chinese Immigrants in Monterey Park." In *Bearing Dreams, Shaping Visions: Asian Pacific American Perspectives*, ed. Linda Revilla, Gail Nomura, Shawn Wong, and Shirley Hune, pp. 33–43. Pullman: Washington State University Press.
———. 1993b. "Asian Americans and Latinos in San Gabriel Valley, California: Interethnic Political Cooperation and Redistricting, 1990–92." *Amerasia Journal* 19:55–68.
Saxton, Alexander. 1971. *The Indispensable Enemy*. Berkeley: University of California Press.
Soja, Edward W., Rebecca Morales, and Goetz Wolff. 1983. "Urban Restructuring: An Analysis of Social and Spatial Change in Los Angeles." *Economic Geography* 59:195–230.
Song, Alfred H. 1980. "The Asian-American in Politics." In *Political Participation of Asian Americans: Problems and Strategies*, ed. Yung-Hwan Jo, pp. 16–20. Chicago: Pacific/Asian American Mental Health Research Center.
Suzuki, Bob H. 1977. "Education and the Socialization of Asian Americans: A Revisionist Analysis of the 'Model Minority' Thesis." *Amerasia Journal* 4:23–51.
Tachibana, Judy. 1986. "California's Asians: Power from a Growing Population." *California Journal* (November): 535–543.
University of California, Los Angeles Asian American Studies Center. 1991. "Public Policy Reapportionment Analysis Project." Unpublished tables.
U.S. Bureau of the Census. 1983. *1980 Census of Population: General Social and Economic Characteristics*. Table 248. Washington, D.C.: Government Printing Office.
———. 1991. *Census of Population and Housing, 1990 Public Use Sample: 5% Sample*. Washington, U.S. Bureau of the Census [producer].
Yoneda, Karl G. 1983. *Ganbatte: Sixty-year Struggle of a Kibei Worker*. Los Angeles: Asian American Studies Center, University of California.

9. The Korean-Black Conflict and the State

Paul Ong, Kye Young Park, and Yasmin Tong

The massive economic restructuring and associated demographic recomposition in Los Angeles since the 1970s have altered the way the state addresses urban racial conflict. The large and growing numbers of Asians, along with their Latino counterparts, have rendered the simple black-white paradigm ineffective. What is replacing established practices is unclear, but it certainly is not based on a dichotomous minority-Anglo configuration. This is not to say that people of color do not have common concerns vis-à-vis Anglos (non-Hispanic whites), who continue to hold political and economic power despite a declining share of the total population. Elements of racism still disadvantage all minorities in U.S. society, and racially motivated violence directed at all non-Anglo groups has been on the rise. Nonetheless, race relations today also encompass clashes among populations of color. Although not new in U.S. history, these tensions and hostilities, once of secondary importance, have moved closer to center stage, making the nature of race considerably more complex. They have added new demands for state intervention, particularly by subnational governmental units and their various associated institutions.

When the state does become involved directly in race issues, through policies such as those related to affirmative action and civil rights, it redefines racial conflict through its dual functions of social change and social control. The details of how the state operates are determined by historical forces (Omi and Winant, 1986; also see Chapters 2 and 10). In the 1950s and 1960s, the state responded to mass movements by minorities and to its changing role in the Third World by dismantling state-sponsored racial oppression and implementing programs to proscribe discrimination. Although the gains were insufficient to offset racial inequalities deeply embedded in and reproduced by larger societal structures, the process yielded major concessions to minorities, including the abolition of racially biased immigration quotas.

Unfortunately, some gains were ephemeral. The economic crisis of the 1970s and 1980s created uncertainty and group competition that fueled racial conflict. In this climate, white backlash congealed into a countervailing political movement of conservative forces supported by a new-right ideology. During the years of Republican power in the White House, the civil rights movement suffered from a series of dangerous retrenchments. When the Democrats regained control of the presidency, this political regression to the right slowed, but it is too early to tell how strongly the current administration can and will reverse the retrogressive momentum of the previous decade.

Despite the role of the state in sponsoring social change, it also operates as a mechanism of social control. Its actions are dictated by the imperative to maintain legitimacy within the existing political-economic structure, as demonstrated by the limitations on the welfare state (O'Connor, 1973). This is partially achieved through channeling racial conflicts to forums sanctioned by the state. By offering concessions, it draws social movements and their leaders into the existing political structure and into the prevailing sets of rules that favor reform over revolutionary change (Mollenkopf, 1983). Within this arena, the tendency is to focus on equality of opportunity rather than equality of outcome, and on interpersonal problems rather than structural defects. In a larger sense, the state serves as a lightning rod, deflecting protest away from challenges to the fundamental social and economic order. Despite the boundaries imposed by political-economic forces and the state's social control function, political struggles within the circumscribed arena are far from meaningless. There is great latitude for action, policies, and programs, all of which have meaningful consequences for minorities and society.

The latitude for action is no less true in a multiracial setting, but the path is very different from that in a biracial setting. Though some institutions have been transformed, the state's fundamental dual functions have endured. To understand the unfolding of these developments and their implications, we examine a case study of the Korean-black conflict in the South Central area of Los Angeles. Many of the issues addressed here have been discussed by other scholars (Chang, 1990; Cheng and Espiritu, 1989; Light and Bonacich, 1988). We add to this literature by updating events to the months after the 29 April–1 May 1992 riot/rebellion in Los Angeles and by focusing on governmental intervention. The research for this chapter is based on interviews with residents, merchants, and program administrators; tabulations of census microdata; and participatory observations of community-based organizations.[1]

Beginning in the 1970s, Korean merchants, many operating "mom-and-pop" stores, have emerged as visible economic actors in South Central, the geographic home for low-income blacks in Los Angeles. The conflict between the two groups is partially embedded in the prejudices held by members of each population, which magnify economic-derived tensions by reinterpreting disagreements and points of friction into ethnic-racial terms. The resulting conflicts include over-the-counter hostilities and group protest. Violence directed at Korean merchants reached a peak during the 1992 Los Angeles riot/rebellion, in which Korean merchants suffered a disproportionately large share of the economic losses. Government-sponsored efforts to address the conflicts have evolved over time, with the 1992 riot/rebellion being a watershed. The strategy to manage race relations was replaced by limited economic initiatives that, unfortunately, balanced the grievances of black residents against the financial interests of Korean merchants.

Structural Foundation of Intergroup Tensions

The emergence of a Korean merchant class in South Central in the 1970s and 1980s is inextricably tied to the larger development of Korean entrepreneurship in Los Angeles. Korean immigrants have the highest level of entrepreneurship among Asian immigrants in Los Angeles (see Chapter 4). In 1990, roughly one in three working adult Koreans was either self-employed or an unpaid family worker.

The diversity of Korean entrepreneurs, ranging from the highly successful to those struggling to survive, is evident in the 1990 census data for adult Koreans in the self-employment sector. Roughly one in five earned an annual income of at least $48,000 in 1989. As a comparison, fewer than one in ten Korean wage workers earned that much. The rewards, however, were hardly uniform. One in three of those in the self-employment sector made less than $12,000 per year, roughly comparable to the proportion for Korean wage workers. There were also considerable differences in personal characteristics. One-fifth spoke English very well; two-fifths spoke English poorly or not at all. While two-fifths had at least a bachelor's degree, a third had at most a high school degree.

The Koreans reached their extraordinary level of entrepreneurship by mobilizing class, ethnic, and familial resources (Light and Bonacich, 1988; Min, 1984). The high rate of self-employment was also the product of limited employment opportunities in the larger labor market caused by language problems, the lack of transferability of education and training received in Korea, and discriminatory practices. Self-employment promised substantial financial rewards, and success was not an impossible dream, as the income data from the 1990 census indicate. Those who "made it" served as powerful and seductive role models, instilling and reinforcing the American dream of economic success based on entrepreneurial spirit.

Interestingly, neither limited English-language ability nor educational attainment strongly influenced the rate of self-employment. While entrepreneurship was a refuge for those suffering significant downward occupational mobility in the labor market, it was also an avenue for Koreans of all backgrounds. The two factors most correlated with the self-employment rate were the number of years in the United States and age, both of which were in turn correlated with the accumulation of capital needed to start a business.

The demands for business opportunities were as varied as the observed economic and personal diversity, ranging from investments in large and profitable firms to investments in small and financially marginal operations. The latter group, which is most relevant for South Central, overlapped with the group of businesses that includes grocery, liquor, and clothing stores. One could start a small establishment with savings and loan amounts within reach of many Korean immigrants. Compared to Korean entrepreneurs in all other sectors, however, Korean entrepreneurs in this sector had less than half the chances of reaching the top income category. Moreover, many had to work hard and long hours to survive, with four in ten working year-round and at least forty-four hours each week.

The availability of capital influenced not only the sector within which a Korean invested but also the geographic location. For Korean immigrants with limited capital, opening a business in a middle-class or affluent community was beyond their immediate reach. Instead, the most feasible option was finding a location where a small-scale store could survive and where the cost of starting or purchasing a business was relatively low. South Central provided such opportunities.

The abandonment of South Central by mainstream capital and corporations and by the public in the 1970s and 1980s, along with the aging of a previous generation of nonblack merchants, created an opening for aspiring Korean entrepreneurs. South Central, home to about a million people, contained some of the poorest neighborhoods in Los Angeles. Although the population changed during the 1970s and 1980s from predominantly black to nearly equally Latino and black (Ong and Lawrence, 1991), South Central continued to be the home of inner-city blacks. Racial recomposition was not the only notable change. South Central is like many other inner-city ghettos in terms of recent economic developments. These communities had been marginalized for most of this century, and structural changes in the urban economy over the last quarter-century made conditions worse, creating, in some situations, an urban underclass (Wilson, 1987). South Central suffered the brunt of deindustrialization of heavy manufacturing in Los Angeles. Between 1978 and 1982, South Central lost seventy thousand high-wage, stable, blue-collar jobs (Soja, 1989). Major companies such as General Motors, Goodyear, Firestone, and Bethlehem Steel closed plants in or around the area (Johnson et al., 1992). According to a study by the

United Way, a total of 321 plants or industries left South Central over a fifteen-year period (Hamilton, 1988–1989).

Few new firms replaced them. Redlining of South Central by major financial institutions, a policy of denying loans to residents merely because of their place of residence, translated into a scarcity of residential loans relative to other parts of Los Angeles, even after accounting for differences in income and other characteristics (Dymski, Veitch, and White, 1991). Although there is no hard evidence, it is quite likely that there was also redlining of commercial loans. This discriminatory practice was part of the gross inadequacy of banking services for the community (Aviles, 1991; Dymski et al., 1991). The lack of capital contributed to keeping the black entrepreneurial class in South Central relatively small, with self-employment earnings far lower than those of nonblacks (Ong, Belcher, and Lee, 1992). Large retailing firms also avoided the area. For example, in 1991 Target had seventy-three retailing discount stores in southern California but none in South Central, and Vons had three hundred supermarkets in the region but only two in South Central (Silverstein and Brooks, 1991). The lack of investment, combined with the flight of jobs, left South Central with a level of economic activity at only a third of the countywide level after normalizing for population (Ong et al., 1992).

Disinvestment occurred not only in the private sector but also in the public sector. Under successive Republican administrations, federal and state government withdrew funds for community-based organizations, thus undermining one of the key institutions in the community. As in many other inner-city communities throughout the nation, the state abandoned the War on Poverty long before poverty was eliminated. The combination of "New Federalism" and declining dollars for community action led to a dispersion of the increasingly scarce moneys for social programs to less depressed neighborhoods (Logan and Harvey, 1987). The lack of attention was duplicated at the local level. While the Los Angeles Community Redevelopment Agency was instrumental in revitalizing the downtown with new, high-rise commercial property, the agency did little for South Central (Davis, 1992).

As a consequence of these economic trends, many blacks became trapped in poverty-stricken, deteriorating neighborhoods with little hope of moving up or out (Norman, 1992, 8). The 1990 census showed that approximately one in three residents lived in households with incomes below the official poverty line, a rate more than twice that for the county. More than a quarter of all households survived on public assistance. Poverty in South Central, however, was not primarily a problem of welfare dependency. The community had a large and growing number of working poor, whose earnings often left a family near the poverty level. The average hourly wage in the South Central area was $9.12 in 1989, 58 percent of the average for Los Angeles County (Ong et al., 1992). Poverty was also tied to joblessness. In 1990, only 59 percent of adults aged twenty to sixty-four in South Central worked, a rate 16 percentage points lower than the county rate.

These broad economic trends set the stage for the appearance of high numbers of Korean merchants in South Central. The absence of large chain retailers meant that smaller operations would not be squeezed out by bigger and more efficient ones. At the same time, increasing poverty, along with a growing crime rate, made old-time merchants want to leave the community. Some were forced to abandon their businesses with no compensation, particularly after the 1965 Watts riot/rebellion, but others found buyers among the Korean immigrants. Once the original cohort of Korean merchants became established in South Central, others followed in increasing numbers.

Although opening a South Central business was cheaper than purchasing a business in other areas of Los Angeles, the costs were nonetheless high. Given the sizable demand for self-employment business by Korean immigrants, buyers competed against one another, and with a fixed supply of businesses, prices rose to the point where the potential for high profits was dissipated. The total cost of starting up a business, which included the purchase price and investments in inventory, could run into the hundreds of thousands of dollars (Duignan-Cabrera, 1993, B8). To raise the funds, some Koreans took great personal risks by mortgaging their homes; thus failure would mean losing not only their business but also their home. The costly investments forced Koreans to operate at the margins, cutting costs by relying on unpaid family workers and cheap co-ethnic labor and by forgoing adequate insurance coverage.

The relative importance of Korean Americans in the South Central subeconomy depends on the frame of reference. In the context of overall Korean entrepreneurship, Korean businesses in this area accounted for a small fraction of all Korean-owned businesses. According to Eui-Young Yu, a sociologist who had closely followed the development of the Korean community, the customer base of Korean-owned businesses in Los Angeles County by the early 1990s was only 10 percent African American and another 17 percent Latino (*LA Weekly*, 3–9 January 1992). Since many of the businesses serving minorities operated outside South Central, it is likely that only about a fifth of the customer base was in South Central.

On the other hand, Koreans operated a visible proportion of the stores in this community. According to some estimates for the mid-1980s, Koreans owned more than two-thirds of the gas stations and about one-third of the small markets and liquor stores in South Central (*Los Angeles Times*, 15 April 1985). Given the continued growth in the number of Korean merchants, the proportions were probably considerably higher by the end of the decade. The economic importance of Korean-owned stores in South Central, then, centered on their prominence in this low-income community, which persisted until 1992. The events of that year, which are discussed in detail later, made the presence of Korean merchants in South Central problematic.

In one sense, the emergence of a Korean merchant class in South Central can be conceptualized as ethnic succession of outside merchants in a low-income, minority community. Koreans were not the first nonblack ethnic group to operate extensively in poor African American neighborhoods. They had been preceded by Jewish merchants, many of whom sold their shops to Koreans (Pleasant, 1992). The succession, however, was not just from Jews to Koreans. There were also smaller numbers of Japanese and Chinese owners, along with some black owners, who also sold their businesses (Takahashi and Hee, 1992). In some cases, these original owners retained control over the property while selling the business operation (Ong and Hee, 1993), thus profiting through both the sales and continuing rents. Many of the absentee landlords were not residents of South Central, so the income generated by these transactions leaked out of the community.

The ethnically based practices of Korean merchants perpetuated the economic leakage and isolated them from the rest of the community. The isolation was reinforced by the fact that most Koreans resided outside South Central and were thus removed from the daily life of the community. The interactions between blacks and Koreans were effectively limited to those between outside merchants and local customers. This restrictive relationship had broader economic consequences. Like the previous generation of merchants, Koreans took their profits and income out of South Central.

One can interpret the role of the Korean merchants in South Central as a middleman minority position (Bonacich, 1973). This group played a commercial role similar to that of some ethnic minorities in Third World colonies: operating retailing outlets that served as the intermediary between the "native population" and those in economic and political power. Certainly, the Korean-owned stores did sell items produced by the large U.S. corporations, thus implicitly acting as their agents and enabling large capital to profit from such sales without having to invest directly in South Central or to interact directly with the residents.

Although the middleman minority concept is a useful starting point for understanding the role of Korean merchants, we see their role as far more complex, given their multiple and sometimes international upstream links. Korean merchants in South Central not only sold goods produced by U.S. corporations but also sold clothing and shoes produced by other Korean Americans and by overseas Korean manufacturers. Consequently, they were part of the global restructuring discussed in Chapter 1 and the restructuring of the garment industry discussed in Chapter 5.

In their drive to adapt to the U.S. economy, the Korean merchants also played a minor role in urban restructuring as it affects South Central. Korean Americans were not party to the disinvestment and abandonment of South Central, but they helped reshape the local economy. The emergence of the Korean merchant class was more than simply a process of a one-to-one replacement. At the very time the community was losing its manufacturing jobs, large retailers, and banking services, other economic activities were selectively maintained or expanded through Korean American investments.

This selectivity can be seen in the abundance of liquor stores and grocery stores with liquor licenses. According to one estimate, there was one store with a liquor license for every seven hundred residents by the early 1990s, a proportion three to four times higher than the ratio for the rest of Los Angeles (Lacy, 1992). Koreans played a significant role in this trend through their purchases and investments in liquor licenses, which made them the intermediary in the sales (Light and Bonacich, 1988, 232–233). The purveying of this self-destructive commodity to an oppressed population was motivated by a search for profits that precluded any social commitment to the overall well-being of the community. The aggregate sum of rational individual actions by Koreans in combination with the exodus of mainstream capital and corporations contributed to the unbalanced economic development of South Central.

Koreans also contributed to restructuring by being active agents of innovation rather than simple passive buyers of existing businesses. The creation of new forms is most apparent in the development of indoor swap meets, the vast majority of which were operated by Koreans (Chang, 1990). These malls operated in large buildings where space was leased to numerous small vendors who sold low-cost clothing, shoes, electronic goods, and other retail merchandise. By the late 1980s, there were more than a thousand Korean-operated booths in indoor swap meets in South Central (Chang, 1990, 98). Similar operations could be found in other parts of Los Angeles, but those in South Central were clearly a product of the absence of large chain retailers.

Interracial Conflicts

The discrete class positions occupied by Koreans and blacks in South Central created a set of interactions potentially filled with conflicts. Many points of confrontation were rooted in economics—the disparate interests of sellers and buyers. In the U.S. economy, the potential explosiveness of market transactions is minimized when fairness is imposed by competitive forces or governmental regulations that prevent monopolistic or oligopolistic behavior. As we argue below, however, South Central residents did not perceive such fairness, but rather shared a sense of being victims of inherent economic injustice. While economics was at the base of potential conflict, the problems between Korean sellers and black buyers were also social because the roles were strongly defined along racial-ethnic lines. The overlapping categorization by class and race-ethnicity was not perceived as coincidental or tangential in importance. Race and ethnicity became a basis for individual and collective action. This tendency was further strengthened by racially based and racially distinct perceptions and misperceptions (Stewart, 1989) and by sharp cultural and linguistic differences that produced a gulf of misunderstanding. Like most Korean merchants, many of those operating retailing stores had a poor command of English.[2]

Regardless of whether Korean merchants provided much-needed services, many South Central black residents saw them as another link in a long historical chain of exploitative outsiders. A thirty-three-year-old cosmetologist who is representative of this view stated, "Blacks see the Koreans as taking their money and making money off them in their neighborhood." In numerous interviews, residents repeated the litany of common complaints: the lack of employment for blacks, exorbitant prices for inferior goods, and poor service.

For some residents, the exploitative relation involved a broader conspiracy by whites and the government. In reviewing the history of outside merchants, one twenty-nine-year-old male cosmetologist stated: "Now that Jews have left and the Asians come in—which the whites have consciously allowed, . . . the whites, or the system, won't allow blacks to get into these business positions." According to another informant, the government was an active agent that allocated Koreans "money to get another family member over as long as they open businesses or something similar." While these arguments are specious, they played a role in casting Korean Americans on the side of whites and the "system."

The judicial system's lenient treatment of Koreans added to the perception of their relative privilege. That was particularly true after the 1991 killing of Latasha Harlins by Korean-born grocer Soon Ja Du and the subsequent trial. What had started as a dispute over a bottle of orange juice in Du's Empire Liquor Market Deli on South Figueroa Street in South Central ended in the shooting death of the fifteen-year-old Harlins. The ruling by Judge Joyce Karlin, a white female, which gave Du probation, became a heated point of controversy. In the eyes of many blacks, the trial was another blatant case of antiblack racism within the justice system.

The potentially conflict-filled relationship was intensified by black perceptions of Korean Americans as racially prejudiced. A twenty-eight-year-old vital statistics clerk stated, "Korean merchants have bought into the attitude that blacks are below human. . . . They look at black people as if they were animals." For one resident, this perceived prejudice explains the actions of Korean merchants: "Korean Americans always watch you. They are very suspicious. They think blacks are thieves." Some residents, however, believed that these prejudices were the product of the larger society, which, according to a forty-year-old manager at a law firm, portrays blacks "as belonging in gangs, uneducated, and as people who steal." Korean Americans, according to a forty-five-year-old hair stylist, "have a negative attitude towards African Americans because of the way television portrays them."

It is difficult to judge how pervasive these anti-Korean sentiments were among South Central blacks. Clearly, the views were not monolithic, for the interviews with residents also uncovered more sympathetic and understanding attitudes toward Korean merchants. Nonetheless, the anti-Korean view was given currency by the opinions expressed and disseminated by the local black newspapers, especially the *Los Angeles Sentinel*. For example, the newspaper published a series of articles in 1986 that accused Asian and Korean merchants of greed, poor services, and high prices and of failing to contribute to the community's social and economic well-being.

One indication that some of the views expressed by the interviewees were widely held by blacks in general comes from a survey of southern California residents by the *Los Angeles Times*

Poll (1993). Although the survey asked questions about the respondents' views of Asian Americans in general, these views are likely to apply to Koreans as well. A large majority (81%) of the black respondents stated that Asian Americans have good or very good access to adequate housing, education, and employment. This response rate is roughly the same as the proportion of black respondents (85%) who stated that whites have good or very good access to these goods. On the other hand, only a third (33%) of the black respondents felt that blacks in southern California had good or very good access. Clearly, most blacks believed that Asian Americans have social and economic privileges that are closer to those of whites than to those of blacks. Moreover, 45 percent of the black respondents stated that Asian Americans are among the two groups with the most racial prejudices. Finally, 39 percent believed that Asian Americans were "getting more economic power than is good for southern California," compared to only 29 percent who believed that this statement applied to whites. Given the underlying economic tensions between blacks and Koreans in South Central, it is likely that anti-Asian sentiments among blacks in that community are even stronger than those found by the survey.

Regardless of the validity of the anti-Korean perceptions, these views, in combination with the history of economic exploitation and racial injustice, played a powerful role in interpreting and magnifying confrontations. A perceived absence of a proper check on the economic power of merchants made every transaction suspect of being an unfair one. Although the Koreans were only actors in a play scripted by larger forces, they were nonetheless the immediate agents conducting business. High prices, poor-quality merchandise, no-return policies, and the like were seen as small but persistent incidents of exploitation. Many of these practices are understandable, given the marginal existence of many Korean stores, which force owners to cut cost and service; nonetheless, those at the receiving end as customers would find it difficult rationally to disregard these practices when confronted with them repeatedly.

Korean Americans also held stereotyped, race-based perceptions, as evident in the statement by a Korean woman shopkeeper:

We are enlightened not to steal, unlike African Americans in this neighborhood. Their parents do not pay attention to their children's education. Especially, since doing businesses in this South Central, I found that they do not have work. Lack of work—they usually do not work. They do not study and therefore they remain children.

The choice of the term "enlightened" is indicative of the way Korean Americans differentiated themselves from blacks. Although racial stereotypes existed, it would be unfair to say that all Korean Americans were prejudiced. Just as the interviews revealed that anti-Korean perceptions were not universal among blacks, it was clear that prejudices against blacks were not shared by all Koreans. Nonetheless, there was a broadly accepted view that the two groups were divided by tremendous cultural differences, which often contributed to intergroup misunderstanding and tension.

The perceptions held by Korean merchants were also shaped by daily exposure to potential crime. Operating in low-income areas obviously carried with it high risks. Shoplifting was regarded not simply as a petty crime but also as a sign of disrespect toward Koreans and a drain on meager profits. Robberies, some of which were violent, were far more serious. At times, the number of incidents was extremely high, and during one tragic month, four Korean merchants were killed. One would be hard pressed to argue that these murders were racially motivated, but some Koreans could not help associating criminal action and race. One Korean male stated, "As blacks have been oppressed for a long time, they have accumulated their hostility toward others, including us." The racial interpretation was reinforced by continuing coverage in the Korean newspapers, which often played up the role of race (Chang, 1990, 199–200). The race-based perceptions, along with the anxiety over the lack of personal safety, made some Korean merchants react defensively to their black customers, thus adding to tensions over daily transactions.

Although over-the-counter conflicts were an important element of Korean-black interaction, racial hostility was not limited to the interpersonal level. Black boycotts of Korean-owned stores were a form of collective action against what the protesters saw as unacceptable business practices. For example, the Organization of Mutual Neighborhood Interests staged a two-day boycott in November 1989 against the Slauson and Inglewood Indoor Swap Meets to protest lack of courtesy, high prices, lack of jobs for local residents, and several other issues (Chang, 1990, 206–207). Boycotts were also triggered by violent occurrences such as the killing of Latasha Harlins. In mid-1991, the Brotherhood Crusade, a vocal black group headed by the charismatic Danny Bakewell, organized a boycott against Chung's Liquor Mart (Holguin and Lee, 1991). Tae Sam Park, the owner, had killed Lee Arthur Mitchell during an attempted robbery. What prompted the protest was a belief that the killing was unwarranted because Mitchell had been unarmed. Feelings were intensified by a lack of action by the judicial system against the owner.

Boycotts were frequently tied to specific incidents, but they had deeper roots in the resentment over racism in general and outside merchants in particular. This sentiment endowed boycotts with a greater political meaning than a simple grievance against any one store or owner. The boycotts took on a symbolic aspect that sometimes became entangled with race. This symbolic importance was not lost on some black activists, who used boycotts to promote their own political agenda, which often included black nationalism.

Korean businesses were also caught in a growing movement to limit against the sale of liquor. Many inner-city residents saw liquor outlets as undesirable because they contributed to alcoholism and served as meeting places for individuals with antisocial behavior (Lacy, 1992, A14). What further inflamed residents was that larger outside economic interests profited by actively promoting sales. The liquor-manufacturing industry developed cheap but potent products targeted at inner-city residents (White and Lacy, 1992). The issue of liquor sales, then, involved not merely personal freedom to consume a beverage but also corporate exploitation.

What started as individual concerns developed into a political campaign both in Los Angeles and in urban areas throughout the nation (Sims, 1992). In South Central, the Community Coalition for Substance Abuse Prevention and Treatment emerged as

a driving force behind this movement. It actively lobbied governmental agencies and elected officials to reduce the number of
liquor outlets, and it organized residents to fight the sale of liquor. Not surprisingly, the movement became enmeshed with
broader issues of racism and exploitation. Consequently, the antiliquor movement, like the store boycotts, assumed political importance beyond the immediate issue.

The controversy over liquor sales need not have been racial.
The Community Coalition attempted to prevent the racialization
of the issue, and its executive director, Karen Bass, worked extensively with Asian Americans to find mutually acceptable options. Nonetheless, keeping events nonracial proved to be difficult because of the way that opposing sides were mobilized.
More often than not, protesters were black (and Latino) residents, some of whom interjected the recurring complaint of outside exploitation.

At the same time, Korean merchants banded together in reactive solidarity to counter the boycotts and the antiliquor movement. Some sought to demonstrate that Koreans were willing to
be responsive to community needs by hiring local residents, contributing to neighborhood scholarship, and adopting a better
code of business conduct. Unfortunately, there were structural
limitations to this response. The larger economic dynamics of
South Central and the ethnic foundation of the Koreans' entrepreneurship precluded radical changes in their practices and
choice of business activities.

The Riot/Rebellion of 1992

The nature of Korean-black conflict changed dramatically during
the riot/rebellion of 29 April to 1 May 1992 in Los Angeles. This
event was spontaneous, albeit highly predictable in retrospect.
Civil unrest exploded in Los Angeles after a jury in Simi Valley,
a white suburb, found four Los Angeles Police Department offi-
cers not guilty of beating black motorist Rodney King. For residents of South Central, as well as millions of citizens throughout
the nation, the verdict was incomprehensible, given the visual
evidence captured on a videotape and broadcast innumerable

times by local and national television. The reaction in Los Angeles was a riot/rebellion of unprecedented proportions, leaving in its wake 43 deaths, 2,383 injured persons, more than 16,000 arrests, and $1 billion in damages and losses (Bobo et al., 1992). Although the riot/rebellion was concentrated in the inner-city neighborhoods of Los Angeles, looting and violence occurred over a large territory ranging from the San Fernando Valley in the north to Long Beach in the south. This civil unrest shared some of the features of the riot/rebellions of the 1960s but differed in its multiracial complexity (Tierney, 1993). The participants in the violence and their victims included whites, blacks, Latinos, and Asians.

Apart from injuries and deaths, some consequences are proving to be long-term. The potential direct and indirect employment losses from the destruction to businesses are enormous: 11,500 jobs with an annual payroll of $240 million (California Employment Development Department, 1993, 67). Many of these jobs are not easily replaceable. The rebuilding has been slow in South Central, where less than a third of all damaged buildings were repaired one year later (Reinhold, 1993). Despite the grand aspirations of Rebuild L.A. (RLA), a nonprofit organization created by Mayor Tom Bradley to coordinate and stimulate the rebuilding of Los Angeles, many of the announced commitments by large corporations for new investments in this community have no substance or will not materialize in the near future (Brooks and Weinstein, 1992). Some areas in South Central will remain devastated into the next century.

Asian Americans, especially Korean Americans, bore a disproportionate share—perhaps more than a third—of the losses during the three days of civil disorder (Ong and Hee, 1993; Tierney, 1993). Koreans far outnumbered all other Asian victims. For example, 235 Chinese-owned businesses suffered some damage or loss (Chinatown Service Center, 1992), compared to more than 2,000 Korean damaged or looted stores. Recovery is not possible for many, because two-thirds were either uninsured or underinsured (Korean American Inter-Agency Council, 1993) and because many Koreans have not received adequate assistance from disaster-relief agencies (Weinstein, 1993). One year after the riot, only 28 percent had reopened their businesses.

Among those still struggling to recover financially and psychologically, there was a pervasive sense of pessimism and a desire to leave Los Angeles.

Korean stores in South Central accounted for more than a third of the total losses to all Korean establishments, with Koreatown being the second hardest hit area. According to one analysis, 761 Korean stores in South Central were looted, damaged, or both, creating a loss of $158 million (Ong and Hee, 1993). Disentangling the reasons why Korean stores were heavily hit is difficult. There is no question that they were easy targets of opportunity with lootable merchandise in large part because of the refusal or inability of the police department to provide timely protection to South Central merchants. Korean owners had neither the political nor the economic clout to prompt the city into action. Moreover, most of these stores were left unprotected, because their owners feared entering South Central during the civil unrest, given the antiwhite and anti-Asian nature of the attacks on persons.

Race also played a direct role: "preexisting racial conflicts provided both the motivation and rationale for such action" (Ong and Hee, 1993, 10). Not only did blacks attack Korean-owned stores in South Central, but Latinos attacked Korean-owned stores in other parts of town. In many respects, Korean victims were no different than business victims of earlier race riot/rebellions who were singled out because they were unwelcome outsiders (Dynes and Quarantelli, 1968).

Even if race did not play a central role in the motivations and actions of the rioters, the devastating outcomes added to the racial tension and mistrust between Koreans and blacks. The events of April–May 1992 are part of a broader escalation of racial conflicts from interpersonal, over-the-counter hostilities to interest-group political clashes and finally to collective violence. This transformation moved the Korean-black conflict closer to the center stage of the discourse on race relations, as can be seen in the coverage by the media. By mid-1992, the Korean-black conflict had pushed its way onto the front pages and the evening news. Although reporters still had a strong tendency to see the riot/rebellion in terms of blacks and whites, there was a growing acknowledgment that contemporary urban racial conflict is "multicolor." In other words, the redefinition of race is unfolding.

State Response

The state's response to the Korean-black conflict was incremental, with the 1992 riot/rebellion serving as a major turning point. Before the civil unrest, intervention relied on managing interracial relations rather than addressing the underlying economic source of conflict. This effort was carried out through organizations such as the Black-Korean Alliance and community-based centers for dispute resolution. The unrest exposed the grave limitations of this approach, and the period following the civil disorder was characterized by political actions that brought about initiatives to improve South Central's economic base. Only moderate reforms were proposed, however, focusing on balancing narrow Korean and black interests while leaving the underlying economic and social problems intact.

The pre–riot/rebellion policy of managing racial conflicts included efforts to incorporate and mobilize the elites in each community, to ameliorate symptoms, and to focus on interpersonal conflicts. Even before Korean merchants moved into South Central, this orientation was well established, as illustrated by the history of the Los Angeles County Commission on Human Relations, one of the primary local agencies handling race-related issues. The commission was founded in 1944, in response to the zoot-suit riots, "to seek out the causes of racial tension and devise all means possible to eliminate them" (Los Angeles County Commission on Human Relations, 1969, 5). This goal, however, quickly proved to be unrealistic, because the commission did not have the power to tackle the profound underlying causes of racial tension. The mission was scaled back a few years later: "To engage in research and education of the public for the purpose of lessening racial, religious and sexual prejudice, and to develop and administer programs and plans designed to promote full acceptance of all citizens" (Los Angeles County Commission on Human Relations, 1969, 8). The commission essentially defined minority-majority conflict in terms of interpersonal relations and, in doing so, defined the problem away from systemic structural racism.

Even with its more modest mission, the Human Relations Commission was ill-equipped to address the Korean-black conflict. Beginning in the mid-1970s, declining local revenues and greater conservative power on the County Board of Supervisors combined to gut the commission's budget, forcing it to reduce its staff of one hundred in the 1970s to only fifteen professionals by the early 1990s (Feldman, 1990; Wong, 1992). These cutbacks occurred at the very time that the demand for services increased: the minority population was growing, along with greater cultural heterogeneity (Ong and Lawrence, 1992; Pearlstone, 1990, 33) and an escalating number of hate crimes (Chavez, 1992). Even when the commission gained public visibility, its recommendations carried little political weight. The commission organized high-profile hearings addressing hate crimes against Asians, the quality of life in South Central, and changing demographics in Los Angeles (Los Angeles County Commission on Human Relations, 1984, 1985, 1991). But the supervisors rarely implemented or acted on the recommendations emanating from these hearings (Wong, 1992).

Given the commission's limitations, other institutional forms emerged to address interracial conflicts. The Black-Korean Alliance (BKA) was established in 1986 with the assistance of Los Angeles County's Human Relations Commission after four Korean merchants were killed in four weeks in April 1986. BKA operated outside the administrative and procedural confines of the county bureaucracy to improve relations between Korean merchants and black residents in South Central. The alliance included representatives from the mayor's office and local small business associations, academics, and workers from the human relations profession, in addition to business, church, and other leaders from the Korean and black communities (George, 1992). The BKA's objective was to establish an interethnic dialogue enabling people to air their differences as well as become more informed about one another.

Along with the BKA, the Asian Pacific American Dispute Resolution Center (APADRC) and the Martin Luther King Dispute Resolution Center (MLKDRC) emerged as key players in the effort to address the Korean-black conflict. These two organizations grew out of a national movement to divert disputes from the civil courts to less costly alternatives. California's Dispute Resolution Act of 1986 enables counties to set aside civil court filing fees to establish and maintain community-based dispute resolution centers. Because the proposed mediation process had applications for groups underserved and underrepresented by the formal legal system (Harrington, 1985, 35), civil rights organizations and activists in the Asian and black communities sought and received funding to establish dispute resolution centers, namely, the APADRC and MLKDRC. With limited funding (an annual budget of less than $100,000 for each), both programs relied on volunteers to handle the forty to seventy-five cases per month involving disputes between landlords and tenants, employers and workers, neighbors, family members, and merchants and consumers (Choo, 1992; Westbrook, 1992). Both groups mediated interracial disputes, including those between Koreans and blacks.

The three organizations did have some accomplishments. The BKA helped develop a merchant's code of ethics and promoted financial contributions to community projects. After the killing of Latasha Harlins, the organization responded swiftly by organizing community forums in local churches on issues of merchant-consumer antagonism, the lack of community reinvestment, pricing, and employment practices (Choo, 1992). Over time, the dispute resolution centers mediated an increasing number of cases involving conflicts between Korean merchants and black consumers. Before the riot/rebellion, these centers were able to resolve a majority of such cases. Moreover, the two centers were moving in the direction of forming joint teams to overcome any appearance of ethnic-racial bias on the part of each organization.

Despite these achievements, the efforts could not eliminate intergroup tension or substantially reduce the level of hostilities. The limitations of the approach of managing racial conflict with the most meager of resources became very apparent during the 1992 riot/rebellion. In the case of the BKA, its ineffectiveness ultimately led to its demise in December 1992, because, to paraphrase the sentiments of some members, "talking was not enough" (Doherty, 1992). Even before the riot, there was considerable tension among its participants, and the fallout from the 1992 riot/rebellion proved fatal. Although the dispute resolution centers continued to operate after April–May 1992 and received funding to form the joint Asian-black mediation team, their resources continued to be grossly inadequate to address the complex economic and social problems that fostered the Korean-black conflict. Of course, it would be unfair to blame any limited set of institutions for society's failure. Both the BKA and the dispute resolution centers had noble intentions and some highly dedicated people, but they had only marginal support at best from the state. The failure was not so much of individual organizations but of the underlying approach to managing racial conflict.

The riot/rebellion instantly transformed the political climate and, with it, the way local government acted. The violence renewed a concern about urban poverty and racial injustice. There was, of course, a conservative interpretation of the events, focusing on criminal acts, unacceptable lawlessness, and law and order as a solution, and there was a leftist interpretation centering on social revolution and radical change. The reaction by local government was much more moderate. Along with an acknowledgment of the need for public safety, there was a growing willingness to listen to the grievances articulated by grass-roots activists and a renewed interest in community economic development. The large-scale destruction required solutions to address both the rebuilding process and the creation of a new economic base.

The policies that emerged were not race neutral, and in relation to the Korean-black conflict they placed Korean merchants at a disadvantage with only limited compensation. This approach can be seen in the mechanisms that the city of Los Angeles adopted to guide reconstruction. Along with incentives to attract new investments, new barriers were enacted to discourage the reestablishment of "undesirable" businesses. Which businesses fell into each category was based as much on politics as on objective criteria.

As stated earlier, liquor outlets were among the most controversial businesses. Even before the outbreak of mass violence, the city had moved cautiously to address the issue. Responding to growing political pressure from South Central residents and organizations, Los Angeles mayor Bradley established the South Central Liquor Task Force in April 1992, ironically only a few weeks before the riot/rebellion. Koreans and blacks were among its members, which included community residents, representatives of businesses, representatives of elected officials, and community activists. Its objective was to limit the number of liquor outlets through enforcing land-use restrictions and using a revocation process to eliminate problem stores. Events quickly overtook the task force.

The riot/rebellion accomplished what the antiliquor movement had been unable to do—the removal of large numbers of liquor outlets. During the unrest, more than half the South Central stores with a liquor license (an estimated 400 of 728) were damaged or destroyed (McMillan, 1992). An analysis of one list (South Central Community/Merchant Liquor Task Force, 1992, 23–26) indicates that an overwhelming majority were owned by Koreans. The widespread destruction enabled the movement to shift from demanding removal of existing outlets to preventing the reopening of the closed operations. In the few months following the riot, the movement was able to gather 34,000 signatures on a petition demanding a reduction in the number of liquor stores in South Central (APPCON, 1992).

Korean merchants resisted this demand, not surprisingly, since the owners stood to lose a substantial part of their investments. The average financial value of a license was about $12,000, with some as high as $25,000 to $30,000 (McMillan, 1992). Although the liquor manufacturers and wholesale distributors also played a role in protecting the "right to sell liquor," they operated in the background through their influence on elected officials (White and Lacy, 1992). Koreans, on the other hand, were on the front line, and their visibility gave a distinctly ethnic appearance to those protecting the interest of liquor sales.

In the battle over the liquor stores, the antiliquor movement made greater gains than their Korean adversaries. Working through the task force and city council representatives from South Central, the antiliquor movement partially achieved its new objective through a special provision in local law (Ordinance no. 167,909). To facilitate reconstruction, the city waived certain fees, eliminated some red tape, and allowed firms to rebuild according to older and less stringent codes. Not all businesses could benefit from these provisions, however. "Establishments dispensing alcoholic beverages for consideration," that is, liquor outlets, along with "swap meets, gun shops, pawnshops, and automobile repair establishments," were excluded. The outcome, then, was a victory for the residents and organizations fighting the presence of liquor outlets.

Although the exclusions did not explicitly target any ethnic group, the de facto effect was to disadvantage a disproportionately large number of Korean merchants. Although corporate-backed operations, such as 7-Eleven stores, had the resources to undergo the rigorous hearing process and to meet newer building code requirements, few Koreans were able to overcome the barriers (Duignan-Cabrera, 1992; Rainey, 1992).

Korean merchants received only minor compensation in the form of financial incentives and programs to help them convert their establishments to other lines of business. The initiative to assist displaced Korean liquor store owners came from the Asian Pacific Planning Council (APPCON), an umbrella organization of social service providers. APPCON accepted the need to reduce the number of liquor outlets in South Central but added that the city must provide "compensation for liquor licensees and assistance for store owners to relocate or convert . . . to another business" (APPCON, 1992).

As a concession to concerns over the fate of Korean merchants, the city implemented two programs. First, it waived charges for connection to the sewer system for those converting to or investing in self-service laundries. The fees could run into tens of thousands of dollars, depending on the number of machines. This incentive was enacted both to help small businesses and to provide a badly needed service in South Central. Although this program was not designed specifically for Koreans, the second program was. The city funded APPCON's proposed Liquor Store Business Conversion Program by channeling $260,000 from the state of California into the effort, and a private foundation added another $100,000. Participation was not restricted to any one racial-ethnic group, but the program was designed so that Korean owners of liquor outlets were the primary beneficiaries. Although the city did acknowledge the needs of Korean merchants through these concessions, the total value of compensation was less than 1 percent of the losses suffered by Korean merchants.

We started with a question of how the state addresses race-related issues in an increasingly multiracial society. The case study based on the emergence of a Korean merchant class in South Central provides some insights. Clearly, the interjection of this group into what had been seen as largely a black-white situation precipitated new economic and social conflicts. From the start, the state used approaches that defined the problems away from a majority-minority framework and avoided fundamental structural issues.

The 1992 riot/rebellion brought about some new initiatives. The restrictions on the rebuilding of liquor stores and the incentives for conversion can be seen as efforts to bring about economic change. But they also represented a reactive adaptation of the state's use of regulatory powers and financial incentives to direct economic development, which had been applied on a much larger scale to benefit corporate America through programs such as urban renewal. The reforms that were adopted for South Central suffered serious constraints. The most obvious limitation is that at best the efforts can only chip away at the underlying social and economic structure of racial inequality, which would be acceptable if the efforts were complemented by more comprehensive changes, but this does not appear to be the case. As stated earlier, the larger rebuilding campaign is not likely even to return South Central to its pre–riot/rebellion state.

Nevertheless, looking at the initiatives concerning the liquor stores solely from an economic perspective misses an important point: the reforms embody a politics that continues to focus on the immediate conflict between Korean merchants and black residents. The outcomes of the process of redressing the grievances of both non-Anglo groups can be partially explained by the Koreans' relative lack of political power, even when they were assisted by other Asian Americans. The underlying political weaknesses of Asian Americans identified in Chapters 8 and 10 certainly were a major contributing factor. Moreover, the bias in the actions chosen by the city may be justified from a historical perspective, since blacks have suffered the greater injustice in U.S. society. Yet such an intergroup comparison has validity only because the debate has been confined to the relationship between two minority groups rather than extended to broader structural issues.

It would be too simplistic and plain wrong to argue that community activists were duped into playing by the rules. Indeed, most were well aware of the need for fundamental change yet were continually frustrated in their struggles to bring it about. This problem is not specific to South Central but prevalent among minority activists throughout the country (Fainstein, 1987). Given the real and pressing daily needs of Korean merchants and black residents and the budgetary and political limitations of local government, the fight over constrained reforms offered the best opportunity for improving local conditions. Without consciously choosing to be willing participants in the process of confining political debate, community activists, through their cumulative daily struggles within the formal political arena, gave legitimacy to the strategy sanctioned by the state. The outcome was that the state succeeded in being a very limited instrument of social change but an effective instrument of social control in a multiracial society.

Notes

1. This chapter draws on open-ended interviews of nineteen Korean merchants and thirty African American customers in South Central conducted by Kye Young Park before the April 1992 riot/rebellion. The interviews with the Koreans were conducted in their shops, and the interviews with the African Americans were conducted in black-owned businesses. The choice of black-owned businesses as sites was based on the assumption that the interviewees would be more open to expressing their opinions in places where African Americans feel relatively empowered. All African Americans were also customers of Korean-owned stores. All interviews were conducted in South Central, which has a noticeable number of Korean-owned shops and is bounded by the following streets: Figueroa,

Vermont, 40th, and 100th. The interviewees were selected to represent a cross-section of merchants and residents. Interviews with community leaders and representatives of agencies were conducted by Yasmin Tong and Paul Ong both before and after the riot/rebellion. Individuals were selected from organizations that participated in efforts to address the Korean-black conflict.

2. We are not arguing that the prejudices and over-the-counter conflicts discussed in this chapter are caused simply by cultural differences or simply by structural and situational sources. As we have stated earlier, structural factors created the class-racial disparities in South Central, which in turn created the potential for conflicts. It is within this context that cultural differences and prejudices came into play. There were other nonblack merchants who faced similar economic conditions but did not receive the same level of hostility or attention as Korean merchants. Even among Korean merchants, we saw differences, with some being able to develop good relations with their customers. Locating and explaining the direct sources of these prejudices and over-the-counter conflicts, however, is exceedingly difficult and beyond the scope of this chapter.

References

APPCON (Asian Pacific Planning Council). 1992. "Proposal for Liquor Store Business Conversion Program." Mimeographed.

Aubry, Lawrence. 1992. Interview of Larry Aubrey, of the Los Angeles County Human Relations Commission, by Yasmin Tong, 20 April.

Aviles, Gilberto. 1991. "The Banking Services Outreach Project, Check Cashing, and Money Orders: A Commentary about Poor People's Access to Financial Services." Master's thesis, University of California, Los Angeles.

Bobo, Lawrence D., James H. Johnson, Melvin L. Oliver, James Sidanius, and Camile Zubrinsky. 1992. "Public Opinion before and after a Spring of Discontent: A Preliminary Report on the 1992 Los Angeles County Social Survey." Occasional Working Paper Series, vol. 3, no. 1. Los Angeles: Center for the Study of Urban Poverty, University of California.

Bonacich, Edna. 1973. "A Theory of Middleman Minorities." *American Sociological Review* 83:583–594.

Brooks, Nancy Rivera, and Henry Weinstein. 1992. "19 of 68 Firms Question Listing by Rebuild L.A.." *Los Angeles Times*, 18 November, pp. A1, A18–19.

California Employment Development Department. 1993. *Analysis of the 1992 Los Angeles Civil Unrest*. Los Angeles.

Chang, Edward. 1990. "New Urban Crisis: Korean-Black Conflicts in Los Angeles." Ph.D. dissertation, University of California, Berkeley.

Chavez, Stephanie. 1992. "Mediators Work to Defuse Racial Tensions." *Los Angeles Times*, 19 April, p. A1.

Cheng, Lucie, and Yen Espiritu. 1989. "Korean Businesses in Black and Hispanic Neighborhoods: A Study of Intergroup Relations." *Sociological Perspectives* 32:521–534.

Chinatown Service Center. 1993. "Riot Relief Project Assists Nearly 300 Chinese-American Families." *Newsletter* 11 (September): 2.

Choo, Marcia. 1992. Interview of Marcia Choo, Director of the Asian Pacific American Dispute Resolution Center, by Yasmin Tong, 22 April.

Davis, Mike. 1992. *City of Quartz: Excavating the Future in Los Angeles*. New York: Vintage Books.

Doherty, Jake. 1992. "Black-Korean Alliance Says Talk Not Enough, Disbands." *Los Angeles Times*, 24 December, pp. A1, A3.

Duignan-Cabrera, Anthony. 1992. "As Some Reopen, Other Stores Caught in Red Tape." *Los Angeles Times*, 25 June, pp. B1, B8.

Dymski, Gary, John Veitch, and Michelle White. 1991. *Taking It to the Bank: Poverty, Race, and Credit in Los Angeles*. Report to the City of Los Angeles. Los Angeles: Western Center on Law and Poverty.

Dynes, R. R., and E. L. Quarantelli. 1968. "What Looting in Civil Disturbances Really Means." *Trans-Action* (May): 9–14.

Fainstein, Susan. 1987. "Local Mobilization and Economic Discontent." In *The Capitalist City: Global Restructuring and Community Politics*, ed. Michael P. Smith and Joe R. Feagin, pp. 323–343. Oxford and New York: Basil Blackwell.

Feldman, Paul. 1990. "L.A. County Agency Tries a Mail Appeal for Money." *Los Angeles Times*, 10 February, p. A1.

George, Lynell. 1992. "Going Between: Mediators Bridge the Culture Gap." *LA Weekly*, 3 January, pp. 14–17.

Hamilton, Cynthia. 1988–1989. "Apartheid in American City: The Case of Blacks in Los Angeles." *LA Weekly*, 30 December–5 January.

Harrington, Christine B. 1985. "Socio-Legal Concepts in Mediation." *Legal Studies Forum* 9:33–38.

Holguin, Rick, and John Lee. 1991. "Boycott of Store Where Man Was Killed Is Urged." *Los Angeles Times*, 18 June, pp. B1, B8.

Johnson, James, Cloyzelle Jones, Walter Farrell, and Melvin Oliver. 1992. "The Los Angeles Rebellion, 1992: A Preliminary Assessment from Ground Zero." Los Angeles: Center for the Study of Urban Poverty, University of California.

Johnson, James, and Melvin Oliver. 1993. "Retrospective Analysis of the Los Angeles Rebellion, 1992." In *Policy Options for Southern California*, ed. Allen J. Scott, pp. 7–31. Los Angeles: Lewis Center for Regional Policy Studies, University of California.

Korean American Inter-Agency Council (KAIAC). 1993. KAIAC *Press Packet: Korean American Inter-Agency Council Announces Results of a Comprehensive Survey Assessing Situation of Korean American Victims Ten Months after the 1992 L.A. Riots*. Los Angeles.

Lacy, Marc. 1992. "Last Call for Liquor Outlets." *Los Angeles Times*, 14 December, pp. A1, A14–A15.

Light, Ivan, and Edna Bonacich. 1988. *Immigrant Entrepreneurs: Koreans in Los Angeles, 1965–1982*. Berkeley: University of California Press.

Logan, John, and David Harvey. 1987. *Urban Fortunes*. Berkeley: University of California Press.

Los Angeles County Commission on Human Relations. 1969. *A Twenty-five-Year History, 1944–1969*. Los Angeles.

———. 1984. *The New Asian Peril: Report of a Hearing on Rising Anti-Asian Bigotry*. Los Angeles.

———. 1985. *McCone Revisited: Focus on Solution to Continuing Problems in South Central Los Angeles."* Los Angeles.

———. 1991. *Hate Crime in Los Angeles County, 1990: A Report to the Los Angeles County Board of Supervisors*.

Los Angeles Times Poll. 1993. "Asians in Southern California." *Los Angeles Times*, 20 August, p. A1.

McMillan, Penelope. 1992. "Task Force on Liquor Stores Is Unveiled." *Los Angeles Times*, 30 June, pp. B1, B8.

Min, Pyong Gap. 1984. "From White Collar Occupations to Small Business: Korean Immigrants' Occupational Adjustments." *Sociological Quarterly* 25:333–352

Mollenkopf, John. 1983. *The Contested City*. Princeton: Princeton University Press.

Nakano, Erich. 1993. Interview of Erich Nakano, Chair of APPCON's Housing and Economic Development Committee, by Paul Ong, 24 June.

Norman, Alex. 1992. "Black-Korean Relations: From Desperation to Dialogue; Or, From Shouting and Shooting to Sitting and Talking." Paper presented at the Conference on Black-Korean Encounters, California State University, Los Angeles, 22–23 May.

O'Connor, James. 1973. *The Fiscal Crisis of the State*. New York: St. Martin's Press.

Omi, Michael, and Howard Winant. 1986. *Racial Formation in the United States from the 1960s to the 1980s*. New York and London: Routledge and Kegan Paul.

Ong, Paul, Wendy Belcher, and Ji-Young Lee. 1992. "The Economic Base of South Central." Unpublished. Graduate School of Architecture and Urban Planning, University of California at Los Angeles.

Ong, Paul, and Suzanne Hee. 1993. "Korean Merchants and the L.A. Riot/Rebellion." In *Losses in the Los Angeles Civil Unrest*, pp. 7–14. Los Angeles: Center for Pacific Rim Studies, University of California.

Ong, Paul, and Janette Lawrence. 1992. *Pluralism and Residential Patterns in Los Angeles*. Discussion Papers, D9202. Los Angeles: Graduate School of Architecture and Urban Planning, University of California.

Pearlstone, Zena. 1990. *Ethnic L.A.* Los Angeles: Hillcrest Press.

Pleasant, Betty. 1992. "A Tale of Two Riots." *Los Angeles Sentinel*, 7–13 May, pp. A1, A16.

Rainey, James. 1992. "Four Liquor Stores Destroyed in Riots Get OK to Rebuild." *Los Angeles Times*, 20 November, p. B4.

Reinhold, Robert. 1993. "Rebuilding Lags in Los Angeles a Year after Riots." *New York Times*, 10 May.

Silverstein, Stuart, and Nancy Brooks. 1991a. "Shoppers in Need of Stores: Lack of Retail Industries and Other Businesses in South Los Angeles, California." *Los Angeles Times*, 24 November, p. A1.

———. 1991b. "Retail Exodus Shortchanges Consumers, South Los Angeles, California." *Los Angeles Times*, 27 November, p. D1.

Sims, Calvin. 1992. "Under Siege: Liquor's Inner-City Pipeline." *New York Times*, 29 November, sec. 3, pp. 1, 6.

Soja, Edward. 1989. *Postmodern Geographies: The Reassertion of Space in Critical Social Theory*. London and New York: Verso.

Soja, Edward W., Rebecca Morales, and Goetz Wolff. 1983. "Urban Restructuring: An Analysis of Social and Spatial Change in Los Angeles." *Economic Geography* 59:195–230.

South Central Community/Merchant Liquor Task Force. 1992. *Final Report*. Los Angeles.

Stewart, Ella. 1989. "Ethnic Cultural Diversity: An Ethnographic Study of Cultural Differences and Communication Style between Korean Merchants and Employees and Black Patrons in South Los Angeles." Master's thesis, California State University, Los Angeles.

Takahashi, Jane, and Suzanne Hee. 1992. "The 1965 Watts Riots and Asian Americans." Mimeographed. Asian American Studies Center, University of California, Los Angeles.

Tierney, Kathleen J. 1993. "Los Angeles, 1992: First Urban Unrest of the Twenty-First Century." Paper presented at the Annual Meeting of the Southern Sociological Society, Chattanooga, Tenn., 1–4 April.

Weinstein, Henry. 1993. "Riot Victims Sue U.S. over Denial of Aid." *Los Angeles Times*, 17 June, pp. B1, B4.

Westbrook, Dennis. 1992. Interview of Dennis Westbrook, of the Martin Luther King Dispute Resolution Center, by Yasmin Tong, 29 April.

White, George, and Marc Lacy. 1992. "Liquor Industry Takes on Activists in Political Arena." *Los Angeles Times*, 15 December, pp. A1, A32–33.

Wilson, William J. 1987. *The Truly Disadvantaged: The Inner City, the Underclass, and Public Policy*. Chicago: University of Chicago Press.

Wong, Jai Lee. 1992. Interview of Jai Lee Wong, of the Los Angeles County Human Relations Commission, by Yasmin Tong, 1 April.

10. Class Constraints on Racial Solidarity among Asian Americans

Yen Espiritu and Paul Ong

Since the pan-Asian concept was forged in the late 1960s, the Asian American population has become much more diversified along ethnic and class lines. Although both ethnic and class divisions affect pan-Asian unity, we believe that class differences pose the greatest barrier to racial solidarity. Unlike ethnicity, class is not simply another line of group demarcation. In the Asian American case, class divisions play contradictory roles, both fragmenting the population and creating a class of professional social activists interested in uniting Asian Americans into a common racial category. Thus, much of what is called pan-Asianism can be understood only by studying this professional class.

Although we examine the relationship between race and class in this chapter, we do not attempt to determine which is the more fundamental variable (Bonacich, 1972; Cox, 1948; Wilson, 1978). Rather than offering a simple, ahistorical answer to this question, we submit that the importance of one relative to the other is determined at each moment in history, depending on various macro and contextual factors. In the Asian American case, the waning of overt racial oppression in recent decades has reified class distinctions among this population. Ironically, these divisions are most evident within the very organizations that purport to promote Asian American racial unity.

Largely on the basis of race, Asian Americans have been lumped together and treated as if they were the same. In expanding their social frame of reference and reorganizing their basic institutions on the grounds of pan-Asianism, Asian Americans unwittingly reify these racial distinctions. At the same time, they also reify class distinctions. Pan-Asian coalitions of social service providers, business owners, political agents, and labor are all organized along social class lines—thereby precluding a broad-based membership. Moreover, class differences correlate with ethnicity, generating internal conflicts over power and control that assume an ethnic appearance. These class distinctions and class-based ethnic tensions undercut the legitimacy of the pan-Asian coalitions and the use of race as their organizing principle, thus weakening the very foundation of these organizations.

Using examples from Los Angeles, we discuss the limits of Asian American racial solidarity, focusing on internal class divisions and class-based ethnic conflicts of pan-Asian organizations. The method is qualitative, relying on information we collected as active participants in some of these organizations. Although there are many dimensions to racial solidarity, we focus on only one: the degree to which group members can act collectively based on a common racial definition. In other words, we are concerned with action, not attitude. To understand the nature and limits of racial solidarity, we examine the very organizations that have adopted race as the basis for their existence. Because these organizations represent the vanguard of the Asian American racial movement, their ebbs and flows inform us of the present and future directions of this movement. We believe that these organizations are intrinsically worthy of examination because their very existence presupposes some degree of consensus. While it is important to quantify this consensus, it is equally important to identify the promoters of the Asian American coalition, and, in so doing, to name the dominant groups and sectors of this race-based movement.

Racial Solidarity and U.S. Racial Politics

Although race continues to be important in modern America, racial oppression has declined over the last half-century. Covert forms of racially motivated state policies continue to exist, but the state is no longer an overt instrument of racial oppression. Since World War II, discrimination based on race has been illegal. The state has also become more willing to enforce existing civil rights laws, some of which were enacted in the previous century, to ensure minority rights in electoral politics. At the same time, private organizations that seek to impose racial subordination through extralegal force have declined in importance. For example, membership in the Ku Klux Klan dropped from a high of 100,000 in 1921 to about 55,000 in 1967 and has continued to decline ever since (Anti-Defamation League of B'nai B'rith, 1982, 87; Bullard, 1988, 15). More important, it is now more difficult for such organizations to act out their aggression with impunity.

Several factors have contributed to the decline of overt racial oppression, including the United States' need for legitimacy as the "leader of the free world" among Third World countries, an expanding economy that made room for both white and minority workers, and the political demands of people of color. Of course, this waning of racial oppression is not a linear, irreversible process. In fact, with the restructuring of the global order and the recurring economic crises in the United States, racially motivated state policies and hate crimes are once again on the rise. In the 1980s, a decade of right-wing politics, the Reagan administration in general attempted to reverse the political gains of the 1960s racial minority movements. The legal attack on affirmative action has been nationwide (May, 1990). Nevertheless, these right-wing initiatives have not completely reversed the political and ideological transformations of the 1960s movements. For example, since the late 1960s, it has been impossible and unacceptable to argue against racial equality; therefore, any "legitimate" politics must at least claim to favor racial equality in the abstract (Omi and Winant, 1986, 140–141). It is this racial climate that has shaped the fortunes of Asian Americans.

Following Michael Omi and Howard Winant (1986), we argue that race has shaped, and been shaped by, U.S. politics. The postwar relaxation of racial oppression has had at least two consequences. The first is a strengthening of minority politics. In the 1960s, political activism among minorities erupted when changes in the legal system failed to eradicate racial inequality in the economic and social spheres, particularly for low-income blacks (Wilson, 1978). The political system became the single most important arena for minorities to vent their frustrations and anger over intergroup differences in income, power, employment opportunities, living standards, and prestige. The civil rights movement and the subsequent radical minority movements (Black, Brown, Red, and Yellow Power) accelerated the demise of state-sponsored racial oppression. Continued activism has also forced the state to implement affirmative action programs to ensure minority representation in employment, public programs, and education (Burstein, 1985; Wilson, 1987). Although these compensatory programs have not been absolutely effective, they have provided a material foundation for a form of minority politics in which race is the basis for making claims on state resources and power. Thus, instead of using race to oppress its minority citizens, the state in the past few decades has provided an incentive for racial solidarity.[1]

The second consequence of the relaxation of racial oppression has had the opposite impact on racial solidarity. The weakening of artificial racial barriers in the economic and political sectors has deepened the class polarization in minority communities, as those who were able to do so took advantage of new job and educational opportunities while the majority remained locked in poverty. In a study of black access to economic rewards, Richard Freeman (1976) argued that the creation and implementation of civil rights laws—along with the expansion of salaried white-collar positions in the corporate and government sectors—have generated unprecedented job opportunities for college-educated blacks but have not improved the life chances of poor blacks. As a result, the contemporary black community is stratified into a relatively small privileged class and a large underclass (Farley and Bianchi, 1983; Wilson, 1978 and 1987). These class divisions fragment the population, undermining racial solidarity.

The Asian American population has also become increasingly differentiated along class lines. The postwar removal of racial barriers in the economic sector increased the number of Asian American educated professionals. The preference for highly educated labor in immigration legislation further widened the class chasm, with Asian immigrants from lower-class backgrounds entering through the family reunification categories and those from higher-class backgrounds entering through the occupational categories.[2] The 1965 Immigration Act also led to an influx of newcomers who are distinct in ethnic composition from the more "established" Asian American groups. In other words, the Asian

American population is fragmented along both class and ethnic lines. Despite the confounding impact of ethnicity, we argue that class divisions constitute the greatest barrier to pan-Asian solidarity.

Of course, class distinctions within minority populations are not new. In the past, middle-class blacks also distanced themselves from lower-class blacks (Frazier, 1957). What is different today is that most of the middle-class blacks no longer reside in the same neighborhoods or participate in the same institutions as lower-class (or underclass) blacks (Wilson, 1987). As vertical intraracial linkages break down, horizontal linkages across racial lines among segments of the middle class grow in importance. This trend is particularly apparent among professionals, who are likely to interact with their class counterparts through work, professional organizations, and social events. These interactions forge and reinforce a common set of values and world perspectives that are embedded in their class segment. Class identity has not supplanted racial identity among professionals: the continuing importance of race is clearly evident in the existence of race-specific associations among lawyers, journalists, scholars, urban planners, and other professionals. Nonetheless, class distinctions have taken the form of class polarization and segregation, undermining racial solidarity.

The Racial Foundation of Multiethnic Organizations

The discussion of race relations has often been hampered by the conceptual ambiguity of "race." In its traditional sense, race is conceived of as a real biological division of human groups. Because physical features are presumed to be innate and immutable, racial groups are often assumed to be permanent entities with easily definable boundaries (Brown, 1973, 19). Race is not only a physical classification, however, but, more important, a social, legal, and administrative categorization. Racial categorization is intimately bound up with power relations (Wilson, 1973). As such, it characterizes situations in which a more powerful group seeks to dominate another and, in the course of so doing, imposes on these people a categorical identity that is defined by reference to their inherent differences or inferiority to the dominant group (Jenkins, 1986, 177–178). As these power relations change, so do the boundaries of racial groups.

In the United States, the classification of racial groups is ever changing. Some social groups defined as races at an earlier time are no longer defined in racial terms. For example, at the turn of the century, the Irish and Italians were considered inferior races by Anglo-Saxon Protestants. This racial designation was dropped as these two groups improved their social and economic conditions (Feagin, 1978, chaps. 4 and 5). Also, a person's race can be determined not only on the basis of physical characteristics but also on the grounds of a socially determined "rule of descent." With regard to African Americans, as skin color became less clear-cut over time, ancestry became more important in the identification process. The ancestry criterion was used to assign people of mixed origin to the black category—even though they may be physically indistinguishable from whites (Harris, 1964, 56). In sum, far from being immutable, physical differences "may be ignored when present, or assumed to be present when they do not actually exist" (Brown, 1973, 18).

Race has become important in the distribution of scarce resources (e.g., jobs, education, housing) that were previously allocated by market mechanisms. Since the Black Power movement of the 1960s, race has been a legitimate means to make claims on the resources of the state. The urban uprisings of the 1960s forced governments to redefine and expand the rights of minorities, leading to increased funding of minority social welfare programs. Civil rights legislation requires federal authorities to look for patterns of discrimination as evidenced by the underrepresentation of disadvantaged minorities. Where such underrepresentation is found, the relevant party must take affirmative action to correct it.

Disadvantaged minorities are defined as those who have been historically subject to racial discrimination and economic oppression in the United States. Federal authorities designate four such minority groups: American Indians or Alaskan Natives, Asian and Pacific Islanders, Blacks, and Hispanics (Lowry, 1982, 48–49). This designation does not take into account the finer ethnic distinctions within the "Big Four." In other words, Puerto Ricans are rarely distinguished from Cubans among Hispanics, and Vietnamese often are not distinguished from Japanese among Asians. Responding to these institutional definitions of group boundaries, formerly distinct but related ethnic groups have united to give themselves more weight in playing racial politics.

While regional and national alliances continue to organize life within Asian ethnic enclaves, movement into the mainstream necessitates a more inclusive organizational structure. Outside the ethnic enclaves, persons of Asian descent find themselves in political and social situations that demand that they act on a racial basis. In particular, because the welfare state bureaucracy treats Asian Americans as a single administrative unit in the distribution of economic and political resources, it imposes a racial structure on persons and communities dependent on government support. As dealings with government bureaucracies increase, political organization along a racial line becomes advantageous—not only because numbers confer power but also because the Asian racial category is the institutionally relevant category in the political and legal systems. In other words, pan-Asian American coalitions are an organizational response to the United States' racial politics (Padilla, 1985).

The development of pan-Asian organizations is the very process through which race has emerged as the principal organizational structure of the Asian American population. Despite their heterogeneity, Asian Americans have established pan-Asian organizations of social service providers, business owners, professionals, political agents, and labor. In a 1984 national roster of Asian American advocacy groups, 52 percent (61 out of 117) were pan-Asian (Nakanishi and LaForteza, 1984, 16–22). Some examples from Los Angeles include the UCLA Asian American Studies Center, the Asian Pacific Planning Council, (APPCON), the Coalition of Asian Pacific Americans for Fair Reapportionment, the Asian Pacific American Chamber of Commerce, the Pacific Asian Women's Network, and the Alliance of Asian Pacific Labor. The raison d'être for these groups is to promote the interest of Asian Americans within racial politics.

The call for racial solidarity is implicit in the names of these organizations, which employ the Asian American label. It is also explicit in their mission statements and activities, which assert that there are generalized Asian American issues that can best be served by generalized Asian American organizations. These Asian American issues range from employment and business opportunities to political representation to stereotypes in the media. For example, the mission of the Leadership Education for Asian Pacifics (LEAP) is to increase the number of Asian Americans in leadership positions; the purpose of the Coalition of Asian Pacific Americans for Fair Reapportionment is to advance the political agenda of the Asian American community; and the concern of the Association of Asian Pacific American Artists is to encourage the use of balanced depictions and realistic images of Asian Americans in the media. As indicated by these examples, pan-Asian organizations promote racial solidarity by defining economic, political, and social issues in racial terms and by presenting a united front against the dominant society. Their very presence provides a setting for persons of diverse Asian backgrounds to establish social ties and to discuss their common problems and experiences. As Asian Americans come together to coordinate, plan, and participate in the activities of these organizations, they become part of a cohesive, interpersonal framework (Weiss, 1974, 242).

Politically sophisticated, these pan-Asian coalitions recognize that organization along a racial line is important for the maintenance and expansion of their interests. By acting on behalf of Asian Americans as a group, these coalitions add legitimacy to this racial classification.

Class Orientation of Pan-Asian Organizations

Like race, the term "class" does not always have the same meaning. The classical Marxian analysis of capitalist society identifies two major classes in conflict: the capitalists, who own the means of production, and the proletariat, who sell their labor to capitalists. On the other hand, mainstream analysis relies on Max Weber's notion of multiple "social" classes (aggregates of individual suppliers of goods or services who share a "market situation") and on the notion of social status that is defined on the consumption side. In recent years, concepts of class have become even more complex within both the Marxist and mainstream analyses (Giddens, 1973; Wright, 1985). In this chapter, classes are seen as strata, from lower to upper. The most common indicators used for ranking them are income, occupation, and level of education. We define a class as a group of people who possess similar goods, services, or skills to offer for income and who therefore receive similar financial remuneration in the marketplace. What we find most useful for our discussion is the notion of the "professional-managerial class," a segment of the population that is sometimes referred to as "educated labor." Typically, members of this class are college-educated people who work in managerial and professional positions, including engineers, scientists, lawyers, teachers, and supervisors (Ehrenreich and Ehrenreich, 1979).

Although Asian Americans are often regarded as a monolithic socioeconomic group, they have become increasingly differentiated along social class lines (see Chapter 4). The Asian American class structure mirrors the structural segmentation of the U.S. economy. Asian Americans congregate in the low-paying service occupations as well as at the top of the occupational hierarchy; some opt for self-employment. This class structure partly reflects the bimodal distribution of the post-1965 immigrants, who include those with very limited skills as well as those with extensive formal training.

U.S. racial politics continues to define Asian American interests primarily along racial lines, ignoring internal class divisions. For example, race-oriented policies and programs operate from the premise that racial divisions are the only significant lines of cleavage in the U.S. social structure. In an effort to achieve political unity among all Asian Americans, community spokespersons also downplay internal class cleavages. But it would be misleading to ignore these class divisions, for they pose an important challenge to Asian American racial unification. Indeed, the very effort to build a movement on the basis of race (i.e., the establishment of pan-Asian organizations) reifies instead of deemphasizes internal class distinctions.

For the most part, pan-Asian organizations are dominated by

the managerial and professional class (Padilla, 1985). This dominance is rooted in the very way the state has responded to the
three forms of minority demands: consumption rights to basic
services such as health care, housing, and education as ways to
compensate for past and contemporary injustices; civil rights
that protect individuals against discrimination and that ensure
fair participation in electoral politics; and production rights, particularly in the form of support for minority businesses. Given
the political nature of government funding for these services, the
ability to deal effectively with elected officials and public agencies has become a desirable qualification for leadership—a development that favors more acculturated and professional persons.
In other words, the political and funding systems require and
reward professionalism, which in turn have led to a proliferation
of well-educated and politically sophisticated Asians in leadership positions. This class bias can be seen in all forms of pan-
Asian organizations, including special interest, advocacy, social
service, and political group.

Dominance by the professional-managerial class can be readily seen in special interest coalitions: the pan-Asian business and
professional groups. Organized along occupational lines, these
pan-Asian coalitions bring together same-class individuals who
share narrow economic interests. One of these organizations,
Los Angeles–based LEAP, is made up primarily of managers,
businesspersons, and professionals. LEAP programs include a
leadership management training institute, a management training program for aerospace employees, and forums for discussion
of leadership issues. When engaged in politics, these coalitions
lobby chiefly for their particular professional interests, and not
the interests of the larger Asian Pacific American community.
For example, founded in the early 1980s, the Council of Asian
American Business Associations in California monitors state and
federal policies and programs that affect its business community.
Similarly, to broaden their visibility and impact, special interest
groups such as the Asian Pacific Bar Association of California
and the Asian Small Business Organization sponsor legislative
days at the capitol in Sacramento. There, group representatives
meet with legislators and department heads to advocate for pro-

grams pertinent to their professional communities. Although
these business and professional coalitions are pan-Asian, their
specific class interests preclude a broad-based membership.

Unlike special interest groups, whose constituency is by definition narrowly defined by class, advocacy groups claim to represent the political and economic interests of all Asian Americans. There is good reason to believe that these groups do
address the concerns of lower-class Asian Americans—in large
part, to legitimize their own existence. But the question of what
issues are represented is different from that of who actively participates in these groups. The answer to the second question is
shaped by changes in the advocacy process. Modern racial politics depends on the existence of political agents who pressure
the state to act on behalf of minorities. As racial politics evolved
from political protest to negotiation of the details of state involvement to the very incorporation of ethnoracial groups into
mainstream political institutions, the advocacy function became
professionalized. Consequently, active participation within the
advocacy coalitions is often limited to those of equal class standing. Although participation is expanding, the leaders and core
members of the pan-Asian advocacy groups continue to be predominantly white-collar workers and professionals.

Social service coalitions, for example, are dominated by professionals. While these coalitions claim to advocate for the welfare needs of the larger Asian American community, their interaction with the rest of the community is limited primarily to
provider-client relationships. In the late 1960s, to vie more successfully for the pool of government monies, social workers from
various Asian groups began to work together. The availability of
government monies professionalized social work. Because the
funding system required professionalism, Asian American social
workers had to be trained and credentialed in order to procure
outside funding. The professionalization of social work eroded
the power of both traditional elites and grass-roots activists.
Articulate and politically sophisticated, the professional social
workers became the de facto representatives of Asian interests,
even though their competence was often limited to social services.

Because the awarding of funds places a premium on grantsmanship, organizations that have professional staffs are likely to prepare the best proposals and thus receive the most funding. Yet these organizations are also likely to be the ones that already have the strongest financial bases. Such a funding system favors professional applicants over less capable ones, often irrespective of their relative objective needs. Thus, in order to receive funding, less established groups frequently depend on the technical assistance of the older, more experienced organizations. This arrangement invariably fosters dependency, for it shifts the fiscal and program management responsibility to the more established persons and organizations.

Social service providers strengthen their professional relationships through social networking. The Asian Pacific Planning Council (APPCON) in Los Angeles County provides an ideal forum for networking. Founded in 1976, APPCON has become the largest federation of Asian Pacific social service agencies in southern California. Numbering more than forty agencies in 1989, APPCON provides a setting for agency representatives to link up resources, share information, and promote one another's interests. Member agencies benefit from such social networking, particularly in the funding process. APPCON is an effective lobbyist in the funding game because its members are tied to multiple levels of funding in the county. They are staff members of advisory boards and panel members on the county and other funding agencies such as the United Way. Thus, for the most part, the daily interactions of Asian American social service providers are with their class counterparts.

In the political arena, Asian Americans have also built coalitions that seek to integrate the interests of diverse groups.[3] The Coalition of Asian Pacific Americans for Fair Reapportionment (CAPAFR) in Los Angeles is one example of the community's organizational response to U.S. racial politics. The purpose of the coalition, founded in the summer of 1990, is to guard the Asian American communities against gerrymandering and to support the creation of electoral districts where Asians will emerge as the dominant population by the end of the century. Although the coalition acts and speaks on behalf of the Asian community, not all segments of the community are equally represented. The coalition has had limited success in inducing community members to participate in coalition-sponsored or associated activities, and the active participants are primarily professionals, students, and legislative aides (Azores and Okamoto, 1990).

The professional-managerial orientation of pan-Asian organizations is reinforced by horizontal linkages at several levels, through both professional and social networking. At a personal level, professional-managerial Asian Americans belong to their respective professional associations, such as the local bar association and academic organizations. Participation in the workshops, conferences, and social activities of these professional groups helps solidify their class values. Horizontal linkages, however, are not limited to individuals but also operate at the organizational level. In Los Angeles, there is an extensive overlap in membership of several of the major pan-Asian organizations; leaders of some organizations are among the most active members in other organizations.[4] The overlap is not just professional, because the organizational linkages function as a basis for social connections, as leaders and members from pan-Asian organizations frequent the social events sponsored by one another.[5] Within-class ties also form when the leaders of pan-Asian organizations enroll in multiracial coalitions that seek to increase the political power of minorities and to enhance the standing of the participating organizations.[6] Since members of these organizations interact primarily with their class counterparts, interracial linkages, like the intraracial linkages, follow class lines. When local pan-Asian organizations establish networks with similar organizations in other regions of the country, horizontal linkages based on class are formed.[7] The horizontal linkages can even be international in scope. For example, one of the activities of the Asian Pacific American Chamber of Commerce (APACC) is to link overseas Asian companies and markets with minority entrepreneurs in the United States.

In sum, the effort to build an organizational structure on the basis of race has reified class distinctions among Asian Americans. Although largely qualitative, the evidence, taken as a whole, certainly affirms the assertion that there is a dominance by the professional and managerial class.[8] This class bias is rooted in the transformation of the role of the state on racial issues, which created positions best filled by articulate and highly educated persons. Of course, social scientists have long called attention to the dominance of middle-class professionals in voluntary formal organizations, particularly in ethnic movements (Yinger, 1985, 173). For example, the civil rights movement was initiated by African American professional groups. Up to the mid-1960s, lower-income African Americans had little involvement in civil rights politics. As William Wilson (1978, 136) reported, "the movement had a class and status bias and it tended to operate with little direct relationship to the black ghetto." We are concerned not with the class homogeneity itself of pan-Asian organizations, however, but rather with its effect on the racial unity sought by these organizations. We argue that the class homogeneity of these coalitions undercuts their legitimacy and the use of race as their organizing principle.

Ethnic Class Conflicts

The other major factor undermining pan-Asian racial solidarity is the ethnic diversity among Asian Americans. The post-1965 wave of Asian immigration has increased this ethnic diversity, making it even more difficult for group members to unite. In the 1960s, there were only four major Asian American groups in Los Angeles County: Chinese, Japanese, Korean, and Filipino Americans. By the mid-1980s, there were at least twenty-five different Asian and Pacific Islander groups in the county. Ten large groups (Cambodian, Chinese, Japanese, Korean, Lao, Filipino, Samoan, Thai, Tongan, and Vietnamese) accounted for 90 percent of the Asian Pacific population, with fifteen other groups accounting for the other 10 percent (United Way, 1988, 1).

The presence of pan-Asian American groups has not led to the obsolescence of single-ethnic groups. On the contrary, single-ethnic organizations continue to proliferate, at times competing with pan-Asian organizations for membership, loyalty, and funds. Within the pan-Asian organizations, constituent communities have also competed for their shares in the benefits of membership: the jobs, money, and services won by their common efforts. As these resources become scarce, the determination of who gets what at times polarizes the pan-Asian coalitions. Under these conditions, historical intergroup enmities and differences in language, culture, and nativity are intensified by intergroup competition.

Although variations in ethnicity play an independent role in weakening racial solidarity, much of the ethnic conflict is in fact based on group differences in resources and class position. Here we rely on Milton Gordon's concept of ethclasses, which are created by the intersection of vertical segmentation along ethnic lines with horizontal stratification of social class (Gordon, 1964, 51). Our concern is not with the class variation within any given Asian population, but rather with the systematic variations in the class distribution among Asian populations. Differences in historical development, immigration history, and contemporary conditions have left Asian groups in the United States with very disparate class profiles. As a result, some Asian groups are more able to participate in and assert control over pan-Asian organizations than are others.

Because they have more professionals and U.S.-born persons, Chinese and Japanese Americans have been most able to assume the leadership positions in pan-Asian organizations (Table 10.1). In 1990, over 72 percent of the Asian residents in Los Angeles County were foreign born. The Japanese were the only community that had a majority of native-born persons (67%). Though the Chinese had a proportionately larger number of foreign-born persons than the Japanese, they nonetheless also had proportionately more U.S.-born persons than the other Asian groups. As stated above, U.S. political and funding systems reward articulate, credentialed, and politically sophisticated individuals. In such systems, U.S.-born Japanese and Chinese professionals benefit more than newly arrived immigrants. The Japanese and Chinese dominance also has a historical dimension: they were here first. In the late 1960s, Japanese and Chinese Americans played a prominent role in the Asian American movement: they were the first advocates and thus first directors of social service agencies; they were the coordinators and instructors of Asian American Studies, and the editors and writers of pan-Asian media (Chun-Hoon, Hirata, and Moriyama, 1973, 85; Spector-Leech, 1988, 12–13). Chinese and Japanese Americans also profited from the liberal affirmative action programs of the time. Because

Table 10.1. Ethnic Distribution of Selected Class and Nativity Groups, in Percent

| | U.S.-Born | | Foreign-Born | |
Group	Managerial	Professional	Service	Operatives
Japanese	62	62	8	3
Chinese	21	25	30	34
Filipino	12	8	27	19
Korean	3	2	15	19
Vietnamese	0	0	10	17

Source: U.S. Bureau of the Census, *Census of Population and Housing, 1990:* PUMS *A Sample* [Computer file] (Washington, D.C.: U.S. Bureau of the Census [producer]).

they got the jobs first, they tend to be more highly placed now than members of newly arrived Asian groups.

The ethnic inequality among Asian groups is reproduced within the pan-Asian organizations. For example, the past and current directors of many of these organizations, such as the UCLA Asian American Studies Center, the Asian Pacific American Legal Center, and the Asian American Drug Abuse Program, are Chinese or Japanese Americans. Although less severe, the lack of ethnic parity is also apparent at the staff level. Interviews with agency administrators indicated that most social service agencies have a multiethnic staff—primarily to attract a multiethnic clientele. Nevertheless, agency directors reserve the management positions for those they deem most qualified. As a result, more established Japanese and Chinese Americans tend to be higher on the job hierarchy than other Asian American groups (Espiritu, 1992, chap. 4). Although the ethnic bias may not affect the policies of these groups, there is no question that some Asian groups exercise greater power over the pan-Asian organizations than other Asian groups.

The irony of this situation is that justification for racial entitlement is often based on the low socioeconomic status of the very Asian groups that have the least power within pan-Asian organizations. These groups include Filipinos, Koreans, and Vietnamese, who are relatively numerous among the ranks of immigrants in the service and operative occupations (see Table 10.1). This practice is possible because of state funding policies that continue to lump diverse Asian groups together. For example, in the early stages of refugee resettlement, the state used the larger Asian American community as a surrogate for the Southeast Asian communities that did not yet exist. As early as 1975, federal agencies turned to Asian American organizations to resettle these refugees and even distributed a publication entitled "We, the Asian American" to refugees in the reception camps. State governments on the West Coast provided the most support for Asian associations' role in refugee resettlement. In 1981, Asian associations accounted for 43 percent of all nonprofit organizations that received refugee social service funding. In Los Angeles, the Asian American Economic Development Enterprise received more than one hundred thousand dollars to provide refugees with employment and vocational training, and the Pacific Asian Consortium of Employment received more than half a million dollars for its services to refugees. In funding Asian American associations to resettle Southeast Asian refugees, government officials linked newly arrived migrants with the larger Asian American community (Hein, 1989).

The lack of equal standing within pan-Asian organizations has become a major source of friction and mistrust, with participants from the less dominant groups feeling shortchanged and excluded. The reaction to the perceived or real inequality is often a reassertion of distinct ethnic identity. In Los Angeles County, Filipino Americans have been most outspoken, claiming that they have been marginalized in several of these pan-Asian organizations. For example, the UCLA Asian American Studies teaching program has not had a Filipino on its permanent faculty throughout its twenty-year history. To a lesser degree, this underrepresentation is also true for other pan-Asian groups, particularly at the leadership level.

One factor in the Filipino-Asian split is the wide cultural distance between Filipinos and the two dominant Asian groups in the United States—Chinese and Japanese. The influence of Spanish colonial rule (1565–1898) on Filipino culture is still apparent, as indicated by the widespread use of Spanish surnames and the strong presence of Catholicism. U.S. colonial rule (1898–1947) also had a profound impact on Filipinos, particularly in ingraining the values of democratic politics and individualism. Shaped by a history of colonization, the cultural orientation of Filipinos stands in contrast to the cultural orientations of Chinese and Japanese. Although distinct, the latter two nonetheless share many elements. It is questionable how important these cultural differences are, especially among U.S.-born Filipinos, Chinese, and Japanese. Yet these differences can be used selectively to rationalize the uniqueness of Filipinos.

Filipinos are also more disadvantaged in the labor market than are Chinese and Japanese Americans. Analyses of earnings indicate that Filipino Americans are much more likely than Japanese and Chinese Americans to be discriminated against—that is, to earn less after accounting for levels of education, age, and geographic location (Chiswick, 1983; U.S. Commission on Civil Rights, 1988). While U.S.-born Filipinos earn about 18 percent less because of their "race," U.S.-born Chinese earn about 2 percent less and U.S.-born Japanese 4 percent less. Filipino American youths are also more likely to be high school dropouts (Azores, 1986–1987).

Because of their disadvantaged position in the labor market and their underrepresentation in higher education, Filipino Americans have a strong claim for protection from the state. But when Filipino Americans are lumped with other Asian American groups, their claim on the state is often diluted because of the relatively high socioeconomic level of the Asian aggregate. Therefore, Filipino Americans have an economic incentive to separate themselves from the Asian American umbrella category.[9] To a degree, Filipino Americans have been successful in gaining special recognition from public agencies. For example, Filipino Americans successfully lobbied for the passage of California Senate Bill 1813 in 1988. This bill requires state personnel surveys or statistical tabulations to classify persons of Filipino ancestry as Filipino rather than as Asian or Hispanic, allowing Filipino Americans to reap affirmative action benefits independent of the Asian grouping. Filipinos are also identified separately in equal employment reports by Los Angeles County and in enrollment counts at UCLA. A more recent example is a conference on minorities and the redistricting of electoral districts sponsored by the Rose Institute of State and Local Government.[10] Rather than joining the Coalition of Asian Pacific Americans for Fair Reapportionment, several of the Filipinos chose to form their own delegation, although they were willing to caucus with other Asian Americans.

Feeling inadequately represented by the pan-Asian coalition, some Filipino Americans have advocated going outside the coalition in pursuit of their goals (Bagasao, 1989). But dropping out is not a viable option for Filipinos. Their major disadvantage is their limited size. Even though Filipinos were the largest Asian American group in the United States in 1980 and the second largest in 1990 (next to Chinese Americans), they are a very small group outside this coalition. Moreover, being a member of the Asian American coalition brings them instant political visibility—if not always benefits. Because of the pitfalls of withdrawing from the pan-Asian coalition, many Filipino organizations in Los Angeles, such as the Federation of Filipino-American Associations and the Search to Involve Pilipino Americans, have opted to stay with the coalition. Although dissenting Filipinos comprise a minority, the dissension has become public, with some Filipinos airing their grievances in mainstream newspapers and to government officials (Bagasao, 1989; Jacaban, 1988). Such public exposure threatens the foundation of the pan-Asian organizations, reducing their effectiveness. Whether the Filipino-Asian split will grow is not easy to predict. Given the limitations and benefits of the pan-Asian framework, Filipino Americans will probably continue to pursue their interests both inside and outside pan-Asian organizations.

Moreover, the pan-Asian coalition is not the only panethnic option available to Filipino Americans. The Latino coalition is another. As a result of the Spanish colonization of the Philippines, Filipinos share many cultural commonalities—including Catholicism—with Latino groups. Filipino and Latino Americans also face many of the same social and economic difficulties, such as low educational participation rates (Azores, 1986–1987). This political course is not without danger, however. First, Filipino Americans are only a fraction of the Latino population in Los Angeles (as well as in other regions). Second, Filipino-Latino alliances have historically ended with Filipinos having even less influence and control of the umbrella organization than they have in pan-Asian coalitions.

In sum, the ethnically biased composition of pan-Asian organizations fragments the Asian American population along class lines and creates a "reactive" ethnicity among the less powerful Asian groups. With the growing ethnic diversity of the Asian populations in Los Angeles and, more important, the reproduction in the pan-Asian structure of socioeconomic differences found in the larger society, ethnic conflicts within pan-Asian organizations will become more prevalent. Like the narrow class orientation, these ethnic conflicts will preclude racial solidarity.

Racial solidarity has not emerged as the central foundation for collective action among Asian Americans in Los Angeles. Although pan–Asian American organizations continue to strive for unity, class cleavages and class-derived ethnic conflicts undercut the legitimacy of these coalitions and the use of race as their organizing principle. David Lopez and Yen Espiritu (1990) have argued that the relative success of Asian Americans in forging panethnic alliances rests in part on the presence of a sizable middle and professional class. We would add that there is a price to this class bias in terms of a recurring question of legitimacy and ethnic-class conflict.

It may be premature to comment on the relative strength of racial solidarity among Asian Americans. What we have witnessed may be a period of transition in which older forms of internal organizations coexist with the emerging form. The very term "coalition," used by some pan-Asian organizations, indicates the incompleteness of the process. Although the future of the pan-Asian organizations is partly determined by exogenous forces such as the rate of immigration and changes in racial politics, their longevity and effectiveness will ultimately depend on overcoming their narrow class dominance and class-ethnic conflicts. Aware of these two flaws, some pan-Asian organizations have begun to diversify their leadership and membership. For example, responding to charges of favoritism and limited representation, the Asian Pacific Planning Council in Los Angeles introduced an outreach program to attract new Asian groups and recently elected a Korean its president. Progress is being made, but it is safe to say that racial solidarity is still an unmet goal. Whether pan-Asian organizations in general can totally overcome the constraints of class remains to be seen.

Although this case study reveals the constraints of class on racial solidarity, it also calls attention to the continuing importance of race—or rather, racial lumping—in uniting Asian Americans. For Asian groups in the United States, a racial identity is not always an identity of choice. Unable or unwilling to recognize the class and ethnic distinctions as insiders see them, the majority of the U.S. public continues to define Asian Americans as a distinct race. This racial lumping leads to counterorganization at the pan-Asian level. In particular, anti-Asian violence draws the largest pan-Asian support. Because anti-Asian violence concerns the entire group, cross-cutting class and ethnic differences, it necessarily leads to protective racial solidarity. Thus we can expect that as racial hostility increases, additional pan-Asian organizations will emerge to monitor, report, and protest it.

U.S. policies also identify Asian Americans along racial lines. When the welfare state bureaucracy treats all Asian Americans as a single administrative unit in the distribution of economic and political resources, it provides compelling material reason for Asian subgroups to consolidate their efforts. Thus the modern state plays a pivotal role in defining and activating racial boundaries (Enloe, 1981; Omi and Winant, 1986). Within this political structure, Asian Americans, like their African American and Latino counterparts, act collectively to make claims on the resources of the state (Olzak, 1983, 362–363). But unlike these two minority groups, Asian Americans do not have a common language, history, or culture. Therefore their racial solidarity is more tenuous, resting primarily on the narrow foundation of exogenously defined race. Asian American mobilization also differs from immigrant-based mobilization, which relies on preexisting traditional institutions to overcome the organizing cost and free-rider barriers to collective action (O'Brien, 1975, 35–42). Lacking these preexisting ties, it is not surprising that pan-Asian organizations depend almost solely on the incentives (funding and power) available from the state, which in turn foster the professional-managerial class bias.

U.S. racial politics has an implication for race relations that goes beyond the intraracial difficulties described above. Because race-oriented programs and policies emphasize group-specific benefits, they undermine the bases for interracial cooperation necessary to create more universal programs. In offering particularistic benefits, these government programs encourage minority groups to seek race-specific policies and to frame their demands in group-specific terms. In the process, racial groups are turned into interest groups, competing against one another for the same limited resources (Weir, 1988, 184). When the resources allotted for racial groups decrease, intergroup competition deteriorates into intergroup hostility. Given their relative class and educational advantages, Asian Americans are often viewed by other minority groups as the most likely to benefit from race-oriented programs. They have also been accused of being part of the white power structure. Whether Asian Americans will simply play the game of racial politics or cooperate with other minority groups to construct more universal programs remains to be seen. Whatever their course of action, it will be partly dictated by the structure of racial politics in the United States.

Notes

Acknowledgments: Partial support for this research was provided by the Institute of American Culture and the Asian American Studies Center, University of California at Los Angeles. The authors made equal contributions to this chapter; alphabetical order determined the order of names.

1. Although race is still codified (as illustrated by the classifications used in the census), this practice evolved out of the need to justify and calculate allocations of resources by race.
2. This distinction is not absolute, because professionals who entered

under the occupational categories eventually sponsored relatives, who tended to come from the same class background, through the family reunification categories. See, for example, Liu, Ong, and Rosenstein, 1991.

3. Asian Pacific legislative aides form a political interest group that is organized informally. They meet several times a year, often in a social setting, such as dinner, to discuss issues of common concern.

4. The Asian American Studies Center of the University of California at Los Angeles is an example of this phenomenon. Community leaders are often invited to give lectures, teach courses, and participate in research activities. Moreover, key staff members and faculty are active in community and advocacy organizations, such as LEAP, the Alliance of Asian Pacific Labor, and CAPAFR. These linkages are further enhanced by the placement of Asian American Studies students and graduates into many of the community and advocacy organizations.

5. These events also attract other members of the professional-managerial class who are not active in pan-Asian organizations but nonetheless believe that racial solidarity among Asian Americans and the sponsoring institutions should be supported. This class bias in attendance can be partially understood as the product of the function of many of these social events, which is to raise funds as well as to build support. The class bias, then, is due to the cost of attending, which can be high—in terms of both out-of-pocket expenses and time—and to the class-defined friendships that the organizers of these events use to recruit supporters.

6. The "New Majority," whose purpose is to alter local policies to address the concerns of people of color in Los Angeles, includes prominent Asians in the leadership and the small core of active participants. The members of the Asian Pacific American Chamber of Commerce (APACC) establish and nurture professional relationships with others of equal class standing, such as members of the Latin Business Association and overseas Asian businesspersons.

7. For example, UCLA's Asian American Studies Center is a member of the Association of Asian American Studies, the Asian Pacific American Legal Center is a part of an emerging national network of legal centers that serve Asian Americans, and the Coalition of Asian Pacific Americans has been in contact with its counterpart in the San Francisco Bay area and New York City.

8. The one possible exception is the Alliance of Asian Pacific Labor (AAPL), which focuses on labor and union issues. Because past

union activities have centered on organizing blue-collar workers, it is not surprising that the founder of AAPL came from the ranks of the "working class." Unlike the college-educated leaders of other pan-Asian organizations, AAPL's founder has only a high school education. Professionals have played key roles in this organization, however; for example, a labor attorney was at one time the chairperson.

9. Southeast Asian refugees also feel that they would be better off outside the "Asian American" umbrella. For example, at a 1990 public hearing on Asian American education at California State University at Fullerton, Southeast Asian representatives argued that as the poorest group in the Asian American minority, Southeast Asians should be placed in a separate category and be given special assistance in the higher education system.

10. "Time to Draw the Line" Conference, 22–23 June 1990, Claremont McKenna College, Claremont, California.

References

Anti-Defamation League of B'nai B'rith. 1982. *Hate Groups in America: A Record of Bigotry and Violence*. New York.

Azores, Tania. 1986–1987. "Educational Attainment and Upward Mobility: Prospects for Filipino Americans." *Amerasia Journal* 13:39–52.

Azores, Tania, and Philip Okamoto. 1991. "Asian Pacific Awareness and Involvement in Redistricting." Asian American Studies Center, University of California at Los Angeles.

Bagasao, Brad. 1989. "Asian Americans No More." *LA Weekly* 1(12):43.

Bonacich, Edna. 1972. "A Theory of Ethnic Antagonism: The Split Labor Market." *American Sociological Review* 37:547–559.

Brown, Ina Corrine. 1973. *Understanding Race Relations*. Englewood Cliffs, N.J.: Prentice-Hall.

Bullard, Sara, ed. 1988. *The Ku Klux Klan: A History of Racism and Violence*. Washington, D.C.: Southern Poverty Law Center.

Burstein, Paul. 1985. *Discrimination, Jobs, and Politics: The Struggle for Equal Employment Opportunity in the United States since the New Deal*. Chicago: University of Chicago Press.

Chiswick, Barry R. 1983. "An Analysis of the Earnings and Employment of Asian-American Men." *Journal of Labor Economics* 1:197–214.

Chun-Hoon, Lowell, Lucie Hirata, and Alan Moriyama. 1973. "Curriculum Development in Asian American Studies: A Working Paper." In *Proceedings of the National Asian American Studies Conference II: A*

Tool of Change or a Tool of Control? ed. George Kagiwada, Joyce Sakai, and Gus Lee, pp. 83–90. Davis, Calif.: Asian American Studies Center.

Cox, Oliver C. 1948. *Caste, Class, and Race.* New York: Modern Reader.

Ehrenreich, Barbara, and John Ehrenreich. 1979. "The Professional-Managerial Class." In *Between Labor and Capital,* ed. Pat Walker, pp. 5–45. Boston: South End Press.

Enloe, C. H. 1981. "The Growth of the State and Ethnic Mobilization: The American Experience." *Ethnic and Race Studies* 4 (1981): 123–136.

Espiritu, Yen Le. 1992. *Asian American Panethnicity: Bridging Institutions and Identities.* Philadelphia: Temple University Press.

Farley, Reynolds, and Suzanne M. Bianchi. 1983. "The Growing Gap between Blacks." *American Demographics* 5:15–18.

Feagin, Joe R. 1978. *Racial and Ethnic Relations.* Englewood Cliffs, N.J.: Prentice-Hall.

Fraizer, E. Franklin. 1957. *Black Bourgeoisie.* New York: Free Press.

Freeman, Richard. 1976. *Black Elite: The New Market for Highly Educated Black Americans.* New York: McGraw-Hill.

Giddens, Anthony. 1973. *The Class Structure of Advanced Societies.* New York: Harper and Row.

Gordon, Milton M. 1964. *Assimilation in American Life.* New York: Oxford University Press.

Harris, Marvin. 1964. *Patterns of Race in the Americas.* New York: W. W. Norton.

Hein, Jeremy. 1989. "States, Social Welfare, and the Adaptation of Political Migrants: The Incorporation of Indochinese Refugees in the U.S." Ph.D. dissertation, Northwestern University, Evanston, Ill.

Jacaban, Melecio H. 1988. "SB 1813 Gives Filipinos Full Benefits of Affirmative Action Law." *Philippine News* 24 (February).

Jenkins, Richard. 1986. "Social Anthropological Models of Inter-Ethnic Relations." In *Theories of Race and Ethnic Relations,* ed. John Rex and David Mason, pp. 170–186. Cambridge: Cambridge University Press.

Kim, Illsoo. 1987. "Korea and East Asia: Premigration Factors and U.S. Immigration Policy." In *Pacific Bridges,* ed. James T. Fawcett and Benjamin V. Carino, pp. 327–345. Staten Island, N.Y.: Center for Migration Studies.

Liu, John M., Paul M. Ong, and Carolyn Rosenstein. 1991. "Dual Chain Migration: Post-1965 Filipino Immigration to the United States." *International Migration Review* 15(3):487–513.

Lopez, David, and Yen Espiritu. 1990. "Panethnicity in the United States: A Theoretical Framework." *Ethnic and Racial Studies* 13:198–224.

Lowry, Ira S. 1982. "The Science and Politics of Ethnic Enumeration." In *Ethnicity and Public Policy*, ed. Winston A. Van Horne, vol. 1, pp. 42–61. Wisconsin: University of Wisconsin System.

May, Lee. 1990. "Activists React to Affirmative Action Losses." *Los Angeles Times*, 18 November, pp. A1, A26–A27.

Nakanishi, Don T., and Bernie C. LaForteza. 1984. *The National Asian Pacific American Roster, 1984.* Los Angeles: Asian American Studies Center, University of California.

O'Brien, David. 1975. *Neighborhood Organization and Interest-Group Processes.* Princeton: Princeton University Press.

Olzak, Susan. 1983. "Contemporary Ethnic Mobilization." *American Review of Sociology* 9:355–374.

Omi, Michael, and Howard Winant. 1986. *Racial Formation in the United States from the 1960s to the 1980s.* New York and London: Routledge and Kegan Paul.

Ong, Paul. 1990. "Tabulation of 1983–86 INS Tape for Southern California." Unpublished. Asian American Studies Center, University of California at Los Angeles.

Padilla, Felix. 1985. *Latino Ethnic Consciousness: The Case of Mexican Americans and Puerto Ricans in Chicago.* Notre Dame, Ind.: University of Notre Dame Press.

Spector-Leech, Garrett. 1988. "Ethnic Community Mobilization within an Urban Environment: An Analysis of Asian/Pacific Community and Advocacy Organizations in Los Angeles County." Master's thesis, University of Southern California, Los Angeles.

United Way. 1988. *Asian Pacific Needs Assessment, 1988.* Los Angeles: United Way.

U.S. Commission on Civil Rights. 1988. *The Economic Status of Americans of Asian Descent: An Exploratory Investigation.* Washington, D.C.: Government Printing Office.

Weir, Margaret. 1988. "The Federal Government and Unemployment: The Frustration of Policy Innovation from the New Deal to the Great Society." In *The Politics of Social Policy in the United States*, ed. Margaret Weir, Ann Schola Orloff, and Theda Skocpol, pp. 149–190. Princeton: Princeton University Press.

Weiss, Melford S. 1974. *Valley City: A Chinese Community in America.* Cambridge, Mass.: Schenkman.

Wilson, William J. 1973. *Power, Racism, and Privilege.* New York: Free Press.

————. 1978. *The Declining Significance of Race.* Chicago: University of Chicago Press.

————. 1987. *The Truly Disadvantaged: The Inner City, the Underclass, and Public Policy.* Chicago: University of Chicago Press.

Wright, Erik Olin. 1985. *Classes.* London: Verso.

Yinger, Milton. 1985. "Ethnicity." *Annual Review of Sociology* 11:151–180.

Conclusion
Edna Bonacich, Paul Ong, and Lucie Cheng

On 22 November 1991, the *Los Angeles Times* reported the following story:

> After a long and distinguished career in the American aerospace industry, during which he helped send the first astronauts to the moon, David Huang might have been expected to retire quietly to his Calabasas Park home. Instead, the 71-year-old engineer has devoted the last 10 years to building an aerospace industry half a world away from Southern California. On Wednesday, he emerged as a central figure in one of the most significant international ventures ever in the aircraft business—McDonnell Douglas' $2-billion preliminary agreement to sell a 40% stake in its commercial aircraft business to a consortium from Taiwan.

David Huang is a U.S. citizen, and his son continues to live in the United States, working as a rocket propulsion engineer at TRW in Redondo Beach. Huang retains strong ties on both sides of the Pacific.

This story is one of the more dramatic examples of the way the new Asian immigration is contributing to the restructuring of the Pacific Rim region. Not only is the immigration a product of the restructuring of the regional political economy; the immigrants are active participants in the process, helping propel change.

All over southern California, as well as other sectors of the nation, the impact of the new Asian immigration is being felt. Women are getting their nails fixed by Vietnamese beauty shop attendants. Thai restaurants are selling a newly popular cuisine. Korean fruitstand operators have transformed the way New Yorkers buy their fresh fruits and vegetables. And, as described in this volume, Filipino nurses have created health care registries, Koreans have constructed swap meets, and Indians are running hotels and motels.

Sometimes the impact of the new Asian immigration is felt

only locally, but sometimes, as in the David Huang case, the ramifications are international. Koreans, Chinese, and Vietnamese, including Chinese-Vietnamese, are helping foster international trade between their homelands and the United States. In the apparel industry, Koreans, sometimes moving from a base in the United States, are setting up contracting shops in such countries as Guatemala, in order to produce there for the U.S. market.

The lines of nationality are becoming blurred. Citizenship no longer means a clear affiliation. Instead, along with a rapidly globalizing economy comes the creation of "global people," who readily move between nation-states as they pursue economic opportunities. Participants in the new Asian immigration are among those who are at the forefront of this process.

There may be some important parallels between the new Asian immigration and earlier migration flows to the United States. For one thing, the new Asian immigration includes an important working-class component, whose incorporation into the U.S. economy resembles that of both earlier European immigrants and, to a certain extent, earlier Asian and Latino immigrants. In all these cases, unskilled or semiskilled workers entered the U.S. economy at the bottom and, through hard work and sacrifice, gradually worked their way up.

The new Asian immigrants also resemble some of these earlier immigrants in the propensity of some of them to engage in small business as immigrant entrepreneurs. In this they are reminiscent of Jewish, Italian, and Greek, as well as Japanese and Chinese, immigrants.

But two aspects of the new Asian immigration make it unique. First is the arrival of highly educated immigrants who are joining the professional-managerial class in large numbers. The size and impact of this new group is unprecedented in U.S. immigration history. Second is the inclusion of immigrants with considerable capital, people who are able to invest in and transform the local economies.

Put another way, the new Asian immigration is far from just a gradual absorption of new numbers of people into the preexisting system. Rather, the new Asian immigration is transforming the economic and political landscape of the United States, especially in southern California. The new immigrants come with fresh ideas, with innovations, with an ambition and drive that is creating, and not just reacting to, local political and economic conditions.

In this volume, we have argued that the new Asian immigration is a product of the larger economic restructuring occurring in the Pacific Rim basin. The tremendous rise of trade in the region, the growth of Asian countries as major manufacturers for export, the resulting dislocations in the U.S. economy as it tries to become more competitive have all stimulated this new immigration and set the stage for the kinds of roles the new immigrants are playing. A globalizing economy is not only changing the relations between countries but also thrusting emigrants and immigrants into new roles. And in the process, those international migrants play a significant part in fostering globalization.

The changes connected with the new Asian immigration have not always been smooth. Conflicts have arisen with other groups, including African American customers of Korean stores, Latino employees in Asian-owned garment factories, and Anglo residents of communities where the new immigrants have settled. In Los Angeles we are witnessing a rise in tensions among groups of color, apart from the more traditional conflicts with the dominant white group. Indeed, conflicts are even occurring within the larger, racially defined but ethnically heterogeneous, Asian group.

Some of the intergroup difficulties Asians are facing have a cultural basis. Coming from very different cultural backgrounds, often also from more culturally homogeneous societies, some Asian immigrants have trouble dealing with diversity. Cultural conflict aggravates already strained economic relations between Asians and other groups of color.

The basic structure of power in the United States still places it heavily in white (or Anglo) hands, and many of the intergroup conflicts arise within this larger context. In the garment industry, for example, Asian contractors are fairly near the bottom of a hierarchy still dominated by white-owned businesses. The evolving history of Monterey Park and the conflict between African Americans and Korean shopkeepers also reflect this hierarchy.

Powerful white institutions also play a direct role in confrontations with new Asian immigrants. Professional-managerial immigrants often encounter a glass ceiling as they pursue upward mobility. Filipino nurses and other Asian professionals face resistance to the use of their native languages. Anti-Asianism stemming from global competition slips over into the U.S. context and leads to local forms of discrimination.

Of course, not all interactions among new Asian immigrants are conflictive. The press tends to emphasize the tensions, ignoring many less headline-grabbing stories of cooperation and the building of cross-ethnic community. The Monterey Park history is an illustration of how different groups can unite to create a politics of interethnic tolerance and respect. Even in the harshest of hostile relationships, the Korean–African American situation, efforts are being made to create new institutions where communication and community-building are possible.

As new Asian immigrants continue to arrive and as their numerical concentration is felt, particularly in regions such as California, their political influence is bound to expand. Will Asians vote as individuals and become absorbed without notice into the political mainstream? Or will they form a voting bloc that helps shape U.S. politics in new directions? And if they do try to organize collectively, will they simply vote to get more Asian representatives elected, irrespective of political orientation, or will they try to stand for a particular type of politics?

As a new Asian American politics is forged, it will be subject to diverse and contradictory trends. On the one hand, many new Asian immigrants come from fiercely anti-Communist backgrounds, and that may encourage the pursuit of right-wing politics in the U.S. context. This tendency could be enhanced by the overrepresentation of Asians in the professional-managerial and business classes, as both small entrepreneurs and large-scale capitalists. On the other hand, Asian immigrants still experience racism, discrimination, and intolerance themselves. Their experience once in the United States can transform any predilections toward the right and shift consciousness toward a more progressive politics. Second and third generations, educated in the United States and exposed to racism without the "excuse" of being "foreign" and speaking English with an accent, may find racism increasingly jarring and discover common ground with other groups of color.

In conclusion, the world economy is changing on a grand scale, and an important aspect of this restructuring is the rise of Asian countries as powerful economic actors. The greater economic integration between Asia and the United States is creating a major population movement of new immigrants to the United States from Asian countries. This movement includes people with a wide diversity of class backgrounds. Unlike most earlier migrations to the United States, which drew heavily on peasants and the urban poor, the new Asian immigration includes important new elements—international capitalists and traders, and highly educated professionals and managerial personnel—as well as the more traditional, working-class immigrants.

The new Asian immigration is forever changing the shape of U.S. economic and political life, particularly in southern California. The impact on local residents is variable, depending on their class position, residential location, ethnic and racial background, and political orientation. Whatever the future brings, we can be sure that this new immigrant community will play an important role in it.

About the Editors and Contributors

Tania Azores received her Ph.D. in urban planning from the University of California at Los Angeles. A lecturer for the UCLA Department of Linguistics and at Loyola Marymount University in the Department of Modern Languages, she is also a research associate at UCLA's Asian American Studies Center. Azores served as the chair of the Asian Pacific American Advisory Committee for the 1980 census.

Edna Bonacich, who received her Ph.D. from Harvard University, is a professor of ethnic studies and sociology at the University of California, Riverside. Her works focus on race, class, and labor. She is coauthor (with Ivan Light) of *Ethnic Entrepreneurs: Koreans in Los Angeles, 1965–1982* (University of California Press, 1988).

Lucie Cheng received her Ph.D. in sociology from the University of Hawaii. She is a professor at the University of California, Los Angeles, and is a visiting professor at the National Taiwan University. She is coeditor of *Labor Immigration under Capitalism: Asian Workers in the United States before World War II* (University of California Press, 1984).

Yen Espiritu received her Ph.D. in sociology from the University of California at Los Angeles. She is an assistant professor of ethnic studies and sociology at the University of California at San Diego and the author of *Asian American Panethnicity: Bridging Institutions and Identities* (Temple University Press, 1992). Originally from Vietnam, she is especially interested in the construction of ethnicity and multiple levels of identity among Asian Americans.

Steve Gold is an associate professor of sociology at Michigan State University. His book *Refugee Communities: A Comparative Field Study*, which deals with Soviet Jewish and Vietnamese refugees in California, was published by Sage Publications in 1992. Gold is currently involved in a study of Israeli immigrants in Los Angeles.

John Horton teaches sociology at the University of California, Los Angeles. He has written extensively on contemporary social and political movements and on class, gender, and ethnic inequalities. He is currently completing a book about the impact of the new Chinese and Asian immigration on the politics and culture of a multiethnic Los Angeles suburb, Monterey Park.

John M. Liu received his Ph.D. in sociology from the University of California at Los Angeles and is an associate professor in the Program of Comparative Culture at the University of California, Irvine. His publications include "Contours of Asian Professional, Technical, and Kindred Worker Immigration, 1965–1988," *Sociological Perspectives* 35 (1992): 673–704; and "A Dialogue on Race and Class: Asian American Studies and Marxism," *New Left Academy* 3 (1986): 139–163.

Paul Ong received his Ph.D. in economics from the University of California, Berkeley. He is an associate professor at the University of California at Los Angeles Graduate School of Architecture and Urban Planning and past associate director of the UCLA Asian American Studies Center. He is the lead author for *Beyond Asian American Poverty* (Leadership Education for Asian Pacifics, Asian Pacific American Public Policy Institute, 1993).

Kye Young Park received her Ph.D. in anthropology from City University of New York. She is an assistant professor of anthropology, Asian American studies, and Korean studies at the University of California, Los Angeles. She is preparing a book entitled *The Korean American Dream: Ideology and Small Business in Queens, New York.*

Leland T. Saito received his Ph.D. in sociology from the University of California at Los Angeles and is an assistant professor in the Ethnic Studies Department and Urban Studies and Planning Program at the University of California, San Diego.

Yasmin Tong received her M.A. in urban planning from the University of California, Los Angeles, Graduate School of Architecture and Urban Planning. Her current research involves ethnic restaurants and institutional responses to interethnic conflict. She lives and works in Los Angeles.

Also in the Series

Gary Y. Okihiro, *Cane Fires: The Anti-Japanese Movement in Hawaii, 1865–1945* (1991)

Sucheng Chan, ed., *Entry Denied: Exclusion and the Chinese Community in America, 1882–1943* (1991)

Karen Isaksen Leonard, *Making Ethnic Choices: California's Punjabi Mexican Americans* (1992)

Yen Le Espiritu, *Asian American Panethnicity: Bridging Institutions and Identities* (1992)

Shirley Geok-lin Lim and Amy Ling, eds., *Reading the Literatures of Asian America* (1992)

Renqiu Yu, *To Save China, To Save Ourselves: The Chinese Hand Laundry Alliance of New York* (1992)

Velina Hasu Houston, ed., *The Politics of Life: Four Plays by Asian American Women* (1993)

William Wei, *The Asian American Movement* (1993)

Timothy P. Fong, *The First Suburban Chinatown: The Remaking of Monterey Park, California* (1994)

Sucheng Chan, ed., *Hmong Means Free: Life in Laos and America* (1994)

Chris Friday, *Organizing Asian American Labor: The Pacific Coast Canned-Salmon Industry, 1870–1942* (1994)